James Herbst

The Politics of Apoliticism

James Herbst

The Politics of Apoliticism

Political Trials in Vichy France, 1940–1942

DE GRUYTER
OLDENBOURG

ISBN 978-3-11-060721-5
e-ISBN (PDF) 978-3-11-061016-1
e-ISBN (EPUB) 978-3-11-060743-7

Library of Congress Cataloging-in-Publication Data 2018965087

Bibliographic information published by the Deutsche Nationalbibliothek
The Deutsche Nationalbibliothek lists this publication in the Deutsche Nationalbibliografie; detailed bibliographic data are available on the Internet at http://dnb.dnb.de.

Cover image: A diagram of the seating arrangements at the Supreme Court in Riom, unattributed newspaper clipping, Box 23, Series GE, Archives d'Histoire Contemporaine des Sciences Po.
Printing and binding: CPI books GmbH, Leck

www.degruyter.com

Contents

1 Introduction

> Treason doth never prosper, what's the reason?
> For if it prosper, none dare call it treason.
> – John Harington

In 1940, a mere twenty-two years after its admittedly ambiguous triumph in the Great War (1914–1918), the French Army experienced perhaps the most abrupt and total defeat ever suffered by a great power. Other great powers have been humbled in war with equal speed; Napoleon's 1809 campaign against Austria comes to mind. Another such case was France itself in 1870. France then, however, had managed to hold out for another year. In contrast, the 1940 catastrophe was unique in its combination of rapidity and thoroughness. In six weeks, France was reduced from one of Europe's two leading military powers – the Soviet army, recently humiliated in Finland, was widely considered to be of doubtful quality – to the status of a client state of Nazi Germany. It was the Third Reich's only fully successful campaign against a great power.

Within weeks, France had not only lost her independence but also her liberty. The collapse of French pluralism[1] was as drastic as her military defeat. For much of the nineteenth century, France had been a byword for rapid changes of regime. Alfred, Lord Tennyson, had mocked them for it in his 1847 poem *The Princess*, only a year before France experienced yet another short-lived shift towards democracy:

> But yonder, whiff! there comes a sudden heat,
> The gravest citizen seems to lose his head,
> The king is scared, the soldier will not fight,
> The little boys begin to shoot and stab,
> A kingdom topples over with a shriek
> Like an old woman, and down rolls the world
> In mock heroics stranger than our own;
> Revolts, republics, revolutions, most
> No graver than a schoolboy's barring out.

From 1875 on, however, France seemed to have settled on a durable pluralistic system. The Third Republic was prone to scandal and rapid cabinet turnover, but it seemed to be, as the former moderate monarchist Adolphe Thiers once

1 Women were forbidden from voting under the Third Republic, as were Muslim Algerians; but there is nonetheless a real sense in which France moved from popular to authoritarian government under Vichy.

https://doi.org/10.1515/9783110610161-001

commented, the form of government that divided the French least.[2] In spite of the resurgence of political divisions in the 1930s, especially after the election of the left-wing Popular Front in 1936, most of the French continued to support parties espousing one version or another of republicanism. In 1940, however, as the *Wehrmacht* approached the fleeing French parliament's new headquarters in Bordeaux, an overwhelming majority voted full powers to Marshal Philippe Pétain, France's only living marshal and a national hero due to his record in the First World War. Pétain was to draw up a new constitution, and, apart from a provision that the result would have to be ratified by the Assembly (honored, as it proved, more in the breach than the observance), nothing guaranteed that the result would be democratic. Indeed, "the Marshal," as he is still popularly known, promptly issued a series of "constitutional acts" that swept away the Republic and replaced it with an authoritarian regime in which he reserved all power for himself. The new regime would be named after the city to which the French government had moved after Bordeaux: Vichy.

Even as the French Army continued to crumble, some political leaders still hoped to hold out in the *reduit bréton* (the Breton peninsula) or in France's vast North African colonies. On June 22, however, Pétain signed an armistice agreement, a day after thirty parliamentarians had boarded the Casablanca-bound *Massilia* in the mistaken impression that the rest of the government would follow them. The Pétain government immediately portrayed this act as one of betrayal, as a panicked flight rather than as an attempt to continue the fight. Soon after, it began to seek to give this portrayal juridical form in the shape of the prosecution for desertion of four of the *Massilia* deputies: Jean Zay, Pierre Mendès France, Pierre Viénot and Alex Wiltzer. They were taken into custody on 31 August 1940. A month earlier, Pétain and Vichy's Minister of Justice, Raphaël Alibert, had established a new court, the *Cour Suprême* (Supreme Court) at Riom, with jurisdiction over former ministers and their immediate subordinates. Pétain, granted power by the same parliament that had launched the Popular Front government in 1936, had begun the process of targeting prominent Popular Frontists for a trial at Riom, which was finally held in 1942.

The intervening eighteen months had not been encouraging for the government's judicial policy. Three of the *Massilia* deputies – Zay, Mendès France, and Viénot – were successfully prosecuted in the course of 1940–41 by a military tribunal at Clermont-Ferrand, but this was the extent of the government's success

2 Michael Butler, *Selling a "Just" War: Framing, Legitimacy, and US Military Intervention* (Basingstoke: Palgrave Macmillan, 2012), 230.

in prosecuting its precursors. The same tribunal – indeed, the same magistrate – who convicted Zay and the other deputies refused even to indict former Prime Minister Paul Reynaud and his Minister of the Interior, Georges Mandel. The Riom tribunal dragged its feet seemingly interminably, to the point that an impatient Pétain overrode the wishes of his new Minister of Justice, Joseph Barthélemy (who had replaced Alibert in February 1941), and instituted a new handpicked *Conseil de Justice Politique* to pass sentence on the Riom defendants. It duly did so on October 15, 1941, but the fact that the Riom court continued to deliberate was an indication of how little credibility the *Conseil*'s verdict possessed, even at Vichy.

Meanwhile, international events had also turned against Vichy. The regime was predicated on the assumption that the war was over and Britain would quickly capitulate or, in the famous words of Vichy's Minister of National Defense, Maxime Weygand, "have its neck twisted like a chicken's."[3] Neither occurred. The establishment of the *Cour Suprême* had taken place in the wake of the British bombardment of the French fleet at Mers-el-Kébir on 3 July, 1940, and consequently at a low point in Franco-British relations; but French opinion continued to be largely favorable to a British victory.[4] In June 1941, the British invasion of Syria began to remove a second component of Vichy's self-legitimation – its continued possession of France's colonies. A series of diplomatic initiatives throughout 1941 gradually brought the United States closer to participation in the war, and made the prospect of ultimate German victory, which had seemed so certain in the summer of 1940, appear to recede still further. The German invasion of the USSR in June 1941, initially highly successful, had bogged down by the autumn. By February 1942, when the Riom court finally convened, it was no longer a triumphant initiative by the victors in France's domestic quarrels so much as a desperate attempt to rescue the government's crumbling legitimacy.

It did not succeed in this goal. The Riom trial was a disaster for the Vichy government. Uniquely among show trials, it failed to result in a conviction, and the 1942 hearings were in fact so embarrassing to the regime that the trial had to be placed on what proved to be an indefinite hiatus. Tardy in its preparation, the trial was also slow in its execution: by the time it was suspended, after a month and a half of hearings, only a minute fraction of the witnesses had been called. By contrast, Philippe Pétain's own trial would take only twenty-three days (July 23 to August 15, 1945). The extraordinary spectacle of a show

3 Michael Curtis, *Verdict on Vichy: Power and Prejudice in the Vichy France Regime* (New York: Arcade Publishing, 2002), 64.

4 Pierre Laborie, *L'Opinion Française sous Vichy* (Paris: Seuil, 1990), 244.

trial that took a year and a half to prepare and failed to accomplish any of its goals demands explanation.

This book will argue that the failure cannot be blamed on the way German demands shaped the trial, because, far from being the result of foreign pressure, Riom was fundamentally about domestic French politics. The German interest in the trial was primarily about demonstrating that France and not Germany was responsible for the war, and it was they who summarily ended the trial when it proved not to consider the question of war guilt at all. This conflict between Nazi and Vichy views of what the trial should accomplish was not a last-minute development. From the beginning, Riom had been designed to show not that France was responsible for the war, but that Vichy's structures of government were right, because the previous structures of government – in particular, the intrusion of politics (that is, debate) into the apolitical realms of administration, justice, defense, and economic policy – had led to the defeat.

This critique of the late Third Republic was not new. A wide variety of political figures, from Édouard Daladier on the left to André Tardieu on the right, had spent the interwar years trying to recast France along more technocratic lines. One group of such like-minded individuals, the *Redressement Français*, would indeed provide the primary inspiration for the trials. Implicit in their analysis, as in the work of many later philosophers of democracy such as Claude Lefort,[5] was the idea that public policy consisted of two separate spheres: the "political" sphere, where public debate was necessary, and the "apolitical" sphere, where an elite consensus had already been reached and further debate would only undermine good government. Pushing sensitive political topics such as economic policy into the apolitical sphere of pure administration held inherent antidemocratic elements, but the interwar *Redressement Français* did not see its activities in that light. Rather, their irritation at the ignorant masses impinging on spheres of which they knew nothing bore a considerable resemblance to today's Dubai Consensus on economic policy. Philosophically, it was closer to the American pragmatist tradition of C. S. Peirce and William James, with their respect for science and limitation of the sphere of legitimate doubt, than to the anti-democratic theorists of Nazi Germany. The members of the *Redressement Français* were merely reiterating the basic insight common to all theorists of democracy that

5 See, for example, Lefort's discussion of the relationship between democracy and rights in Claude Lefort, *The Political Forms of Modern Society: Bureaucracy, Democracy, Totalitarianism*, ed. John B. Thompson (Cambridge: Polity Press, 1986), 239–272. Lefort was much better aware of the problematic nature of separating rights from debate; the objective of his analysis was to create the possibility of a left-wing politics based on a respect for, rather than a Marxist rejection of, the idea of human rights.

a limitless sphere of debate vitiates that debate by forcing a constant revisiting of the fundamental postulates without which the debate itself becomes impossible. Until 1940, the French disagreed on exactly what the "apolitical sphere" might cover, but it was not undemocratic to argue that it existed. The result of the defeat of 1940, however, was to raise the stakes of this disagreement about apoliticism. Arguing, for example, that the military should be free from political interference now carried the implication that those who interfered were responsible for the defeat, and were consequently not merely wrong, but treasonous.

Riom's failure, then, was the result of Vichy's highly ambitious effort to inculpate its precursors collectively as not only politically wrong but criminal. This in turn was the result of the very sincerity of the beliefs of Vichy's leaders that their Popular Front precursors had engaged in policies that were not deliberately intended to undermine the nation but that nonetheless led to the defeat. Vichy consequently redefined treason to include negligence – that is, bad policies – in addition to deliberate assaults on the nation's interests. Those who formed Vichy's legal policies sincerely believed that its political trials were not political at all, and, in fact, that it was the victims of these trials who were guilty of placing party politics above the commonweal. It was this sincerity that led to the extraordinarily ambitious venture that was Riom, which was intended to demonstrate to the French that their new leaders relied on objective means like the law rather than on political sloganeering.

This ambition made Riom a venture unprecedented in French history. No previous regime had ever attempted to try its precursors as a group; indeed, since Louis XVI, every successive deposed ruler had departed into exile without trial. The Fourth Republic would copy Vichy's efforts to secure a judicial condemnation of the previous regime, but prominent Vichyites like Pétain, Pierre Laval and their subordinates were tried as individuals (albeit before a court set up specifically to try all Vichy-era Ministers and State Secretaries). They were, moreover, generally accused of offenses well-established in the legal codes, even if the punishment of *indignité nationale* was a novel one.

Even outside France, it is difficult to find precedents that match Riom. The Bolsheviks did not feel the need to try their hated precursors Alexander Kerensky and Pavel Miliukov together (or at all); the Nazis, after one abortive experiment (the Dimitrov Trial), sought to kill rather than try their precursors. The Spanish dictator Francisco Franco's Bellón Commission,[6] which sought to demonstrate the illegitimacy of the Second Spanish Republic that preceded him, and his

6 Julius Ruiz, *Franco's Justice: Repression in Madrid after the Spanish Civil War* (Oxford: Oxford University Press, 2005).

Causa General, which tried many rank-and-file Republicans, formed the only close precedents in recent European history. Franco, however, made no attempt to hide the military nature of his rule, and the *Causa General* was an openly military tribunal. Moreover, much of the Republican political leadership, including Lluìs Companys, the president of Catalonia, and Manuel Azaña, the last president of the Second Republic, had already succeeded in fleeing abroad after the civil war. In its scope and ambition, therefore, the Riom trial broke new ground.

Nor was the legal theory of the Riom trial directly comparable to those of the more famous show trials that preceded it. Rather, it stood totalitarian legal theories on their heads. The Soviet show trials of the *Yezhovshchina* or purge era, 1936–8, were part of the Stalinist government's mid-1930s reversion towards more conventional norms, including what had previously been denounced as bourgeois legality. Even so, they were openly political in a way that Vichy could never have adopted.

In a curious way, however, this hyperpoliticism approached Vichy's apoliticism from the opposite side. The Stalinist effort to produce a total politics – that is, the politicization of all areas of society – and the Vichyite effort to remove politics from society both ultimately stifled democratic debate. The Stalinist prosecutor Nikolai Yezhov's efforts to show that opponents were "historically" rather than factually wrong paralleled Vichy's efforts to establish a definition of treason that focused on consequences rather than intent. Both the USSR and Vichy saw the historical process as determined by abstract factors that could and should be predicted by historical actors who, whatever their intentions, were criminal if they failed to understand what was to come. Both consequently reduced the political sphere, the sphere of legitimate debate, to something radically smaller than exists in functional democracies.

Similarly, the goals of transitional justice, of the Nuremberg Trial and of the post-1989 lustration trials (that is, trials of the members of the fallen Communist regimes) in Eastern Europe, appear at Riom as if in a mirror image. Traditional studies of transitional justice[7] focus on the transition from dictatorship to democracy. The Riom Trial, in contrast, aimed at demonstrating that a certain set of policies were the only correct ones – at subtracting democratic discussion from national debate. This book will demonstrate that in the eyes of the Riom magistrates, as well as in those of the government, the newly established *Cour Suprême* would be nothing less than a replacement for the indefinitely suspend-

7 Jon Elster, *Closing the Books: Transitional Justice in Historical Perspective* (Cambridge: Cambridge University Press, 2004).

ed Parliament in terms of the ability to assess the validity of the policies conducted by the executive. Riom did not cause the break with the pluralistic past, but it was an important element of the government's program for executing the break, and it consequently reveals with unusual lucidity the goals that cause the break. As a performative event designed to demonstrate a break with a past regime, Riom should be considered one of the first transitional justice trials, and one whose concerns prefigured those of the better-known *épuration* or purge trials of the Vichy leaders themselves.

In emphasizing the continuity between transitional justice trials during and after the Second World War, this book stands in a long tradition of historiography[8] of continuities between the Vichy and Republican years, while also providing a mechanism (the disruption of the national community) to explain how these continuities took on a much more vicious form during the Vichy years. This historiography of continuity first emerged in response to the so-called "parenthesis" argument – the idea that Vichy constituted a parenthesis imposed from abroad and without foundation in French society.

The parenthesis argument was originally a deliberate Gaullist misinterpretation of the Vichy years as constituting an excrescence without legitimacy or antecedents in French history. This initial argument was essentially a legal rather than a historical one. During the war itself, the Gaullist legal scholar René Cassin denounced the legality of the pivotal transfer of powers to Pétain on three grounds. Firstly, Vichy was the outcome of a conspiracy which had been prepared for years before the war (a simplistic view of Vichy's origins, but an extremely common one at the time). Secondly, with the German troops advancing on Bordeaux, the deputies were incapable of making a free and reasoned decision (and many deputies were not present). Thirdly and most importantly, parliament did not have the power to abolish the Republic.[9] This argument was always rather dubious, since, if the Vichy government lacked the legitimacy of democratic continuity, the Gaullist administration in London was even more precariously based. In the immediate aftermath of the war, however, the argument had the considerable advantage of enabling a national reconciliation of sorts, and sweeping under the carpet a disreputable episode in French history. It coexisted with a violently opposed but similarly comforting apologia, the "shield" argument, according to which Vichy's primary motivation had been to guard the

8 The best summary of changing French attitudes towards the history of Vichy is Henry Rousso's famous four-part chronology in Henry Rousso, *Le Syndrome de Vichy: De 1944 à Nos Jours* (Paris: Points, 1990).

9 Marc Agi, *René Cassin, Prix Nobel de la Paix, 1887–1976: Père de la Déclaration Universelle des Droits de l'Homme* (Paris: Perrin, 1998), 133–134.

French against the worst aspects of the occupation. Vichy had thus been a knowing or unknowing counterpart to De Gaulle in London, France's "sword."

In the 1970s and 1980s, public interest in Vichy revived in the wake of a series of landmark works on the subject, especially Robert Paxton's *Vichy France: Old Guard and New Order,*[10] and of the release of Marcel Ophuls' documentary *Le Chagrin et la Pitié*, made in 1969 but not released until the election of François Mitterrand, the Fifth Republic's first Socialist president, in 1981. The following decades saw an explosion of interest in Vichy so dramatic that the historian Henry Rousso aptly called it a "syndrome."[11] Paxton's initial suggestion that the majority of the French supported the new authoritarian regime was quickly refined by John Sweets, who pointed out the difference between supporting Pétain and supporting Vichy.[12] At the same time, however, a wave of new historiography on the interwar period suggested that the era was marked by the development of a distinctively French Fascism,[13] and even suggested that this fascism was primarily a phenemenon of a certain section of the French Left.[14] A new picture of the French people in the wartime years emerged, stressing a quiescent[15] attitude in which the primary form of "resistance" was merely a consensus that it was necessary to be rude to the Germans[16] in much the manner suggested by Vercors (Jean Bruller)'s famous resistance novel *Le Silence de la Mer,*[17] in which a French family refuses to speak to the apparently sympathetic German soldier billeted upon them. One British historian, Robert Gildea, went so far as to suggest that not only did the French retreat into the selfishness and materialism of the *Système D* during the war years, but that resistance might not even have been the correct solution, given its general ineffectiveness and the propensity of the

10 Robert Paxton, *Vichy France: Old Guard and New Order, 1940–1944* (New York: Columbia University Press, 2001). See also Henri Michel, *Vichy, Année 40* (Paris: R. Laffont, 1966), and Eberhard Jäckel, *La France Dans L'Europe De Hitler*, trans. Denise Meunier (Paris: Fayard, 1968). There is an excellent summary of this generation of historiography in Jean-Pierre Azéma, "Vichy et la Mémoire Savante," Jean-Pierre Azéma and François Bédarida, *Vichy et les Français* (Paris: Fayard, 1992).

11 Rousso, *Syndrome Vichy.*

12 John F. Sweets, *Choices in Vichy France: The French under Nazi Occupation* (Oxford: Oxford University Press, 1986).

13 Zeev Sternhell, *Ni Droite ni Gauche: L'Idéologie Fasciste en France.* (Paris: Éditions du Seuil, 1983); Robert Soucy, *French Fascism: The First Wave, 1924–1933* (New Haven; London: Yale University Press, 1986); Robert Soucy, *French Fascism: The Second Wave, 1933–1939* (New Haven; London: Yale University Press, 1995).

14 Philippe Burrin, *La Dérive Fasciste: Doriot, Déat, Bergery: 1933–1945* (Paris: Seuil, 1986).

15 Pierre Laborie, *L'Opinion Française sous Vichy.*

16 Philippe Burrin, *La France à l'Heure Allemande: 1940–1944* (Paris: Seuil, 1995).

17 Vercors, *Le Silence de la Mer* (London: Les Éditions de Minuit, 1942).

Germans for shooting hostages.[18] Another suggested that even the French who exiled themselves to Britain during the war tended towards *maréchalisme*, or personal support for Pétain but not his policies.[19] Meanwhile, public perceptions of France's conduct during the war, which in the 1960s and 1970s had lagged behind the developing historical consensus, now began to outpace it. Scurrilous[20] books circulated that rehearsed the divisions in the Resistance itself[21] and suggested that icons of the Resistance such as Jean Moulin and Raymond and Lucie Aubrac had in fact been traitors,[22] prompting a debate among historians on the relationship between journalism and history.[23]

As historians and public alike became more cynical regarding claims that the country "resisted," suggestions of continuity between the Third Republic and Vichy (and even between Vichy and the Fourth Republic[24]) became more and more common. (This is not to suggest that such suggestions were new. Indeed, one of the most striking features of the historiography of Vichy is the way it has kept recycling arguments about responsibility for the dictatorship or for the French defeat that originated as interwar arguments about the correct direction for the country.[25]) Historians increasingly discovered the roots even of Vichy's most problematic elements in the Third Republic. Michael Marrus and Robert Paxton suggested that Vichy's antisemitism was already present in abun-

18 Robert Gildea, *Marianne in Chains: Daily Life in the Heart of France during the German Occupation* (New York: Picador, 2004).
19 Nicholas Atkin, *The Forgotten French: Exiles in the British Isles, 1940–44* (Manchester University Press, 2003).
20 For more accurate appraisals of Moulin, see Alan Clinton, *Jean Moulin, 1899–1943: The French Resistance and the Republic* (Houndmills, Basingstoke: Palgrave, 2002), and François Bédarida, Jean-Pierre Azéma, and Daniel Cordier, *Jean Moulin et le Conseil National de la Résistance: Journée d'Études sur le Conseil National de la Résistance, Sorbonne, 9. Juin 1983* (Paris: Centre Nationale de la Recherche Scientifique, 1983).
21 See, for example, the idiosyncratic resistance activist Henri Frenay's effort to paint Moulin as a Communist fellow traveler in Henri Frenay, *L'Énigme Jean Moulin* (Paris: R. Laffont, 1977).
22 For an extensive discussion of these rumors, see Eric Conan and Henry Rousso, *Vichy: An Ever-Present Past* (Hanover: University Press of New England, 1998).
23 *Ibid*; Gérard Noiriel, *Les Origines Républicaines de Vichy* (Paris: Hachette, 1999).
24 E.g., Julian Jackson, "Mal embarqué bien arrivé: The Strange Story of François Perroux," in Hanna Diamond and Simon Kitson, *Vichy, Resistance, Liberation: New Perspectives on Wartime France* (Oxford: Berg, 2005).
25 Compare, for example, Duroselle's praise for the notion of republican efficiency in Jean-Baptiste Duroselle, *France and the Nazi Threat: The Collapse of French Diplomacy, 1932–1939* (New York, NY: Enigma, 2004), with André Tardieu's contemporary arguments: François Monnet, *Refaire la République: André Tardieu, une Dérive Réactionnaire (1876–1945)* (Paris: Fayard, 1993).

dance in the prewar years,[26] while historians of women have shown that the regime's legitimating ideas of social order drew on longstanding notions of gender difference.[27] The longstanding notion of French interwar "decadence"[28] has thus expanded in the domestic sphere even as it has increasingly come under attack as an explanation for the military defeat.[29]

The old differentiation between the "good French," who held respectable antifascist views in the interwar period that would later form the basis of their resistance activity, and the minority of "bad French," who had always been defeatist and probably pro-German, is no longer tenable. Michel Winock is in a minority in contrasting positive, "open" nationalism with negative, "closed" nationalism.[30] The leading work on French antifascism has found little connection between antifascism and resistance,[31] while the leading work on religious groups in wartime France – once seen as a primary basis of support for the regime – has suggested that the role of the churches, after an initial rallying to Pétain, was essentially a positive one.[32] Examples could be multiplied indefinitely.[33]

This book does not seek to overturn the hypothesis of continuity between the Third Republic and Vichy, but, building on the breakdown of the differentiation between "good" and "bad French," it does seek to refine it. Rather than suggesting that the defeat tilted France down one of multiple routes already embedded

---

26 Michael R. Marrus and Robert O. Paxton, *Vichy France and the Jews* (New York: Basic Books, 1981).

27 Miranda Pollard, *Reign of Virtue: Mobilizing Gender in Vichy France* (Chicago, IL: University of Chicago Press, 1998); Francine Muel-Dreyfus, *Vichy and the Eternal Feminine: A Contribution to a Political Sociology of Gender*, trans. Kathleen A. Johnson (Durham: Duke University Press, 2001).

28 The term is Duroselle's. Jean-Baptiste Duroselle, *La Décadence, 1932–1939* (Paris: Imprimerie Nationale, 1979).

29 Occasionally this contrast is explicit, as in William Irvine, "Domestic Politics and the Fall of France in 1940," in Joel Blatt, *The French Defeat of 1940: Reassessments* (New York: Berghahn, 2006).

30 Michel Winock, *Nationalism, Anti-semitism, and Fascism in France*, trans. Jane Marie Todd (Stanford, CA: Stanford University Press, 2000).

31 Gilles Vergnon, *L'Antifascisme en France de Mussolini à Le Pen* (Rennes: Presses Universitaires de Rennes, 2009).

32 W. D. Halls, *Politics, Society and Christianity in Vichy France* (Oxford: Berg, 1995).

33 This notion that prewar politics did not determine wartime action should be differentiated from the older "immunity thesis" of French politics, which argued that the country was temperamentally opposed to Fascism (and, by extension, that Vichy was indeed a "parenthesis"). See the works by Soucy and Sternhell cited above, which attacked this thesis, as well as the excellent review of the literature on the "immunity thesis" in Chris Millington, *From Victory to Vichy: Veterans in Inter-war France* (Manchester: Manchester University Press, 2012).

in its political discourse, we will argue that the defeat destroyed French pluralism. Although those responsible for Vichy's political trials were already predisposed towards the kind of militant apoliticism that the trials exemplified, it was the defeat itself that gave their views such an anti-pluralistic cast that it became impossible for them to consider their opponents as part of the political nation. When one's opponents were seen not merely as misguided but as responsible for one of the greatest catastrophes a great nation has ever endured, it was no longer possible for different political forces to coexist without violence. We will show that support for a trial of those deemed responsible for the defeat was near-universal in 1940, and that this support was incompatible with the basic democratic principle of a loyal opposition. Vichy represented, not one possible path for the nation, but the *end* of the unitary nation and the beginning of a cold civil war.

The central importance of 1940 can be seen with particular clarity in an idea that was absent from the trial: the idea of natural law, which seems like a natural match for the trials' apoliticism because it posits the notion that there are natural rights that supersede the deliberations of governments. Although the individuals whose work inspired the formation of the *Cour Suprême* had previously envisioned legal reform that would give France an equivalent to the US Bill of Rights, including an explicit reference to the sanctity of property rights, they did not attempt to prosecute the Popular Frontists for having nationalized industries or even for having declared a "vacation of legality" during the sit-down strikes of 1936. They accepted that these matters were legitimately political and could not be monitored by courts. Indeed, the fact that the French legal system of 1940–1944 was more biased towards positivistic conceptions of law (which imply that any legislation passed by a legitimate government is also legitimate) than towards naturalistic conceptions of law has frequently been blamed for French magistrates' willingness to enforce antisemitic legislation.[34] Vichy's politics of apoliticism expressed itself not in a blanket attack on the socialism of the Popular Front, but in a specific attempt to show that socialist policies were responsible for the catastrophe of 1940.

To hold the Popular Front Prime Minister Léon Blum responsible for the defeat, although probably incorrect,[35] was at least a somewhat reasonable position

34 See, e.g., Alain Bancaud, *Une Exception Ordinaire: La Magistrature en France, 1930–1950* (Paris: Gallimard, 2002). For a contrasting view that questions the relevance of the positivistic/naturalistic distinction, see Liora Israël, *Robes Noires, Années Sombres: Avocats Et Magistrats En Résistance Pendant La Seconde Guerre Mondiale* (Paris: Fayard, 2005).

35 The consensus of most of the historiography on the defeat is that the Popular Front reforms were not responsible. See Robert Frank, *Le Prix du Réarmement Français: 1935–1939* (Paris: Pub-

to hold. To put him on trial was a different matter. In 1995, the author of one of the most respected biographies of Pétain, Guy Pedroncini, could still reiterate (quoting Pierre Massé) one of the main assertions of the Riom Trial: "The forty-hour week was a bad response to Hitlerian rearmament."[36] The problem with Riom was not that it made this accusation, but that, by making it in a juridical setting, it turned it into an accusation of treason. Yet treason was also what the opposition to Vichy thought had occurred. The difference was only in the choice of suspects, and it is still far from certain that Vichy was historiographically wrong in some of its choices – choosing to blame politicians rather than generals, for example.[37]

Vichy's desire to transfer authority from politicians to courts can be seen in the structure of the new institutions it created, which were a supplement and extension of the existing legal system rather than a replacement for it. Prior to 1940, the French court system was composed of three main branches. The first two, headed by the *Conseil d'État* and the *Cour de Cassation*, handled administrative and ordinary law respectively. In addition, there was a third, less regularly-convoked branch: the *Haute Cour*, which handled political justice, such as prosecutions of current and former ministers. The *Haute Cour* was not a regular court, but Parliament sitting as a judicial organ – the equivalent of the US Congress's role in the impeachment process. Vichy's new *Cour Suprême* was a body, drawn heavily from current and former judges, that replaced the *Haute Cour* in the judicial process. It therefore represented, not an expansion of the political justice system, but the incursion of the regular court system into the political justice process.

Two other bodies would also have an impact on the trials discussed in this book. One, the *Conseil de Justice Politique*, was an ad-hoc body convened in 1941 under German pressure in an effort to hasten, but not supplant, the *Cour Suprême*. This led to the odd spectacle of the *Cour Suprême*, when it finally embarked on the Riom trial in 1942, presiding over defendants who had already been sentenced by the *Conseil*. The *Conseil* was an openly political body, but, as we will see in later chapters, it was also highly unrepresentative of Vichy's general conception of the justice system.

---

lications de la Sorbonne, 1982), as well as the literature on the Riom Trial, especially Henri Michel, *Le Procès de Riom* (Paris: Michel, 1979), and Frédéric Pottecher, *Le Procès de la Défaite: Riom, Février – Avril 1942* (Paris: Fayard, 1990). For a less sympathetic view, however, see *Richard Vinen, The Politics of French Business: 1936–1945* (Cambridge: Cambridge University Press, 1991).

36 Guy Pedroncini, *Pétain: La Victoire Perdue (1919–1940)* (Paris: Perrin, 1995), 9.

37 *Ibid, passim.*

Finally, the third major judicial organ discussed in this book was the military tribunal of Clermont-Ferrand. Institutions that had already existed under the Republic, France's military tribunals were designed to preside over trials that concerned issues of military justice, such as, in this case, desertion. The only political figures sentenced by the military tribunal of Clermont-Ferrand were young parliamentarians who had waived their parliamentary immunity to conscription in 1939 in order to volunteer for the front, but who had rushed to Bordeaux during the military collapse of 1940 in order to take part in the parliamentary debates that ultimately ended the Republic, and who then headed to French Morocco aboard the *Massilia* in order to continue the French war effort there. As military officers, they were vulnerable to charges of abandoning their post; but, as parliamentarians who had elected to leave France on the *Massilia*, they could also have been targeted with political charges. Vichy's decision to use the preexisting system of military tribunals to try them was therefore, once again, an example of the extension of the regular justice system into the sphere of political justice.

The individuals who created this judicializion of politics were convinced even before the war that opposition to their ideas was objectively wrong; and they had never had much support for the idea of politics. Yet, until 1940, they had continued to support a democratic and humanistic framework, whereas, after the defeat, politics became treason. On both sides of the political spectrum, the events of May-June 1940 led to an immediate reappraisal of the consequences of political disagreement and to the disappearance of the concept of a loyal opposition.

Democracies have survived without loyal oppositions. The case of Italy after Aldo Moro's cooptation of the Socialists comes to mind; for some twenty years, the main parliamentary opposition was the Communist Party, with which, at the height of the Cold War, few politicians were prepared to negotiate. No democracy, however, has ever been able to withstand a situation in which there was a general consensus – and this consensus was indeed general, held by opponents of Vichy's trials as well as by supporters of them – that its opponents' policies, even if they were not deliberately aimed at helping a national enemy, were nonetheless so obviously bad for the country that a neutral court could easily find enough evidence to convict them of treason. It was this judicialization of politics that constituted one of the main constitutive elements of the new post-democratic regime.

That the regime sought to put its opponents in jail is unsurprising. It was, after all, a dictatorship; and it is a defining element of dictatorships that they do not allow their opponents to criticize them unmolested. What is unusual about Vichy's persecution of its political opponents in its first two years was the consistency of its efforts to find a legal fig-leaf for their imprisonment. It would have been easy for Vichy to criminalize opinions with retroactive effect, or even simply to imprison those it disliked without bothering with a trial; the latter is, after all, what ultimately happened to several of the individuals this book will discuss. If the regime shrank from such measures, it would also have had the option to keep individuals considered dangerous under house arrest, and to restrict their access to the press. This was the ultimate fate of the former Popular Front Finance Minister Vincent Auriol, for example, before he escaped to England. Instead, however, the regime chose to seek to legitimate itself through what appeared outwardly to have some characteristics of a fair trial. That is why the regime made the otherwise almost unbelievable blunder of giving orators of the quality of Daladier, known as the "bull of Vaucluse" for his rhetorical vehemence, their day in court.

Vichy was, as Stanley Hoffman has argued,[38] a revenge on the men of 1936. Like Alexander in Dryden's poem, Vichy was remarkably fond of fighting all its battles o'er again. It was not, however, a mere changing of the political guard, but a reshaping of French politics towards a new model that would replace the perceived disorder and venality of parliamentary politics with the rigid obedience of hierarchy. It was an authoritarianism of the middle ground, one which would seek to appeal to the *juste milieu* of French society by reassuring it that their opponents were not merely wrong but traitors.

All regimes, regardless of political complexion, necessarily engage in some form of legal exclusion from the political arena. What made Vichy a dictatorship was the very abruptness and unexpectedness of the defeat, which enabled a large section of the political nation – who, as we shall argue, held very similar views to Vichy's regarding the nature of the political arena – to be suddenly excluded from it. If Blum had always been a leader of the opposition, there would have been no need to try him, just as Alcide De Gasperi's monolithically Christian Democratic postwar Italy only descended into political violence when it seemed that there was a real chance that the Communists would take office. It is worth remembering that even McCarthyism was the direct product of a military defeat, the most severe that America ever suffered in the course of the Cold War. That was, of course, the loss of China, which Republicans saw as an opportunity to differentiate themselves from the Democrats after a failure to offer clearly distinct policy alternatives cost them the 1948 election. The loss of China was, of

38 Stanley Hoffmann, "Aspects du Régime de Vichy," *Revue Française de Science Politique* 6, no. 1 (1956).

course, a much less severe defeat than the fall of the Maginot Line; and McCarthyism was far less dictatorial than the National Revolution.

What we are suggesting, then, is that Vichy's slide into dictatorship was the product of the abrupt and unforeseeable fracturing of the political community. Even those who differed from Vichy held similarly anti-pluralist conceptions of justice when it came to assigning responsibility for the national disaster. As we will see repeatedly throughout this book, Vichy represented a breach *within* a national reformist consensus. Other reformers also believed themselves to be absolutely, juridically correct, albeit with far fewer pernicious consequences.

The flaw in this reformist consensus, then, was the belief that there existed somewhere in France an abstract Nation, with objectively determined demands and needs, and that this Nation's government could rationally be arranged by a group of persons of good will and foresight. This problem with this analysis, of course, was the supposition that such a group of objective technocrats existed, or rather Vichy's own failure to understand that their own set of beliefs were political views and not objective truths. One is reminded of François Furet's famous argument that the violence of the French Revolution stemmed from the difficulty of reconciling the abstract and unitary nation with a specific body of representatives, with the result that numerous different groups could sincerely believe that they were the one and only representatives of the true France and that all competing groups were traitors. Furet, however, was following the legacy of Alexis de Tocqueville, who had contrasted French democracy (which was unstable because it was based on absolutism and the notion of the unitary nation) with Anglo-American democracy (which was stable because it was based on liberalism and the notion of the federal state). We will argue, however, that such an interpretation cannot explain the Riom trial. Not only was the *Cour Suprême* that presided over that trial modeled in part on the US Supreme Court, but the primary ideologue behind the trial, the journalist, historian and economist Lucien Romier, was in part inspired precisely by the desire to imitate what he saw as the best parts of Anglo-American political practice.

Romier saw in American politics a kind of anti-ideological ideology, which rejected specific doctrines while affording religion a prominent place in public life. This in turn appealed to Romier's anti-doctrinal brand of Catholicism, which sought to heal the traditional breach between religion and modernity. Throughout the nineteenth century, mainstream French Catholicism had been anti-Republican, having deemed the French Revolution's Civil Constitution of the Clergy (which confiscated church property and turned the clergy into state employees) an intolerable affront. This, indeed, was the attitude of the Catholic Church in general, epitomized by Pope Pius IX's 1864 Syllabus of Errors, which denounced the evils of modernity root and branch.

Yet there had always been another, more moderate strain in French Catholicism, epitomized by the quiet majority of priests who agreed to abide by the Civil Constitution. The rationalism of St Thomas Aquinas never ceased to be the official ideology of the Catholic church, and it provided an alternative Catholic model for individuals interested in the derivation of the idea of individual rights from natural law. Another alternative model was Germany's Center Party, which had little choice but to stand up for minority rights since Catholics in Otto von Bismarck's Germany were themselves an oppressed minority. After 1900, this branch of French Catholic thought increasingly gained ground, inspired by the non-practicing Catholic Charles Péguy. Although he died in 1914, Péguy's thought came to incarnate the First World War spirit of "sacred union" and of placing nation over politics.

During the interwar period, the ideology of liberal Catholicism was further buttressed by a social element. Charity had, of course, always been part of Catholic thought, but from the 1920s on, the Catholic philosopher Emmanuel Mounier created a new ideology of social Catholicism called Personalism. Personalism, which differentiated itself from both the collectivism of socialist thought and the impersonal nature of bourgeois society, sought to provide a distinctively Christian basis for individual rights. As with so many aspects of French political thought, personalism had an ambiguous relationship with Vichy; but Mounier himself welcomed the new order,[39] and was welcomed by it to the extent of being offered a post at Vichy's training academy at Uriage.[40] The moderate strain of French Catholicism would find its full voice after the Second World War in the form of the new *Mouvement Républicain Populaire* (MRP), France's equivalent of the many Christian Democratic movements that dominated postwar politics across western Europe. The MRP never attained the outright dominance Christian Democrats enjoyed in postwar Germany or Italy, and its influence, already in decline during the late Fourth Republic, received a sharp blow in 1958 with the creation of the Fifth Republic. Thereafter, Gaullism became the dominant force on the French democratic right. Nonetheless, the MRP, which at its peak after the 1946 election was the largest French political party, must be considered a fundamental part of France's postwar democratic stabilization.

The appeal of the modern as something that transcended political boundaries between Catholics and Republicans, therefore, was critical to the new Catholicism and, indirectly, to Vichy's political trials. The idea of modernity as a

---

39 Debbie Lackerstein, *National Regeneration in Vichy France: Ideas and Policies, 1930–1944* (Farnham: Ashgate, 2012), 40.

40 John Hellman, *The Knight-Monks of Vichy France: Uriage, 1940–1945* (Montreal: McGill-Queens University Press, 1993), 34.

force that unifies by ignoring its own political nature has been forcefully defended by Bruno Latour in *Nous n'Avons Jamais Étés Modernes* [We Have Never Been Modern].[41] Latour's work centers on an analysis of the modernist project as the creation of the seventeenth-century debate between Thomas Hobbes and Robert Boyle – representing, respectively, the political and the empirical – regarding the sources of knowledge legitimation. Latour describes the resulting hybrid as the modernist "Constitution," which seeks to keep the poles of nature and analysis completely separate while causing the proliferation of a myriad of hybrid categories (including, famously, the hole in the ozone layer) which were both political and scientific. In this sense, the basis of Vichy was a very extreme version of this constitution, in which the "scientific" sphere (economists, whose doctrine of neoliberalism represented absolute scientific truth) was in service to the "social" sphere (men blessed with – in Romier's words – *prévoyance*, or extraordinary foresight).

It is in this sense that we can say that the famous dichotomy between traditionalists and modernizers at Vichy – between *jeunes cyclistes* and *vieux romains,* as Romier himself jocularly put it – is meaningless; for Romier was both, and his Maurassianism (that is, his support for some of the ideas of the influential monarchist and ultra-conservative Charles Maurras) did not conflict with his pursuit of technocracy. The fundamental problem consists in the notion that there was anything innocent about the notion of technocracy in wartime France. Adam Tooze has demonstrated[42] that there was no real ideological distinction in the Nazi regime between Albert Speer and Heinrich Himmler, the technocrat and the ideologue; both were engaged in sometimes separate but always complementary efforts to keep Germany in an unwinnable war for as long as possible. A similar argument can be made for France, since the fundamental Latourian problem of the Modernist Constitution was the same everywhere, and the categories of "traditionalists" and "modernizers" equally unilluminating. Speer and Himmler embarked on a purely ideological (or, in Latour's terms, Hobbesian) solution as Romier and his conservative counterpart Raphaël Alibert embarked on a purely technocratic (or Boylean) one. In practice, the two extremes approached one another.

Latour's work is an invaluable aid to understanding the problem that Romier was trying (and failing) to confront. We must, however, go one step further by rejecting the notion that the natural sciences are the only possible source of

---

41 Bruno Latour, *Nous n'Avons Jamais Été Modernes: Essai d'Anthropologie Symétrique* (Paris: La Découverte, 1991).

42 J. Adam Tooze, *The Wages of Destruction: The Making and Breaking of the Nazi Economy* (New York: Penguin Books, 2006), *passim* but especially 552–589.

the kind of technocratic move he describes. Alessandro Pizzorno[43] has suggested that the source of the modern idea of politics is the Gregorian Revolution of the thirteenth century, which, by dramatically expanding the claims of religion over noble and imperial actors, provided a basis for conceptualizing a new sphere of action in order to aspire to which it was necessary to provide a vision fulfilling certain basic requirements. Specifically, this new notion of "absolute politics" required a certain vision of the future beyond the ken of normal foresight ("transcendental knowledge"); control over the law; control of "devotion", or the ultimate ends of society that transcend individual lives; and the ability to designate enemies (i.e. something like the political theorist Carl Schmitt's famous friend-enemy distinction).

In this light, it becomes clear that what the individuals behind the Riom trials were claiming, presumably without being aware of it, is what Pizzorno would call "priestly" control over politics. That is, they was asserting that, because of their superior understanding of the ultimate ends of society (the national interest), provided by a "transcendental knowledge" that enabled them to make predictions about the future of Europe, they had the right to use France's legal structures to designate as enemies individuals who, whether through malice or incompetence, had violated that interest. It was, in Pizzorno's sense, a religious assertion – that is, using the Schmittian transformation (in which modern politics descends from premodern theology), a political one. But it cloaked itself behind a disguise of apoliticism.

It does not greatly matter whether we use the term "technocratic" to describe this assertion, as long as we bear in mind that it was not really "technocratic" in the conventional sense – that is, making claims based on a purely technical knowledge. Rather, it was based on what Pizzorno calls "transcendental knowledge" and Romier called *prévoyance*. If we allow for the extremely porous boundaries of academia in Romier's time, it might be called a technocratic theory based on the social rather than the natural sciences. In political terms, it might be called a right-wing version of James Scott's "high modernism,"[44] divorced from its characteristic faith in progress.

It might be argued that we are splitting hairs here, and that, since what Romier was doing was quite clearly political whether he realized it or not, there is no useful difference to be found between "hyperpolitical" dictatorships like Maoist

---

43 Alessandro Pizzorno, "Politics Unbound," in Charles S. Maier, *Changing Boundaries of the Political: Essays on the Evolving Balance between the State and Society, Public and Private in Europe* (Cambridge: Cambridge University Press, 1987), 27–62.

44 James C. Scott, *Seeing like a State: How Certain Schemes to Improve the Human Condition Have Failed* (New Haven, CT: Yale University Press, 1998).

China or Pol Pot's Cambodia (both of which preferred the ideological to the technical, and, indeed, openly persecuted intellectuals on a massive scale) and "hypopolitical" dictatorships like Vichy (which sincerely believed themselves to be upholding the basic nature of economic reality against invidious socialist fictions whose partial implementation had caused the sensational collapse of 1940). There is a great deal of truth to this claim; but it is not the whole truth. For all of its antisemitism and violence, Vichy France was not Nazi Germany, and the reason for this stemmed directly from its hypopolitical nature. Vichy held an open trial at Riom in large part because Romier demanded it, and Romier demanded it because he knew that Vichy's claim to legitimacy was predicated on proving that their path was the only path. In other words, the regime's claim to uphold the rule of law mattered even when it was more honored in the breach than the observance.

While Riom – and therefore that claim to legality – did not in itself lead to the downfall of Vichy, it nonetheless provides an excellent example of the regime's internal conflicts. Moreover, it led directly to the dismissal of François Darlan, the return of Laval, and the relative sidelining of Pétain and his circle (including Romier). Over the past forty years, there has been a backlash against the notion that Laval represented a fundamentally different face of Vichy than Pétain did. In a practical sense, it is certainly true that there was little to choose between them. But if Laval was merely a different set of clothes over the same body, it was nonetheless the difference between a gaudy robe and a set of rags. It was a difference that mattered to public opinion at the time.

The National Revolution ended in 1942 for many reasons other than Riom. The occupation of the Unoccupied Zone, the loss of France's colonies, and the fact that it was growing increasingly obvious that the regime had backed the wrong horse in the global war were all of greater significance in Vichy's loss of popularity. Riom, however, represented the end of an experiment. Thereafter, the regime turned increasingly to open repression to maintain itself. Even without the Liberation, it seems implausible that the Vichy of the *Milice* could have survived indefinitely.

In *On Violence*,[45] Hannah Arendt makes a useful distinction between power, which implies mass (albeit not necessarily majority or even plurality) support, and violence, a strictly physical concept implying the use of the technical means of destruction. Most of the literature on Vichy France acknowledges that, at some point between Pétain's *vent mauvais* (ill wind) speech of 1941

---

45 Hannah Arendt, *On Violence* (New York: Harcourt, 1970), chap. 2. This distinction can be found in many of Arendt's works.

and the beginning of the STO (*Service du Travail Obligatoire*, or forced labor) in 1943, a transition took place that can be summarized in Arendt's language as a shift from government based on power to government based on violence.

None of this, of course, is intended to apologize for Vichy's brutality, which was extraordinary even in its early years. Rather, it is intended to explain the ideology, or anti-ideology, that motivated the brutality. Hypopolitical regimes can also commit inhuman acts of violence; consider imperial regimes, which frequently displayed a similar antipathy to "playing politics." In colonial Zambia, for example, the British government reacted to Jehovah's Witnesses they suspected of anticolonial sentiment by denouncing them for playing politics.[46]

There has been a longstanding tendency to separate out the technocratic and the political elements of Vichy, and to apologize for certain aspects of the regime with the suggestion that they were "apolitical" or "technocratic." Julian Jackson, for example, has summarized the *Redressement Français* leader Ernest Mercier's politics as merely "a pious hope that disinterested men of goodwill would unite around his ideas."[47] This pious hope, however, led to juridical violence. When the 1994 verdict against the collaborationist Paul Touvier found that Vichy had no "precise ideology" but only a "constellation of good sentiments,"[48] it was missing the point: it was precisely the notion that "good sentiments" were different from "ideology" that was the problem. All democracies, and indeed all societies, have areas of thought regarding which genuine bipartisan consensus can exist; but the *claim* to nonpartisanship is inherently anti-pluralistic, for, if the concept in question were genuinely subject to a resolution that would not exclude a substantial segment of public opinion, there would be no reason even to make such a claim in the first place.

Indeed, if there is any lesson to be drawn from the profoundly unedifying story of Vichyite apoliticism, perhaps it is simply that the abnegation of politics can produce results almost as bad as a deliberate commitment to stamping out the beliefs of others. The alternative to radicalism is not withdrawal to an imagined technical sphere, but a more extensive pluralism. To an American today, as we survey our polarized and gridlocked institutions – so similar in their difficulties to those of the Third Republic – it is a thought in equal measure comforting

---

46 Karen Elise Fields, *Revival and Rebellion in Colonial Central Africa* (Princeton, NJ: Princeton University Press, 1985), 207.

47 Jackson, *France: The Dark Years*, 53.

48 Robert Gildea, *France since 1945* (Oxford: Oxford University Press, 1996), 74.

and disturbing to reflect that this may simply be what real democracy looks like when it seeks to express the wishes of a divided people.

* * *

Although there have been four monographs on the Riom Trial,[49] in addition to numerous articles[50] and works that touched on the subject, most of these works drew primarily or exclusively on published sources and the trial transcript. The most scholarly of these works was also the first; André Michel's 1979 *Procès de Riom* added to the above-mentioned sources a number of other procedural records collected at the time by the Ministry of Justice. These records, which Michel himself played a large role in converting into archival form, can be found in cartons BB30/1718 and BB30/1719 at the *Archives Nationales*. To Michel's work and the subsequent and less scholarly works on the trial must be added the 1973 *Procès de Riom* by Christiane Rimbaud and Pierre Béteille.[51] As Beteille was himself a prominent magistrate who had served at Riom as a clerk (*greffier*),[52] this book should be considered in part a primary source.

The major methodological drawback of these works, questions of interpretation aside, is that they all omitted from consideration a large portion of the sources relevant to the trial. The trial transcript is a highly partial and misleading guide to what happened at Riom, because it omits the first stage of the trial: the *instruction*, a civil-law procedure which involves collecting and sorting evidence for the trial proper. Because the Riom Trial was cut short by its embarrassingly public failure, the vast majority of the witnesses and testimony assembled during the *instruction* do not appear in the trial transcript. Moreover, the witnesses who did appear during the trial, who were virtually all military men, were not representative of those called to testify before the *instruction*, who were a much more diverse body of individuals.

---

49 Michel, *Le Procès de Riom*; Pottecher, *Le Procès de la Défaite*; Elisabeth Bokelmann, *Vichy contra Dritte Republik: Der Prozess von Riom, 1942* (Paderborn: Schöningh, 2006); Jean-Denis Bredin, *L'Infamie: Le Procès de Riom, Février-Avril 1942* (Paris: B. Grasset, 2012). See also Julia Bracher, *Riom 1942: Le Procès* (Paris: Omnibus, 2012), which is primarily a source collection but also contains some secondary work on the trial.

50 See, particularly, Alain Bancaud, "Le procès de Riom: service et renversement de la justice," in Marc Oliver Baruch and Vincent Duclert, eds. *Justice, Politique et République – De l'Affaire Dreyfus à la Guerre D'Algérie* (Brussels: Complexe/IHTP/CNRS, 2002).

51 Pierre Béteille and Christiane Rimbaud, *Le Procès de Riom* (Paris: Plon, 1973).

52 His career was a complex one. See Jacky Tronel, "Pierre Béteille, Un Magistrat Sous Surveillance..," *Histoire Pénitentiaire Et Justice Militaire*, August 28, 2010, accessed September 20, 2018, https://prisons-cherche-midi-mauzac.com/des-hommes/pierre-beteille-un-magistrat-sous-sur veillance-4356.

In order to gain a full idea of what the Riom Trial was supposed to be, therefore, it is necessary to consult the *instruction* records themselves. These are enormously voluminous. The painstaking Daladier, who had himself trained as a lawyer, assembled some fourteen boxes of material related to the trial and its aftermath (Series 486AP, Boxes 36 through 49),[53] the majority of them copies of *instruction* testimonies with annotations by Daladier and his lawyers. Daladier's *chef de cabinet* or first secretary, Roger Genebrier, also collected material relevant to the trial, now collected in the GE series at the *Centre d'Histoire des Sciences Po.* The other defendants were less careful than Daladier in preparing for a trial that for a long time seemed as if it would never come, but the personal papers of Reynaud (Series 74AP, distinguished by a very large number of press clippings), Mandel (544AP), Auriol (552AP), Blum (570AP), Zay (667AP) and Mendès France (Series E1, *Alliance Israélite Universelle*) are also of interest. The papers of Pierre Cot (Series PC, *Archives d'Histoire des Sciences Po*), in contrast, are too abbreviated to be of much use.

Next in importance are the various official archives on the subject of the trial, which Michel in particular exploited in part, but only in part. He was instrumental in assembling Barthélemy's papers on the trial into a series (AN Series 72AJ, Boxes 411 and 412), but made less use of the *Cour Suprême*'s own papers (Series 2W), or of the prosecution records on the Clermont-Ferrand trials, conserved today at the *Archives de Justice Politique* at Le Blanc in Indre under the names of the various defendants (Zay, Mendès France, Vienot and Wiltzer). Pétain's personal cabinet also assembled some sparse documentation on the trial (Series 2AG, Box 522), although, unfortunately, a good deal of the government's deliberations on the matter seem to have been verbal and were not recorded. The postwar trial *in absentia* of Raphaël Alibert, Vichy's first Justice Minister, also garnered some useful material, conserved today in Series 3W, Boxes 46 and 47.

Finally, there is the history of the origins of the trial. The sources for these are, of course, infinite, depending on interpretation; and those with different interpretations of the origins and meaning of the trial might also believe a different source base to be relevant. Since most contemporaries believed that Romier was the main inspiration for the trials, the archival sources examined for this book focused on him. His personal papers are conserved in Series 407AP, and the papers of Henri Cacaud, the secretary of the *Redressement Français* movement of which Romier was the primary ideologue, are also illuminating. (The departmen-

53 All archival series in this passage are from the *Archives Nationales* except where otherwise mentioned.

tal archives of the Puy de Dôme contain material on the Romier family, but none of direct interest for the trial.)

In general, however, the most important material for writing the prehistory of the trial are not archival. Riom was not a direct consequence of the debates of the interwar period, but its nature was nonetheless profoundly shaped by those debates, which were public and therefore largely printed. Much the most illuminating source for Romier's ideas, therefore, is not his personal papers but his voluminous publications, both journalistic and monographic. Of these probably the best-known at the time was his first major non-historical work, *Explication de Notre Temps*, which was published in 1924 and quickly became the bible of a certain kind of conservative reformist.[54]

This is thus a standard archival history in terms of its source base, and the major challenges to writing it were also standard. Even with the new (in fact old, but largely unused) sources I was able to access, there are always others that would have been useful. For example, it would have certainly have been desirable to examine the German sources on the trial had time permitted, although their correspondence with the French (reproduced in Reynaud's personal papers as part of the evidence assembled for the trial of Otto Abetz, the German ambassador to Vichy) gives a good idea of German intentions – which in any case have never been the subject of historiographical controversy. Other sources simply do not exist, such as the minutes of the *Conseil de Justice Politique* that was set up to provide a solution to the issue when it seemed as if the *Cour Suprême* would dawdle indefinitely, or the minutes of the Vichy cabinet itself. Finally, any research question is limited by its nature even before the archival work begins. Because this is a book about trials of Third Republic leaders rather than all political trials under Vichy, it omits the trials of Resistance groups as well as the *in absentia* trials of the individuals, most notably Charles de Gaulle himself, who came to form Free France.

54 For its prominence, see Richard F. Kuisel, *Ernest Mercier: French Technocrat* (Berkeley: University of California Press, 1967), 65.

2 "No other explanation seemed possible"

> No longer was there any "legitimate diversity of opinions." Men condemned each other to death as traitors because they did not see the future in the same way."[1]

It is impossible to escape the centrality of the defeat of 1940 in discussing the origins of Vichy's political trials. Before 1940, the French had opposed or supported the politicians in power for many very different reasons. After 1940, they continued to oppose these individuals for much the same reasons; but the stakes had changed. The result was radicalization of the consequences of opposition; but, as the list of crimes and of criminals was different for different individuals, so was the nature of the trial envisaged. The ideologues of *jamais plus* (never again, i.e., that the First World War should never be repeated) and the admirers of Nazi Germany, for example, both saw the declaration of war as the cardinal sin of the late Third Republic; so they wanted a trial of those responsible for the war. At the same time, however, virtually everyone else who wanted a trial was far more interested in trying those responsible for the defeat. This, moreover, was merely one of many differences of opinion. There were as many potential trials as there were French citizens. The flip side of the coin, however, was that the notion of a trial, in itself, enjoyed remarkably broad support.

Vichy's show trials did not take place in a vacuum. Whereas, for example, the trial of Nikolai Bukharin occurred in a society where the public sphere had been largely eliminated and foreign opinion was a relatively minor cause of concern, Vichy had to deal with a foreign occupier, a reliance on foreign recognition (especially that of the United States) for imports and legitimacy, and a nation accustomed to political participation. The German government had its own views on the trials, or at least on that at Riom, and intervened forcefully at a number of times in the course of the proceedings; for example, its intervention was one of the main factors in the suspension of the Riom trial. This impact, however, appears to have been felt increasingly strongly as the trial developed, rather than being an urgent concern *ab initio*. If the trials had not existed, Germany's later conduct suggests that she would have invented them; but, in the summer of 1940, internal forces were paramount.

There is considerable controversy surrounding the question of how public opinion saw the trials. The conventional view in France's Resistance-dominated postwar historiography was that the trials were an endogenous development

---

1 Maurice Merleau-Ponty, *Humanism and Terror: An Essay on the Communist Problem*, trans. John O'Neill (Boston: Beacon, 1969), 37.

https://doi.org/10.1515/9783110610161-002

within Vichy government circles. This served the double function of undermining the trials' legitimacy while exculpating the public, furthering the Gaullist myth of Vichyite "parenthesis" that a nation of resisters had always opposed. Thus, for example, John Sherwood's 1970 biography of Mandel ascribed the right-wing press campaign of the summer of 1940 to outright government manipulation.[2] Similarly, Mendès France's autobiography acknowledged that the country "had the impression of being poorly defended" and attributed the press campaign to a government effort to divert this impression onto scapegoats.[3]

Examples could be multiplied. In fact, Mendès France's statement pointed towards a sad reality of the summer of 1940. The popularity of the notion of trying those responsible for the defeat was not confined to supporters of the National Revolution, of Vichy, or even of Pétain. Left-wing and Gaullist thinkers also believed that the country had been betrayed – albeit, of course, not by the same groups or individuals. In her memoirs, for example, Simone de Beauvoir explained her initial reaction to the news of the German breakthrough against General André Corap that began the process of military collapse: "Had there been treachery? No other explanation seemed possible."[4] Even in 1960, she still believed that "generals and other notables" had "sabotaged the war because they preferred Hitler to the Popular Front."[5] Similarly, in 1946, Maurice Merleau-Ponty asked of Pétain: "Plot, premeditation, or coincidence?" The rest of the paragraph makes it clear that the signature of the armistice was one of the events that Merleau-Ponty thought might plausibly have been designated as a "plot." Nonetheless, more prudent and more interested in broad social forces than Beauvoir, he finally decided that Pétain was probably guilty only of being formed by his military and "pre-Fascist" prewar environment, rather than of deliberate treason. For him, however, treason-by-incompetence was treason enough.[6]

Merleau-Ponty, writing in defense of the postwar *Épuration* (purge) trials of former Vichyites, had in fact arrived at Vichy's legal theory via the back door:

2 John M. Sherwood, *Georges Mandel and the Third Republic* (Stanford: Stanford University Press, 1970), 266.

3 Pierre Mendès–France, *Liberté, Liberté Chérie (1940–1942): Suivi de Roissy-en-France: Recit d'un Vol du Groupe Lorraine (3 Octobre 1945)* (Paris: Fayard, 1977), 76. Translations of primary sources are mine except where otherwise indicated.

4 Simone de Beauvoir, *The Prime of Life*, trans. Peter Green (Cleveland: World Publishing Company, 1962), 347.

5 *Ibid.*, 370. The slogan "Better Hitler than Blum" was frequently alleged to be current on the French Right.

6 Maurice Merleau-Ponty, *Sense and Non-Sense*, trans. Patricia Dreyfus and Hubert Dreyfus (Evanston, IL: Northwestern University Press, 1964), 111.

like Vichy (and Stalin), he had thrown out the notion of *mens rea* (criminal intent) in favor of what the Vichy *réquisitoire* (list of charges) had called *impéritie* (negligence). In this, however, he was in a distinct minority. Beauvoir's attitude, while more naïve, was also more typical. The result was that the postwar *épuration* trials – like some of Vichy's own lesser trials – tended to rest more on refutable claims of peculation and venality, as well as on the traditional definition of treason as cooperation with the enemy, than on vast philosophical notions of being on the wrong side of History.

If most people in 1940 wanted a trial of some kind, therefore, they nonetheless disagreed sharply regarding the question of who was to be tried. De Gaulle, speaking on 9 September 1940, reacted to the wave of arrests then in progress by acknowledging that the idea of a trial to determine responsibility for the defeat was popular. "It is understandable that public opinion wants punishments," he admitted, but the fact that the trial seemed to have been arranged with a view to determining responsibility for the war rather than for the defeat was unacceptable: "For the self-proclaimed governesses at Vichy, acting under Hitler-the-chambermaid and Mussolini's whip, it is a matter of making [the public] believe that France was wrong to enter the war and that those who led her to it must be punished," he thundered. The government's real motive, in his view, was to cover the guilt of surrender by pretending that the war was criminal to begin with. At the same time, he unwittingly agreed with a number of Vichy's own justifications for the Riom trial. "The guilty parties are simply those who, due to their positions, were responsible for preparing for war and did not do so," he said, adding that they might be "ministers or great leaders." "France will certainly one day hold a trial of those responsible, but there is every reason to believe that some of today's accusers will figure then among the accused," he concluded. In other words, De Gaulle's denunciation of the trial was remarkably similar to Vichy's defense of it – albeit with the protagonists changed. Vichy's shift from a trial of those responsible for the war to a trial of those responsible for the defeat satisfied most of his demands. It is worth noting in this context that a copy of De Gaulle's speech ended up in the *Cour Suprême*'s own records.[7]

Even before the war, accusations of siding with the enemy had become common on both sides of the French political spectrum. It was a natural reaction for the disaster to turn accusations of anti-national feeling to become accusations of treason. This reaction was so strong that it still appears in documents written years after the fact, and long after the wave of trials that followed the Liberation. It was, however, stronger still at the time. The issue then was not whether to try

7 Transcript of de Gaulle speech of 9 September 1940, Box 2, Series 2W, AN.

those responsible for the disaster, but rather whom to try. Answers to this question, however, varied widely. In general, they diverged along two axes. De Gaulle's speech hinted at one of them: the question of responsibility for the war versus responsibility for the defeat. The fact that Pétain, the new dictator, was a career soldier raised a second question: that of civil versus military responsibility.

We can see these concerns at work in the letters that private citizens addressed to the newly formed *Cour Suprême* in the course of August 1940. The most obvious impression these letters give is one of an understandable sense of shock. Secure in the reassuring bosom of a France whose wartime propaganda had emphasized safety over struggle,[8] many had not known of even the more obvious of her military deficiencies. The fact that the Maginot Line only covered part of the border, for example, came as a painful surprise to many. A certain Adrien Berget, retired, who emphasized that he was a former teacher of history and geography, testified to his "painful surprise [...] at not having learned [until the defeat], with some 30 million French people [...] that the Maginot Line stopped at Montmédy." He bemoaned the fact that "the little savings possible for a retired person" had been invested in apparently pointless bonds and subscriptions for the national defense.[9]

Wild and implausible rumors circulated, fueled by Pétain's comments that France had lacked war materiel and by the revelations about the Maginot Line. Berget, the author of the above letter, claimed to have heard that the failure of the Maginot Line to cover the whole border was due to the need not to violate the treaties of 1815![10] A man named Maillart claimed to have seen a secret Franco-Swiss treaty negotiated by Reynaud in early May 1940; Reynaud, he said, had exported iron to Germany via Switzerland.[11] More mundanely, some correspondents had heard that the deficiencies of materiel were due to corruption at the highest levels of the old regime. Berget thought he had heard of a street named after Cot; based on this rather tenuous fact, he speculated that the money spent on aviation had been wasted on worthless land for the benefit of the well-connected. On the other hand, the rest of his letter, in which he cites the fascist Jacques Doriot as a source, makes his political inclinations clear and his denunciations of Popular Front figures perhaps less surprising.[12]

---

8 For the soporific effect of this presentation, see Pierre Laborie, *L'Opinion Française sous Vichy*, 119–120.

9 Adrien Berget to *Cour Suprême*, 28 August 1940, Box 1, Series 2W, AN.

10 *Ibid.*

11 Maillart to *Cour Suprême*, undated (around September 1940), Box 1, Series 2W, AN.

12 Berget to *Cour Suprême*, 28 August 1940.

One rumor, which originated in the radical right-wing press, concerned the future punishment of the accused. It was a common developing trope among these journalists to portray Vichy's treatment of the accused as weak or even complicit, a continuation of the lax punishments for political offenses they saw as typical of the Third Republic. A letter from Jean Martet quoted one such report almost verbatim: "We have heard that a court of justice will be assembled, but that the scale of possible sentences range from a 16 franc fine to lifetime exile."[13] He commented that the first punishment was ridiculous – as indeed it would have been for anyone actually convicted of treason – and demanded the death penalty.

The scale of penalties was literally accurate, as far as it went; the *Cour Suprême*'s judgments were to be conducted on the basis of an article of the Third Republic's criminal code that provided punishments ranging from a fine of sixteen francs for the most minor offenses to life imprisonment for the most serious. The exaggeration lay in implying that the two ends of the spectrum were equally likely, when, in fact, there was never any possibility that those the government chose to prosecute would receive anything other than the most severe sentence provided by the law. Like all good propaganda, it was truth mixed with a small but judicious amount of falsehood. From a very early stage in the proceedings, the collaborationist press was already portraying the trial as an unnecessarily delayed half-measure.

Martet also thought, again following the right-wing press, that, a month and a half after the armistice, the judicial proceedings should have been at a more advanced point. He feared that those responsible would flee abroad (as Cot, presumably one of his suspects, already had). His solution to the problem was almost endearingly absurd: "It would have been better, for example, to print a simple announcement in the press allowing everyone to designate the person he deems guilty. A few days later, we should have arrested the highest-placed among [those designated] and given them ten days to defend and justify themselves."[14] Ridiculous though the proposal may appear to those familiar with Vichy's legalism, this dichotomy between the slow movements of the courts and the rapid developments in public opinion would be an enduring problem for the trial. Vichy wanted to distinguish itself from what it saw as the failings of democracy by choosing a mode of procedure with no role, even indirect, for public opinion; but this goal, although itself designed to demonstrate the breach with

---

13 Jean Martet to Philippe Pétain, 10 August 1940, Box 1, Series 2W, AN.
14 *Ibid.*

the previous regime, conflicted with the trial's performative element of showing how that breach would operate in practice.

Meanwhile, the rumors continued to spread. Georges Marlio, who described himself as an unemployed sub-prefect, claimed that during the winter of 1936–1937 he had been in touch with an envoy from German Minister of Aviation Hermann Goering who wanted to negotiate an alliance with France, but that Blum had rejected the notion.[15] (The President of the German *Reichsbank* or Central Bank, Hjalmar Schacht, had indeed visited Paris in the fall of 1936, but it is not clear why he would have chosen someone as low-ranking as Marlio for his interlocutor.) Another overly imaginative individual claimed that there had been a secret Germano-Soviet Pact since 1936.[16] Even well-connected figures could be taken in, and not only in the heat of the moment. In November, none other than General Charles Huntziger, the commander-in-chief of Vichy's land forces, wrote to ask that the second-hand claims of an officer concerning the correspondence of an industrialist named William Loth be investigated. Loth had apparently asserted that he had sent drafts of prototype inventions to Popular Front Minister of Aviation Pierre Cot; Cot had failed to return the manuscripts, but suspiciously similar inventions were then tested in Germany.[17] It was a situation in which claims, not merely of negligence, but even of actual treason seemed plausible at every level of government.

The identities of those accused of treason, however, varied widely. Sometimes, as for Berget, the correspondent's attitude corresponds clearly to that of a political grouping or newspaper; this is particularly true of those who were most vehement in denouncing Blum and Cot. For others, however, it is evident that the writer had thought the matter through for him- or herself, and come to a conclusion that does not readily support any specific political line. A "Jean Franc" (presumably a pseudonym) wrote in August 1940 that the French nation currently had confidence in the new court, but that this confidence would only continue if the court prosecuted ex-President Albert Lebrun (for having chosen the wrong ministers), Daladier (for having chosen the wrong generals), and, most interestingly, the members of the *Conseil Supérieur de la Guerre* (Supreme War Council).[18] Since the oldest member and guiding influence of the Supreme War Council for most of the 1930s was none other than Pétain, it is evident that "Jean Franc"'s righteous indignation can best be described as broad-spectrum. The letter also furnishes a salutary reminder that most people had presumably

15 Letter from Georges Marlio, 11 August 1940, Box 1, Series 2W, AN.
16 Unsigned letter, 12 August 1940, Box 1, Series 2W, AN.
17 Letter from Charles Huntiger, 26 November 1940, Box 1, Series 2W, AN.
18 Letter from "Jean Franc," undated (probably August 1940), Box 1, Series 2W, AN.

not actually read the constitutional act establishing the court, even though it was reproduced in the newspapers. "Jean Franc" certainly had not, since the court's jurisdiction was limited to ministers and former ministers and their immediate subordinates.

The heterodoxy of this collection of ideas, which borrows from a number of different political agendas, is typical. In August 1940, a doctor named P. Vignard wrote a bloodthirsty letter to the new court asserting that France demanded "all of the heads." He then listed a series of bullet points expressing what he deemed to be the responsibilities of the defeat. His third point accords fairly well with the attitude of the radical right-wing press:

> 3. The Sabotage of National Defense
>   a. Breach with Italy
>   b. Deliveries of All Kinds [underlined] to Spain.
>   c. Waste and failure to properly allocate to their Goal the billions borrowed and voted for National Defense

Vignard also denounced the "inertia, laziness, cowardice before the Enemy of High-Ranking Soldiers," thereby differentiating himself from Vichy's attempts to fix the blame solely on civilians (and the Republican-affiliated former Commander in Chief Maurice Gamelin). He also, however, employed one of Vichy's most cherished talking points: the idea that those responsible had in some way manipulated or lied to Parliament to deceive it about the real gravity of the situation. "Each of these 5 acts besides the last [i.e. the previously mentioned inertia, laziness and cowardice of the military] for which the Responsibilities are numerous has had its principal actor: its poisoner of opinion and of Parliament of which he carried the votes," wrote Vignard. So far, then, he appears to have absorbed his ideas wholesale from the collaborationist press. He turns, then, to a very different note: "A Supreme Court that only pays attention to the End point: the Declaration of War will not give Satisfaction."[19] In other words, he wanted a trial of those responsible for the defeat, not (or at least not only) those responsible for the war.

This kind of selective reading of the collaborationist press was common. In particular, to the extent that it is possible to draw conclusions from the letters sent to the *Cour Suprême*, it seems likely that the idea of a trial of those responsible for the defeat was far more popular than the idea of a trial of those responsible for the war, even though the latter was generally espoused by most of the radical right-wing newspapers to which so many of the correspondents referred.

19 Letter from P. Vignard, 1 August 1940, Box 1, Series 2W, AN.

The two individuals most associated with the idea of a war guilt trial were Reynaud and Mandel; but Reynaud barely appears on the list of those denounced to the court, and Mandel scarcely more frequently. Instead, Blum was by far the most common target of opprobrium, demonstrating that the memories of the interwar period had lost none of their divisive potential. He frequently appears, generally coupled with the leftist Popular Front Minister of Aviation Pierre Cot, on letters which, like Vignard's, were directed *against* the idea of a war guilt trial. A Mme Crussard, for example, wrote to the president of the *Cour Suprême* on 31 July (thus, immediately after it had been established) to emphasize that responsibility for the war belonged to the Germans:

> Be careful, Mister President [of the Court], *deign* to be careful that in your Court of Justice not a word escapes anyone that can be taken so [i.e. as a declaration of French war guilt]. Investigate those who are responsible for having built us such a mediocre system of alliances ; investigate those who are responsible of having so poorly prepared us for war, for having made France incapable of defending herself (Pierre Cot who demolished our aviation, Blum who demolished work in France – 40 hours [a week] while the Germans did 72 ! – those are true culprits). But be careful of the words that will be pronounced. Every Frenchman should pull his tongue out rather than by a single word to aid the Germans to free themselves of the responsibility of the "desire" for war, of which the entire weight rests on them.

Crussard emphasized what was at stake. Not only would the court lose its authority in the eyes of public opinion if it suggested that France was responsible for the war, but "America too will listen." Therefore, she called for extensive guidance to the press: "Let your orders to all the 'talkers,' to all the newspapers be severe."[20]

A similarly selective reading of the right-wing press appears in a letter from a man apparently named Giener (his signature is difficult to parse), who also wanted the trial's emphasis to be transferred from responsibility for the war to responsibility for the defeat. "The whole press claimed that we didn't have enough planes or antitank guns. Of all these, quantities were delivered to the Spanish," he (inaccurately) claimed. In his view, Blum's factory reforms had restricted the authority of hierarchical superiors. Moreover, since the communists were now officially declared public enemies, it was necessary that "those who were hand in hand with them in 1936 should be investigated." These accusations were not dissimilar to the actual focus of the Riom trial as it transpired. Giener, however, was worried that it was being prepared with other ideas in mind: "They seem to want more to prosecute opposition to the current Government and the fact of having

20 Crussard to President of the *Cour Suprême*, 31 July 1940, Box 1, Series 2W, AN.

started and continued the war, than the fact of not having given FRANCE an army permitting her to conduct a policy worthy of her. In September 1939, everyone was pro-war. People said "it can't go on like this." Today they [want] to throw the responsibility on two or three [people]. It's absurd and under the German bootheel, it isn't proper."[21]

This reminder that the trial was taking place "under the German bootheel" is another recurring theme, both in the trial records themselves and in the court's correspondence. A certain Henri Strict, for example, wrote directly to Alibert to suggest that, while the basic idea behind the *Cour Suprême* was a good one, its operations should have awaited a durable peace treaty: "The institution having been established[,] its functioning should have been adjourned until the day when France will have recovered her sovereignty." "What complications if the archives are thrown open wide[,] for serious political and military questions will arise," he lamented. "Will you hear the accused, whom you will blame for having wanted or declared war, respond to you by drawing up a list of accusations against Germany when German boots sully three-quarters of our territory?"[22] Strict encapsulated Vichy's dilemma in a nutshell by noting that a trial under *huis-clos* (closed to the public), while it would avoid the disgraceful spectacle of a country condemning itself for war while under enemy occupation, would look bad to public opinion; but he overlooked another problem, which was that Vichy's legitimacy was based on using the trial to demonstrate a break with the overly "political" system of the past, and that this project necessitated a strict time frame.

Other letters placing emphasis on the idea that the trial would (but should not) be one of war guilt were more sympathetic to the defendants. Raymond Brugère, former French Chief of Mission in Yugoslavia, wrote to comfort Daladier, claiming that a war guilt trial would be "against France still more than against yourself; it would to my eyes add considerably to our mistakes and to our misfortunes, as well as our lack of dignity, to add with public complicity or public silence to the legend that the war Hitler wanted could have been avoided or delayed and that the responsibility for its outbreak falls, with the exception of the Foreign Ministry, on the French government that was then in power."[23] It is worth emphasizing that Brugère evidently assumed that Daladier, and not, for example, Reynaud or Mandel (who were the primary German targets), would be the focus of a war guilt trial. For some individuals at least, therefore, the trials rep-

21 Letter from Giener (?), 8 August 1940, Box 1, Series 2W, AN.
22 Henri Strict to Raphäel Alibert, 7 August 1940, Box 1, Series 2W, AN.
23 R. Brugère to Edouard Daladier, 15 September 1940, Box 1, Series 2W, AN.

resented a choice between what the Germans wanted (a war guilt trial, which implied trying Mandel and Reynaud) and what French public opinion wanted (a trial of those responsible for the defeat, which, for many right-wingers, implied trying Blum at a minimum, along with other members of the Popular Front).

Of course, there were still those who were capable of the mental gymnastics necessary to blame Blum for the war, even though he had left power two years before its beginning. A "Charlot" wrote to the court in August to demand when it would finally prosecute "the Great Malefactor, *the primary author of the war* [emphasis in original], Léon BLUM, the man of the vacation of legality, of strikes, of occupations of factories, of the scandals building the Exhibition, of the debacle of the franc, of communal processions, of the division among the French that incited Hitler to affront us, to occupy the RHINELAND." (The original version is almost unpunctuated, which is perhaps a hint as to the level of education of its author.) It seems possible that "Charlot" associated the Popular Front with some traumatic memory, which accounts for the intensity of his hatred. His denunciation of "that filthy [Albert] Sarraut [who had served as Prime Minister during the transition to the Popular Front government in 1936], he who permitted the first red procession on the Boulevard Saint-Germain, with hordes yelling the [revolutionary song] 'ça ira...' insulting the properly dressed persons on their balconies, demanding the 'scaffold' for good Frenchmen,"[24] perhaps explains the nature of this memory.

There were, then, occasional correspondents who did consider the question of war guilt to be part of the court's proper remit. For example, in January 1941, an otherwise anonymous "Mayor" claimed to have heard a worker asserting that "If they don't condemn those responsible for the war, there will be a catastrophe."[25] However, even when correspondents were clearly thinking more about the question of war guilt than of responsibility for the defeat, they were as likely to mention Daladier as a culprit as Reynaud or Mandel. After all, Daladier had presided over the declaration of war; Reynaud and Mandel had merely been in favor of a pro-British foreign policy. A mother who lost her only son in the war, for example, wanted Daladier "and Co" shot or hanged.[26] There were thus not two possible trials, but three – a French-inspired war guilt trial, a German-inspired war guilt trial, and the most popular option as well as the one that ultimately transpired: a trial of those deemed responsible for the defeat.

As important as was the question of the objective of the trials, its timeframe was considered equally critical. As we have seen, the fact that it took the govern-

24 "Charlot" to *Cour Suprême*, 3 August 1940, Box 1, Series 2W, AN.

25 Letter from "Maire," 22 January 1941, Box 1, Series 2W, AN.

26 Marie Legrand to *Cour Suprême*, 10 August 1940, Box 1, Series 2W, AN.

ment a month and a half to assemble the *Cour Suprême* was in itself deemed problematic; and its legalistic nature would ultimately lead to even more considerable delays. This did not please audiences interested in quick justice; it contrasts with the post-liberation trials of Vichy's leadership, the most prominent among whom were generally tried quickly or not at all.

An unsigned and undated letter from August 1940, for example, demanded that the trials be as swift as Hitler's wars. (This comparison between German efficiency and French sloth was a common and perhaps natural one in the wake of the defeat.) "The country that has been duped and betrayed by its politicians, such as [the Radical politician Édouard] Herriot, [the Socialist politician Joseph] Paul[-]Boncour, etc., sold to the Jews, has given all its confidence to its savior Marshal Pétain, but this will quickly change if he does not quickly obtain rapid, immediate and brutal penalties against those who uselessly spilled French blood," the anonymous author from Algiers threatened redundantly. The link between legitimacy and willingness to punish "traitors" was thus explicitly developed, and, from his or her point of view, it would be better to offer a perception of speed than a perception of legalism: "They say that the pretrial phase will be long because they need to examine mounds of documents. The impeccability of justice is a laudable quality, but it is necessary to avoid formalism."[27]

The perception of unnecessary delays, which appeared as soon as the court was constituted, even led to occasional suggestions that the government was deliberately shielding the defendants and potential defendants. A certain Gamiery, who emphasized that he was an officer and had received the *croix de guerre*, complained that so far only "a few stars" such as Cot and Cot's successor at the Ministry of Aviation, Guy La Chambre, had been touched, but that their immediate subordinates (a repetition of the language found in the constitutional decree establishing the *Cour Suprême*) were also guilty, not only of the defeat, but also of stealing public funds. "For if the ministers[,] certainly, are guilty, all those who lied to them and knowingly led them astray are the *guilty* of our defeat and also merit the High Court, despite the influence they still have on our revered leader, Marshal Pétain," he added snidely.[28]

What emerges most clearly from the letters to the *Cour Suprême* is the extraordinarily confused circumstances of the summer of 1940. This was not a mere repetition of talking points handed down from a newspaper or a demagogue. The angry demands of the correspondents conflicted with those of the right-wing press, those of Vichy, those of the defendants, those of the incipient resist-

27 Unsigned letter, undated (probably mid-August 1940), Box 1, Series 2W, AN.
28 Letter from Gamiery, undated (probably early September 1940), Box 1, Series 2W, AN.

ance movement and above all those of each other. They were divided primarily, but not only, by the questions of whether the trial should be of military figures or civilians and whether it should concern itself with war guilt or responsibility for the defeat. On one thing, however, everyone agreed. There should be a trial – and most of them wanted it as soon as possible. As the summer turned into autumn, impatience was already brewing.

Those who wrote to the *Cour Suprême* were presumably those who were likeliest to find it legitimate; but the desire to condemn those responsible for the catastrophe was far from limited to them. One potent node of support for such a trial came from the Communist Party, which had hardly had good relations with those in power in the spring of 1940 in any case. The official line of the Communist Party immediately after the defeat was that the disaster had revealed that the party line of opposition to the war, adopted after the Nazi-Soviet Pact of 23 August 1939, had always been correct. Now, only those with the foresight to have denounced the war in advance could legitimately enter government. This was a chain of reasoning that implied that what mattered was responsibility for the war, and excluded responsibility for the defeat; thus, the initial Communist reaction, unsurprisingly in an era when the USSR was still allied with Germany, overlapped with the argumentation of the ultra-collaborationists and the Nazis. Indeed, a police report destined from the summer of 1940 and intended for the eyes of the *directeur général de sûreté nationale* (general director for national security)[29] revealed that “the prosecution of those responsible for the war” was a common theme of this propaganda.

The report admitted that this line of argument had some popularity: “[the] argument found a favorable audience among the public, inasmuch as it raised the problem of responsibility for the war and was dispersed in the centers where the retreating Government was constrained to sit.” In other words, this line of propaganda was already active as the government fell back on Bordeaux. In the words of the police report, the Communists were determined to draw “every possible advantage” from the collapse; thus, they did not hesitate to denounce those responsible for the war on the one hand, and of the “traitors who handed the French over to Hitlerism” on the other. Communist opposition to the war was hastily rewritten as a prudent denunciation of risk in order to reconcile these two positions. “It is also suggested that our defeat is due to our lack of military preparation, and that it amply justifies a change of government,” explained

---

29 *Étude au sujet de la Propagande Communiste, au cours des mois de Juin, Juillet et Août 1940*, 1 September 1940, Box 55, Series 2W, AN. Subsequent citations from Communist tracts are taken from this document, which in turn was part of the documentation the *Cour Suprême* assembled on Communist activities.

the report; this new government would have to be Communist-led because “that was the only party that foresaw the catastrophe.”

A tract from 21 June 1940 went into more detail on the supposed causes of the catastrophe. Now they were said to have begun at the time of the Munich Agreement, when Daladier and then-British Prime Minister Neville Chamberlain were accused of having “thrown France into a frightful adventure and of having wanting ‘Sadowas’ because they were preparing ‘Sedans’.” (Sadowa was the 1866 defeat of Austria-Hungary that had freed Prussia’s hands for war against France, which, in 1870 as in 1940, had reached its turning point in a French defeat at the border town of Sedan.) This rather incoherent line of argument, which was necessary to tie together the French Communist Party’s abrupt shifts of policy before the war, only made sense if it carried a direct implication that Daladier was not merely misguided but a traitor in the literal sense. Indeed, the police report waxed indignant at the fact that the communists “were not afraid to affirm that they had deliberately, [sic] wanted to hand France over to the Germans and Italians, which explains the treason of Sedan and the disaster of the Army of the North, preliminaries to a fascist peace.” Similarly, the report denounced as “a sometimes specious argument” another communist tract which alleged that “our current rulers are traitors” because of their abandonment of Austria and Czechoslovakia and their subservience to the City of London. It is worth underlining the irony that the police were angry that the communists had accused of treason individuals whom they themselves would soon be putting in prison.

Seen from a certain light, these assertions were hardly surprising. All of these tracts originated in the Occupied Zone, where an uneasy truce reigned between the Communist Party and the German administration. For tactical purposes, it suited the Germans well enough to have a popular body denounce Frenchmen as responsible for the war; and the Communist leadership was also, for the moment, satisfied with this *modus vivendi*. This may in part explain the Party’s line on the trials, since it was of a peace with a general reluctance to denounce the occupying power. The police, for example, noted a rumor spread by northern Communists that Pétain’s cabinet did not have German approval. One tract on “the two Frances” even asserted that the two zones were similar, since the same shortages and anti-Communist repression reigned in both zones.

Tracts from the Occupied Zone, then, represented the official line of the Communist Party, which explains their sometimes tortured efforts to make Communist policy before and after the Nazi-Soviet Pact appear to be consistent. In the unoccupied zone, on the other hand, the Communist Party was proscribed. Communist tracts that appear there generally lacked the imprimatur of the central organization. They consequently lacked the northern tracts’ defensive preoccupation with justifying their previous policy and could focus all of their energies on attacking those they deemed responsible for the defeat. They were also, for the same reason, less coherent.

The ability to operate outside German control enabled Unoccupied Zone tracts to make even clearer what they thought of the new Pétain government. By and large, they were not fans. A 26 June tract called “Red South” (with the subtitle, which the police report noted was significant, of “France-Erect”) denounced the new government as imposed by Hitler and called for a revolution. Another tract denounced the armistice as shameful, and asserted that the fact that bourgeoisie chose Hitler over the French people could be seen from the fact that “Paris was yielded without a fight.” (This was a common left-wing grievance regarding the defeat, as Paris had held out for a year in 1870–71. That resistance had led to the Commune, and left-wingers were generally convinced that the failure to defend Paris had been motivated by the desire to avoid a repetition of this incident.) At the same time, Communist activists in the south made their views on the prospective trial at Riom clear as soon as it had been announced. Tracts appeared on the walls of that city to “ridicule this High Jurisdiction.” The police cited a representative example:

- Down with the comedy of Riom!
- Young Frenchmen, you will not work for the Hitlerite army!
- Hang the traitors!
- Down with Pétain!
- Long live the Republic!
- Long live Liberty, unite yourselves!

However, this opposition to Pétain and to his trials did not imply opposition to the idea of a trial of those responsible for the defeat or of the war. Most inclined towards the latter category. For example, a tract entitled “Officers, Judges, Soldiers, Guards, etc,” directed at persons who helped imprison Communists, “risks a simplistic comparison, evidently well-made to impress the reader, between the importance of the crimes committed by these militants and the gravity of the responsibilities of those who declared war.” In other words, opposition to the Riom court did not imply opposition to a war guilt trial, even during a period when the president of that court would later claim that it was generally assumed that it was supposed to preside over a war guilt trial.

The Communists, then, were almost as divided as the general population, in addition to facing the additional divisions caused by the occupation line and the impact of the Nazi-Soviet Pact. Also like the general population, however, they were consistent on one thing: the necessity of trying those responsible for the defeat. Like De Gaulle, like the resistance intellectuals cited above, and like the individuals who wrote letters to the *Cour Suprême*, they agreed on the trial and differed only regarding who would be tried. That would be a matter determined by those who happened to be in power in 1940.

3 Certain ideas of France

The man who came to power in 1940, and who consequently bore the ultimate responsibility for the trials that followed it, was Marshal Philippe Pétain. His military reputation was great, and he is still popularly known in France as "the Marshal." (His Free French counterpart, Charles de Gaulle, is "the General.") His supporters saw him as the archetypal Frenchman, and one famous Vichy propaganda poster bore his photograph with the legend "Are you more French than he?"[1] He was initially very popular, and it has become a cliché of Vichy historiography that in 1940 there were "Forty million Pétainistes"[2] in France – that is, the entire population of the country.

Pétain[3] was born in 1856, during the Second Empire. He turned 58 in 1914 and was preparing to retire; his career seemed at a dead end when the First World War broke out. War, however, garnered him an enormous reputation, especially during the Battle of Verdun in 1916, when he became known as a general who – unlike his predecessors – was careful of the lives of his men and reluctant to waste them in the massed infantry charges against machine guns that marked so many First World War battles. On 15 May 1917, after General Robert Nivelle's disastrous offensive on the Chemin des Dames had left the French Army on the brink of collapse, Pétain assumed the supreme command of the French armed forces.

1917 was a pivotal year in French history, and Pétain played a critical role in it. His strategy, often summarized as "waiting for the tanks and the Americans," was centered on the need to preserve France's manpower and her central place in the alliance against Germany. He was largely successful in both goals, and this success, combined with his earlier triumph at Verdun, was sufficient to make him one of France's most revered soldiers in the interwar period.

He was not, however, the only person responsible for France's reversal of fortune; nor was he even the person most associated with this reversal in the public mind. He was not even France's most prominent military officer. That honor belonged to Ferdinand Foch, who also achieved the supreme rank of Marshal, and who was chosen ahead of Pétain for the role of commander-in-chief of the Allied forces in 1918. Yet even Foch was less associated with victory than

1 Anthony Rhodes and Cyril Buffet, *La Propagande dans la Second Guerre Mondiale*, trans. Henri Gueydon (Paris: Presses de la Cité, 1989), 145.

2 Henri Amouroux, *Quarante Millions de Pétainistes: Juin 1940-Juin 1941* (Paris: R. Laffont, 1977).

3 The best book on Pétain's wartime experience is Guy Pedroncini, *Pétain: Le Soldat et la Gloire 1856–1918* (Paris: Perrin, 1989).

https://doi.org/10.1515/9783110610161-003

France's prime minister during the critical years of 1917–1918: Georges Clemenceau, "The Tiger." Clemenceau's great political achievement was to keep the nation united in its hour of trial and to isolate antiwar politicians from the scope of legitimate politics – what modern political scientists call the Overton window. One such politician, Louis Malvy, was even tried for treason. The specific neologism used to condemn his dissent from the national consensus, *trahison des devoirs de sa charge* [treason against the duties incumbent upon him], would later figure in the indictment of Third Republic leaders under Vichy.

Moreover, the crisis of 1917 was not the only one that called into question the nature of French national unity. During the crisis of 1923–4, the French occupation of the Ruhr and the resulting international run on the value of the franc created another kind of standard for national unity – this time economic. Raymond Poincaré, who successfully stabilized the franc, offered another icon for nationalist sentiment.

Pétain's position as the natural heir of the legacy of 1917, therefore, stemmed not solely from his achievements but also from his longevity. Of the heroes of that year, he was the only one still alive in 1940. If Foch, for example, had lived as long as Pétain did, he would have survived until 1946. Instead, both he and Clemenceau died in 1929, while Poincaré (who in any case was a more divisive figure) followed them in 1934. This left the field clear for Pétain to emerge as the monopolist of the memory of 1917's legacy of national unity. During the disaster of 1940, when Prime Minister Paul Reynaud decided to invite a senior soldier into his cabinet to shore up the crumbling nation, Pétain was the obvious choice – so obvious that he rapidly replaced Reynaud. On 22 June 1940, he signed an armistice with Germany, and on 10 July, Parliament voted him full powers to rewrite the constitution. The vote was crushing – 569–80 – but besides the fact that the 1875 Constitution had banned any change in France's form of government, the decision was made in circumstances of panic and with many prominent parliamentarians absent from the scene. The resulting government, however, could at least claim to be closer to legality than the possible alternatives, like De Gaulle's Free French government in London, which called for continued resistance against Germany.

The result was that, between 10 July 1940 and the Liberation of 1944, France lacked a government whose legitimacy was universally recognized. The defeat had opened the possibility of a drastic shift in the boundaries of what was politically acceptable. For the moment, however, most French citizens looked to Pétain for guidance. At a time when so much seemed discredited by the defeat, he seemed to many to be the closest thing to a national institution that had survived. Pétain would define the limits of France's Overton window, and like most of the French, he would do so by assigning responsibility for the defeat by means of the judicial process. He would not, however, do so in an apolitical framework, in spite of some of his supporters' claims. Pétain had political views of his own, and the fact that he, and not Foch or Clemenceau, had survived to be the symbol of 1917 was to have far-reaching consequences.

It is a truism to say that nothing happened in early Vichy France without Pétain's imprimatur. Three years later, that would no longer be the case; as the Germans and the French public lost faith in him, Pétain's room for maneuver diminished. In 1940, however, Pétain was still at the height of his popularity, and Vichy was in a very real sense his personal government. At the very least, it is certain that he could have vetoed any proposal he disliked; so the mere existence of the Riom trial, as well as the subsidiary Clermont-Ferrand trials of lesser Popular Front figures, is evidence of his assent.

Like almost every Frenchman, Pétain had an active personal interest in the question of responsibility for the war and the defeat. Indeed, his interest was more personal than most, since he had been Minister of War in 1934 and the main inspiration for France's defense policy throughout the 1930s. This naturally raised the question of his personal responsibility for the defeat, which would be a constant theme of the defense arguments during the trials.

Given these preoccupations, it is not surprising that Pétain's primary concern in the summer of 1940, like that of Commander-in-Chief Maxime Weygand, was to save the honor of the army. "The honor of the army" was in fact a rather tendentious term; in a country where the army was synonymous with the (male) nation in arms, its "honor" could only be differentiated from that of the nation if the term "army" was reduced to meaning the professional officer corps. It was this group that Pétain, as well as Weygand, sought to protect by forcing the government to undertake an armistice (which could be presented as a political decision) rather than a military capitulation (which was the option preferred by most of Germany's conquests, since it opened to door to further resistance from abroad, but which would underline the military's responsibility for the disaster). Pétain's role in these matters is well known; but we will focus on a somewhat less well-documented incident that shows how, from the moment of the defeat itself, Pétain immediately worked to reformulate the national consensus that someone was criminally responsible for the defeat into a specific attempt to inculpate prominent politicians. As we have seen, the popular debate about 1940 turned on a number of axes, one of the most important being whether civilians or the military should bear the brunt of the responsibility. Pétain's priority from the beginning was to ensure that it would be the former.

On 26 May 1940, when Pétain was still Vice-President of the Council of Ministers in Reynaud's cabinet, he addressed to Reynaud a letter (later published in the wartime hagiography of Pétain by General Émile Laure, the head of Pétain's military cabinet)[4] regarding Reynaud's decision to fire General Corap. While the letter is not as well-known as some of Pétain's other statements of opinion about the causes of the defeat (such as his famous speech blaming it on the lack of men, arms and allies), it contains considerable detail lacking in other sources.

Firstly, it is obvious that he was already involved in the national debate over the causes of the defeat as early as May, and that it was not a side issue: Pétain made it explicit that he was addressing "the question of responsibility" and that "the military leaders are not alone in having explanations to make." The fact that he allowed Laure to print the letter in a book published in 1941 suggests that he continued to hold the views contained therein. Secondly, one of his primary concerns – he may have had others that do not appear in the context of a letter on the specific issue of General Corap's dismissal – concerned saving the army's reputation. It would not be difficult to extrapolate on the basis of this letter alone what Pétain thought of the Dreyfus Affair, during which an innocent Jewish officer had been accused of espionage to protect the military's reputation. The army, Pétain commented, was one; any opprobrium cast on a single member of the army affected all of its members – and, by extension, himself.

The key word of the letter was "discipline." On the 26th of May, a stabilization of the military front did not appear entirely out of the question, so it is conceivable that Pétain only meant the kind of military discipline that he had imposed during the 1917 mutinies; but this was also the attitude that the trials would apply to the home front. Honor, reputation and discipline were intertwined; only the correct allocation of blame could protect hierarchy from being fatally undermined.

Perhaps the most interesting aspect of the letter, however, is how it reveals how Pétain was initially in touch with the public debate. Once he became head of state, many visitors noted how his prominence tended to leave Pétain isolated from new information. Michel Clemenceau recounted at Pétain's 1945 trial how, even though Clemenceau lived in the Occupied Zone, Pétain had asked him for information about the Unoccupied Zone, explaining that he lacked access to any reliable sources on the subject.[5] Vichy's second Justice Minister Joseph Barthélemy, similarly, observed that Pétain was surrounded by flatterers who refused to give him bad news.[6] In May 1940, however, Pétain still had access to popular rumors. He believed that French public opinion had begun to believe that the in-

4 Auguste Marie Émile Laure, *Pétain* (Paris: Éditions Berger-Levrault, 1941), 430–431.
5 Transcript of Pétain's trial, audience of 28 July 1945, p. 92, Box 49, Series 496 AP, AN.
6 Barthélemy, *Ministre de la Justice*, 69.

cipient defeat was due to the presence of "traitors." The crowd, in his view – and we have seen that it was a correct one – was baying for blood.

In short, all of what would later become the government view on the question of responsibility for the defeat is present in this letter. Some kind of reckoning would become necessary as soon as the immediate emergency had passed. The generals, if not blameless, needed to be protected so that the honor of the army could be saved. The politicians, on the other hand, could safely be blamed for the "abandonment of effort" that was the real cause of the defeat. Here Pétain's curious combination of lip service to Catholic verbiage coupled with a complete disregard of its message came to the fore. What was needed was a national *mea culpa*, but Pétain and the high command would naturally be excluded from the *mea*. From the very beginning of Vichy, Pétain had a very distinct idea of who should be blamed, and this idea coincides too well with the actual course of events under Vichy to be an accident.

Pétain, then, bore a general responsibility for the trial that must not be underestimated. Nor can his age excuse him: two of the best-known historians of the Vichy period have concluded, regarding his responsibility for Vichy's antisemitism, that "In 1941, Pétain *knew*."[7] The fact that he was in power limited the scope of the trial: it ensured that Riom could not focus on military responsibilities for the defeat.

At the same time, however, the fact that Pétain was ultimately responsible should not mislead us into believing that he was responsible for the specifics of the way the trial developed. Pétain lacked the personal expertise to weigh in on matters relating to the trial. He had virtually no understanding of matters juridical, especially compared to standards under the Third Republic, a regime dominated by lawyers. His subordinates, especially those with actual knowledge of law, did not always display privately the mawkish respect for the Savior of France that was expected in public.

Pétain was not a Napoleon or an elder Moltke – brilliant polymaths who merely happened to find their primarily vocation in the military. Pétain was, in the sense used in other contexts by his subordinate Lucien Romier, a "technician" or specialist rather than an "aristocrat" or polymath – that is, although he was undoubtedly a brilliant general, his wider perspectives were very limited. Barthélemy later recounted an anecdote from a cabinet meeting that exemplifies this problem:

---

7 Marrus and Paxton, *Vichy France and the Jews*, 86.

> One day when, in the Council [of Ministers], I was vigorously reproaching [Deputy Prime Minister] M. Laval for being fixated on bread, wine, meat [...], I finally said: "Man does not live by bread alone. *Non in sole pane vivit homo.*" The Marshal interrupted me: "Oh, that phrase is so beautiful. Who said it?" "It's in the Gospels, *Monsieur le Maréchal.*"[8]

It is, of course, a commonplace that Pétain's support for Catholicism was purely theoretical; but what we should retain from this story is that his own Minister of Justice had very little respect for his non-military expertise.

There remain the other cabinet members, particularly those personally close to Pétain, who was notoriously easy to influence. Indeed, when members of the defense teams of those imprisoned at Riom tried to contact persons at Vichy, they frequently cited Pétain's personal entourage as a roadblock. Barthélemy, for example, commented to Reynaud's defense lawyer, Jacques Charpentier, in December of 1941 that "Personally, I am in favor of dismissing the case, but the Marshal's entourage is opposed."[9] This, of course, may be a mere excuse. It may also be an example of the common practice of blaming the ministers to avoid attacking the king. Given Pétain's lack of knowledge of legal matters, however, he necessarily must have relied on others to help shape his government's judicial policy. It is to those others we must turn to explain the philosophy behind the trial. Many of Pétain's subordinates would play a role in the trials that was arguably more crucial than that of the aging Marshal, and they had ideas of their own about what the lesson of 1917 meant for reestablishing national unity in 1940–1942.

One possible response to the events of 1917–24 was to claim that Clemenceau's opponent Malvy had been right after all, and to turn against war altogether. Those who adopted this course were pacifists. They were prominent across the political spectrum in interwar France, and it would be misleading to portray them as a monolithic movement. Many of them, however, shared certain ideas in common. They tended to be pro-German, an attitude that went naturally with pacifism because it was clear that the next war would probably be against Germany. Frequently they railed against undue influence from France's former allies, building convoluted conspiracy theories about the role of the City of London or of "international Jewry" in Anglo-American political life. Some of France's best and brightest trod this path in the interwar period, including famous authors like Louis-Ferdinand Céline (the pen-name of Louis Ferdinand Auguste Destouches) and Robert Brasillach. Many of them would become vocal supporters of collaboration, and Brasillach was to be executed after the Liberation be-

8 Barthélemy, *Ministre de la Justice*, 67.

9 List of grievances by Reynaud(?), 14 July 1942, Box 24, Series 74 AP, AN.

cause his pro-German attitude had come to be considered treasonous. In the preparation for the Riom trial, those who espoused these ideas generally came to support the idea of trying those responsible for the *war*, in distinction to the causes of the *defeat*. Most of the radical collaborationist newspapers of the Occupied Zone espoused these ideas, although, as we have seen, it was entirely possible for the readers of these newspapers to adopt more conventional views of the trial that focused on the origins of the defeat rather than those of the war.

Of Vichy's own future ministers, the most prominent voice against war had been Pierre Laval, who was to become the symbol of collaboration. Laval was convinced from the beginning of the war that it was a tragic mistake, and probably illegal to boot. He also had motives for personal vindictiveness against the Popular Front defendants at the Riom trial, as he was one of the men of the early 1930s who constituted the "dispossessed" (*déclassé*) political group that Stanley Hoffmann's analysis situated as one of Vichy's key supports.[10] This exclusion was not one that Laval took lightly. He was, as Barthélemy remarked in another context, "extremely prone to holding grudges,"[11] and he took his exile from office as an insult.

On 7 June 1940, at a meeting of the Senate's Army Commission, Laval had tried to speak as a member of the Senate Comittee on Foreign Affairs to raise an alternative to Reynaud's policy but was rebuffed.[12] It seems probable that he was about to raise the question of an armistice. Laval had thus seen in action for himself what was to become the German interpretation of war guilt: Reynaud's supposedly criminal refusal to consider an earlier armistice. If this attitude influenced the Vichy attitude at all, it surely influenced Laval most. The fact that the Germans forced his recall to office immediately after the Riom trial failed to raise the issue of war guilt confirms this interpretation.

It is possible that Laval played a role in originating the use of the formal legalism of the *Cour Suprême* as a means of both marking and easing the transition to the new regime. The Americans thought so at the time, but it is unclear what their sources may have been: "Laval, it is said, hoped that the court would take the place in the public judgment of the free institutions which had been abolish-

---

10 Stanley Hoffmann, "Collaborationism in France during World War II," *The Journal of Modern History* 40, no. 3 (1968): 390.

11 Barthélemy, *Ministre de la Justice*, 103.

12 *Minutes of the Senate Army Commission*, 7 June 1940, Box 8, Series 2W, AN.

ed."[13] As a lawyer himself, Laval was naturally biased towards legal patterns of thought.

Barthélemy, however, did not have a high opinion of his legal instincts, commenting in his autobiography that "Laval does not possess the juridical spirit to any degree."[14] Laval, moreover, was not even in office for much of the period when the Riom trial was being prepared. On December 13, 1940, Pétain had had him removed from his position – an event that aroused considerable controversy then and later, but that seems to have been motivated by a conflict of personalities. Laval had always been an atypical figure at Vichy. He had the reputation of being a political "fixer," one of the last remnants of the old regime – a politician in a regime dedicated to abolishing the political.

In the months that followed his dismissal, the court gradually ceased to investigate the causes of the war, instead choosing to focus exclusively on the causes of the defeat. The court's interest in questions relating to the war credits vote of 2 September 1939, which launched France's involvement in the war, tapered to a close in late 1940 and early 1941,[15] a few weeks after the coup against Laval. The evidence therefore suggests a gradual tapering of political pressure on the court to investigate the causes of the war, rather than an explicit change in orders from above. Either way, the pacifists had lost the battle for Riom. From then on, the trial would be what public opinion wanted it to be – a trial of the causes of the defeat.

It has always been assumed[16] that Laval's return to power in 1942 was in large measure the product of the failure of the incumbent government to manage the trial in a way the Nazis wanted, and, in particular, their failure to condemn Reynaud and Mandel. While this would be consonant with Laval's pacifism, it is worth noting that, even prior to December 1940, the court had never made any serious attempt to prosecute Reynaud and Mandel for the crime of "bellicosity" (that is, seeking a war with Germany), even though this was what both the Germans and the Paris collaborationist newspapers wanted. Rather, to the extent

---

13 Coordinator of Information, Western European Section, *French 'War-Guilt' Trial at Riom*, 3. The title shows how much difficulty even contemporaries outside France had in differentiating "war guilt" from responsibility for the defeat, even though, as we have just seen, the difference was crucial to public opinion at the time.

14 Barthélemy, *Ministre de la Justice*, 105. The comment should be taken with a grain of salt. Barthélemy hated Laval with a passion and blamed him for his dismissal.

15 See, e.g., Testimony of Jean Jardel, 27 December 1940, Box 39, Series 496AP, AN. Robert Coulondre was questioned in May 1941 regarding the origins of the war (among other matters), but this initiative came from Daladier, not the magistrates: Testimony of Robert Coulondre, 2 May 1941, Box 38, Series 496AP, AN.

16 See, e.g., Charles Sowerwine, *France since 1870* (London: Palgrave, 2001), 189.

that it dealt with the question of responsibility for the war at all, it had focused on the legalistic question of whether the war credits vote of 2 September 1939 had constituted parliamentary consent to a declaration of war, as well as whether the war cabinet of 23 August 1939 had been misled regarding France's chances of winning such a war. This implied prosecuting Daladier, the prime minister during the outbreak of war, and not Reynaud or Mandel. The government did make a half-hearted and ineffective effort to force the court to prosecute Reynaud and Mandel by expanding the court's remit to include peculation; but, even if Laval was the inspiration for this development, it fell considerably short of what the Germans and the right-wing press wanted. Even among those who believed that the crime was war rather than the failure to win the war, there was considerable room for divergence regarding personal responsibilities.

In short, Laval's obsession with the causes of the war rather than with its outcome made him an outsider at Vichy. His priorities may have played a role in the early months of trial preparation, but they were not central to the way the trial ultimately developed. By early 1941, the pacifists had clearly lost the battle for the soul of Vichy. Even before that point, the surely deliberate choice to resuscitate for the Riom trial the phrase used to try Clemenceau's opponent Malvy – *trahison des devoirs de sa charge*, treason against the responsibilities of one's position – offered a clear indication that the trial would not be about the decision to go to war, but the Popular Front's supposed straying from the national interest.

Like Laval's pacifism, this idea also derived from the crisis years of 1917–24, but those who uphold it had drawn an entirely different lesson from the events of that troubled period. As far as they were concerned, the lesson of 1917–1924 was that the national interest lay in preparing the nation to resist the German threat, and that the way to do so lay through economic reform. They had seen how the war had ultimately been decided by economic strength rather than battlefield *élan*, and how France had lost her dominant position in Europe because of her susceptibility to pressure from the international currency markets. Their heroes were Clemenceau, who in 1917–8 had held the nation together by imposing a unitary idea of the national interest that excluded a compromise peace, and Poincaré, who in 1924–6 had defended the franc.

In these individuals, Clemenceau's ideas lived on – but he was no longer present to speak for or interpret them. Clemenceau's own political affiliation was difficult to pin down, but since his youthful experiences under the Second Empire, he had always been a sincere believer in the Republic. He had been one of the leaders of the Dreyfusards, who had protested against France's antisemitic establishment (especially the French Army) in the name of a Jew wrongfully convicted of espionage. Dreyfusards were left-wing by definition. By the First World

War, however, Clemenceau was best known for his action against strikers, and the war generally solidified this impression. Clemenceau stood for the expansion of executive authority at the expense of parliament, which in the French context was a basically right-wing notion, associated with such figures as Napoleon I and III – not to mention Marshal Patrice de Mac-Mahon, the second president of the Third Republic, whose Moral Order had nearly strangled the nascent democracy in its crib. By the interwar period, therefore, many of those who believed most passionately in Clemenceau's message of republican unity were right-wingers.

This was a novelty. The French Right had originally been defined by its opposition to Republicanism, and many still doubted the sincerity of their democratic commitment. Since the foundation of the Third Republic, the French Left had defined itself in considerable measure in defensive terms, as a loose association of individuals committed to the continuation of democracy in France. They took it for granted that right-wingers could not be sincere Republicans. By the 1920s, however, many right-wingers saw this view as being obsolete. For the new conservatives, Clemenceau's message of unity implied that "rallying around the Republic" no longer meant the exclusion of the right. Rather, they believed that the First World War and the unity of the trenches had put an end to division within French society. In their view, "national union" was a totalizing entity; those it excluded were precisely those who refused to believe in its existence. Class warfare had no place in the new France.

Not all of the people who admired Clemenceau or believed in national unity and modernization, however, were right-wingers. Indeed, many of the figures who would later stand trial at Riom, including Daladier and Blum, had been associated with the new postwar generation of modernizers. Vichy was a civil war, not merely among Frenchmen, but among those who believed that the nation's government needed less politics and more unity. The question of unity naturally brought to the fore the question of which groups this union should exclude.

This prefigured the later question of responsibility for the defeat, albeit with lower stakes. Being less urgent, however, did not make the question any less meaningful. Long before 1940, men like Romier – who was later to play a key role in organizing the Riom trial[17] – were arguing that France's independence, her very survival, was conditional on strengthening her economy and defending her currency. The practical result was to transform a dispute about economics into a fundamental test of patriotism.

---

17 See *infra*, chap. 4.

Romier was the chief ideologue of the *Redressement Français*, an anti-political group that flourished in the late 1920s and was primarily devoted to the cause of economic reform. Indeed, Robert Kuisel's classic biography of the movement's leader, the businessman Ernest Mercier, concluded that Mercier at least was genuinely apolitical, even though Vichy adopted many of the *Redressement*'s aims.[18] This was certainly the movement's self-perception, and there is no reason to doubt its sincerity. Nonetheless, the *Redressement Français*' policy prescriptions were anything but anodyne. They would, in fact, form the main ideological basis for Vichy's political trials.

Because the *Redressement Français* saw itself as appealing to all men of good will, there is a certain danger in generalizing about the movement's views. The founding member Raphaël Alibert, for example, whose career is of particular interest to us because he went on to draft the law establishing the *Cour Suprême* at Riom, was a monarchist, whereas the official stance of the *Redressement* was Republican. At the same time, however, the public pronouncements of the *Redressement*, many of which have been conserved in the personal papers of Henri Cacaud, the movement's secretary, offered a lowest common denominator on which all members (and, indeed, all good Frenchmen) were supposed to be able to agree. As one of the movement's pamphlets put it:

> The *Redressement Français* is not a political party. It does not include any politicians. It is not the serf of any doctrine, of any group. It is and must be above political parties.
>
> The *Redressement Français* is not dominated by any philosophical or religious idea. It does not hide any secret intentions.
>
> It wants to unite all those of [interpellated in pen: good] will into a methodical and disciplined organization. It wants to be an organ of action and of practical implementation.[19]

In other words, its program was predicated in its entirety on the supposition – which is a great deal less banal than the historiography has hitherto supposed – that all the political wills of the country could be combined and disciplined. The language of "goodwill" was ominous, for it implied that an adherence to, for example, socialism could only be the product of ignorance or malice. The ideology of the *Redressement Français* was technocratic, perhaps, but only in a very specific and highly exclusionary sense. Its adherents may have been technicians, but this did not mean that their technical recommendations stood outside politics. Pétain himself, who briefly advised the group on military matters, is an ex-

18 Kuisel, *Ernest Mercier*, 145–146.

19 Note on the financial crisis, 1926, Box 1, Series 485AP, AN.

cellent example of this. He was France's most respected living soldier, but he was also far from an apolitical figure.

This in turn meant that, even as the *Redressement* claimed to welcome individuals of any political persuasion, its "apolitical" diagnosis of the state of France in the 1920s excluded a large portion of the political spectrum. The *Redressement* believed the parliamentary system to be in crisis, even during the brief window between the reconciliation with Weimar Germany at Locarno in 1925 and the beginning of the Great Depression in 1929, when the underlying state of France seemed relatively healthy. This presupposition of an underlying solidity was, in fact, the original basis of the diagnosis of a political crisis. It is in this light and this light only that we can understand how the men of Vichy came to understand French problems as the consequences of a bankrupt political system destroying the fruits of the labors of the private sector.

The basic outlines of the *Redressement Français*' explanation of the problem can be seen in a pamphlet issued in 1926,[20] when the biggest problem with the French economy was not a Great Depression which did not as yet exist, but the continued failure to stabilize the franc. Yearning for the national union that the Great War had supposedly engendered, the movement found it in this support for an apparently apolitical symbol of the nation – its currency. This support served as the launching point for a more general attack on a small minority of "politicians" who were undoing the good work of France's businessmen and *fonctionnaires*, or bureaucrats. (It is worth noting that magistrates are bureaucrats in civil law systems like France's.)

In the pamphlet's own words:

> Bad politics lead to bad administration.
>
> High public functions are more and more reserved for parliamentarians. The top-ranking bureaucrats, poorly paid and poorly treated, drift away from their duties. Many bureaucrats neglect the service for which they are paid in favor of exercising political functions in ministerial cabinets. They obtain medals there, they are promoted rapidly.
>
> Politics rules all spheres: legislative, executive, judicial. It slithers from top to bottom.
>
> Ministers, instead of being responsible only to those the nation has elected, appear before [party] congresses and committees full of partisans who place above all the triumph of their party.

The pamphlet proceeded to ask a pointed rhetorical question: "Is this political situation the reflection, the consequence of the economic situation?" They an-

20 *Ibid.*

swered with a resounding No: the core of the country was healthy, as could be seen in the continued progress in every technical domain, from agricultural fertilizers to commerce. “In every sphere, one sees brave and active men working hard. It is to these men” – here we finally reach the point of the pamphlet – “that the ‘*Redressement Français*’ addresses itself.”

This attack on the political involved a clearer political position than the *Redressement* was willing to admit. In particular, it meant defending Poincaré, who had stabilized the franc in 1924, and attacking Herriot, his main political rival at the time. At the time, however, the crisis of the franc really did appear to be a problem of political inadequacies that could be set right by confident “technicians” (in the very specific sense that we are using here). Consider, for example, Stephen Schuker’s effort in *The End of French Predominance in Europe*[21] to place the blame for the mismanagement of the economic negotiations with Germany on Herriot – a very similar diagnosis to that adopted by the *Redressement Français*.

With the benefit of hindsight, it is possible to discern many weaknesses in the economic orthodoxy of the 1920s; and French economic orthodoxy was arguably worst of all. The economic historian David Glasner, who has a relatively positive view of the state of the economics profession in the 1920s,[22] has nonetheless characterized the response of the Bank of France to the Great Depression as “insane” and as having provoked a major contraction in the world’s money supply at the worst possible moment.[23] This contraction, motivated by the Bank of France’s desire to stockpile gold to protect the franc at the level established by Poincaré, casts a very dim light on the *Redressement’s* economic views. This is, however, a retrospective analysis that fails to grasp the complexity of the situation. The *Redressement* was correct to say that the contemporary opposition to the Bank of France was motivated more by politics and sloganeering – it was said to be a stronghold of the *deux cent familles*, the two hundred rich families that supposedly ran the French economy – than by an academic critique of its monetary views, which, catastrophic though they were, were not far outside the mainstream of contemporary thought.

---

21 Stephen A. Schuker, *The End of French Predominance in Europe: The Financial Crisis of 1924 and the Adoption of the Dawes Plan* (Chapel Hill: University of North Carolina Press, 1976).
22 See, for example, his work on Hawtrey, the economist Winston Churchill cited as exemplifying the “treasury view”: David Glasner, “Hawtrey’s Good and Bad Trade: A Centenary Retrospective,” SSRN, December 19, 2013, accessed September 21, 2018, http://ssrn.com/abstract=2369028.
23 David Glasner, “Eureka! Paul Krugman Discovers the Bank of France,” *Uneasy Money*, November 04, 2013, accessed September 21, 2018, https://uneasymoney.com/2013/11/03/eureka-paul-krugman-discovers-the-bank-of-france/.

The *Redressement*, then, was "technocratic" in the sense that it wanted to transfer influence over government to individuals who had acquired prestige in fields other than politics. It would be a great mistake, however, to extrapolate from this that the *Redressement Français* wanted technocrats to *lead* the government. The pamphlet cited earlier continues by specifying the nature of the political involvement it expected from businessmen: "Without a doubt politics are not your task [...] But you can choose to complete your work men who will care for it well. You have the right and even the duty to keep watch over what they do, according to your ideas, your legitimate interests, your projects. Never has politics had so much of an impact on economic interests."

According to the *Redressement*, then, certain actions within society were objectively better than others. Politics had no role in determining the nature of these actions, but, because a *bad* political framework could destroy their fruits, it was necessary for those who possessed the innate ability to perform such actions to interfere in politics – not personally, to be sure, but via their duly elected representatives.

As to how this was to be accomplished, there is no reason to believe that anyone in the *Redressement Français* contemplated a dictatorship at this point. Nor was a dictatorship the inevitable result of their actions, for, although they made it clear that bad politicians could destroy the work of good businessmen, there was no indication that such politicians' incompetence was actually treasonous. It was 1940 that would make *impéritie* – incompetence – a form of treason. It is also true, however, that 1940 brought to fruition germs that were already present in the movement; for, beyond the not very inspired suggestion that businessmen should vote for individuals who represented their interests – and, in light of its self-presentation as an apolitical movement, the *Redressement Français* could not state explicitly who these individuals were – it is evident that the movement had no real idea of how to implement its proposals. It offered no more than a banal appeal to act "by popularizing around you the essential ideas of republican government and social progress." At the same time, however, the movement offered no real suggestion as to how a basically anti-pluralist notion of policies above politics could take root in a pluralist system without destroying it.

To be sure, even at this early date, the *Redressement Français* did have one suggestion that they thought might be helpful in resolving the dilemma they dimly felt. The government could adopt what they took to be the American system of transferring power to apolitical courts. Of particular interest is a pamphlet[24] issued by that organisation in 1927, before Romier had formally joined the movement, but when Alibert already figured among its leading lights. Yet the views the pamphlet espouses are much closer to those later attributed to the moderate conservative Romier than those normally associated with the monarchist Alibert. It is highly probable that Romier was already advising, or at least inspiring, the *Redressement Français* on an informal basis, but it is also evidence that, when it came to the fundamental questions regarding the direction reform should take, the difference between Vichy's technocratic and ideological wings was more apparent than real.

The pamphlet is of particular interest in that, although nominally devoted to administrative reform, it begins by explaining in detail a proposed reform of the judicial system. This makes sense in the light of the extraordinary fluidity and capaciousness of the notion of the "technical" at the time, which could enable a body devoted to apolitical improvement to propose a major change in France's structures of government under the guise of administrative reform. The first of the pamphlet's proposals is therefore what the historian Guy Thuillier has called a "Supreme Court along American lines," to be called the *Cour Suprême de Justice*. This, as it happens, was the name given to the Riom court – not as trivial an overlap as it might appear, given that the fact that the proposed court's name would change from from the more traditional *Haute Cour* to *Cour Suprême* in the course of Alibert's 1940 draft laws[25] suggests that serious thought was given to the matter of nomenclature. Indeed, the basic conception of a court that would be above politics clearly survived the fifteen years that elapsed between the 1927 pamphlet and the opening of the Riom trial, as we shall see when we examine the court's self-image and its intended function.

All of these ideas stemmed from the *Redressement*'s desire for a return to 1917, for a union of impartial individuals against those who undermined the unity of the nation. In 1917, these supposed underminers had been pacifist socialists like Malvy and the Radical politician Joseph Caillaux; and this animus against socialism continued into the *Redressement*'s interwar work. The movement claimed to be "above all motivated by a great desire for *social peace*" (emphasis in original).[26] As was generally the case in interwar French politics, this was code for an opposition to socialism or to Marxism, which were seen as im-

24 Difficult to find in the original, but summarized in some detail in Guy Thuillier, "La Réforme de l'Administration vue par le Redressement Français en 1927," *La Revue Administrative* 43, no. 253 (January/February 1990).

25 Draft of law establishing the *Cour Suprême*, marked "1ère version," undated, Box 1718, Series BB30, AN.

26 Note on the financial crisis, 1926, Box 1, Series 485AP, AN.

pairing the unity of the nation by their emphasis on class warfare. The importance of anti-communism in radicalizing conservative opinion in interwar Europe has been much remarked; one thinks, for example, of the crucial role of Italy's *Biennio Rosso* (Two Red Years, the term used to describe the 1918–1920 wave of strikes) in paving the way for Benito Mussolini. It is therefore worth emphasizing that there were never any indications that the *Redressement Français* contemplated recourse to violent extremists as a way of breaking strikes with cudgels, as so many Italian moderates did in the immediate postwar years.[27]

Nor did the movement ever seek to associate itself with a new, nationalized brand of socialism, as so many Fascist and crypto-Fascist movements in and outside of France tended to do. On the country, while the *Redressement Français*' emphasis on modernity might afford a superficial resemblance to Fascism, the similarities were skin-deep. We have seen that, far from treating capitalists as the enemy even in a rhetorical sense, the movement sought to appeal specifically to them; and class struggle was itself among the elements of French politics that the *Redressement Français* deemed to be premodern. In the pamphlet cited above, for example, the movement described itself as abnegating "the outdated ideology and verbiage of politics, the old labels and [added: the] old formulae that no longer correspond to reality." Class struggle was one of these old formulae, which had been exposed as outdated by the possibility of national union that the war had demonstrated.

Opposition to Marxism, then, was one of the movement's founding principles. The personal papers of Henri Cacaud, the secretary general of the *Redressement Français*, contain an undated note[28] on the division of political parties which groups them into three basic categories: aristocratic, republican, and "Marxist – Communist." Of these, the republican group was certainly the most favoured, but the aristocratic grouping also seemed preferable to the Marxists and Communists, who were denounced as seeking to destroy individuality. It is worth remarking, given the subsequent importance to the Riom trials of the notion of an inchoate ministerial responsibility to something other than their democratic mandate, that responsibility under an aristocratic system was parsed as follows: "Those who exercise the public powers have no responsibility before the people, they are responsible only to their own conscience." It is in this light that we can perhaps understand the *Redressement Français*' refusal to incorpo-

27 Charles S. Maier, *Recasting Bourgeois Europe: Stabilization in France, Germany, and Italy in the Decade after World War I* (Princeton, NJ: Princeton University Press, 1988).
28 Note on division of parties, undated, Box 1, Series 485AP, AN.

rate Marxists of any stripe into the category of those whose *volontés* could be considered *bonnes*.

It is important to understand that this opposition to Marxism, in the context of the rise of Stalin in the USSR, was in itself anything but antidemocratic. It would not be quite accurate to say that the *Redressement Français* challenged the self-presentation of the French Communists as the new Jacobins and the only true heirs to the French Revolution;[29] rather, this self-presentation was completely incomprehensible to them. Thus, for example, a mid-1920s article in the group's newsletter that reprinted the Rights of Man and of the Citizen for the edification of their readers was immediately followed by an article headed "Strikes – political blackmail."[30]

The movement's 1928 "Statement of Political Engagement,"[31] which was supposed to define the common views of its members, expanded upon this notion. Since property was a basic right, it was not subject to dispute, and those who questioned the absolute nature of this right were simply outside the pale of reasonable dispute. Thus, for example, the movement called for "Liberty for all, Equality before the Law, Political Rights (*le Droit Commun*)" – all respectable republican premises – and wanted a "confident National Union as broadly-based as possible," but since this union was supposed to defend property, the franc, family, and national security, it is evident that the socialists (and probably even the more left-leaning Radical Socialists) could not be invited. This was their own fault, since the rights being defended were absolute; thus, for example, the movement hoped that a "Statute of the French [male] Citizen" which would define individual rights – presumably including the right to property – would avoid "depressing internecine struggles." In other words, a national unity of ideas was to be obtained on the basis of forcing (or persuading) the opposition to abnegate their own.

As far as the *Redressement Français* was concerned, therefore, socialism was not a point of view; it was simply objectively wrong. Yet their opposition to socialism did not make them a mere tool of the capitalists against the workers, nor was their claim to the middle ground – or, rather, to no political ground – any less sincere. They should not be confused with Zeev Sternhell's duplicitous advocates of *Ni droite ni gauche* (neither right nor left),[32] French Fascists who claimed to offer a middle path between socialism and capitalism. The *Redresse-*

29 Daniel R. Brower, *The New Jacobins: The French Communist Party and the Popular Front* (Ithaca, NY: Cornell University Press, 1968).
30 Newsletter, undated (1926?), Box 1, Series 485AP, AN.
31 "Acte d'engagement politique," 1928, Box 1, Series 485AP, AN.
32 Zeev Sternhell, *Ni droite, ni gauche*.

ment was even willing to criticize what they saw as conservative as well as socialist deviations from the Objective Truth. For example, they denounced as demagoguery right-wing proposals to solve France's public deficit problem by spending cuts alone.[33] Indeed, they were even willing enough to countenance workers' organizations as long as they did not seek to adopt views that the *Redressement Français* deemed incorrect. Around 1926, for example, one of the movement's position papers offered high praise of the advanced state of the British trade unions[34] – not a trivial concession in the year of the General Strike. This suggests a certain willingness to countenance labor organizations as long as, like the British Trade Unions Council, they were non-Marxist.

Indeed, one of the most consistent features of the *Redressement Français* was the way in which it consistently drew inspiration from the Anglo-American world. This might seem a surprising stance for an organization whose members would in considerable part go on to be associated with a government whose foreign policy was based on subservience to Germany and the end of the longstanding British alliance. It is perfectly logical, however, if one bears in mind that what the *Redressement Français* desired above all was a situation in which the major parties were united against movements that were "demagogic" – that is, that wanted policies that were clearly (according to the *Redressement Français*) out of touch with reality. The America of the 1920s, with its mass of conservative Southern Democrats, appeared to provide such a model.

To be sure, the USA of that time had sufficient discreditable elements to make it an attractive model for a whole range of Europeans, including the early Nazis, who admired what they saw as an admirable solution to race relations. There is, however, no reason to believe that these were the elements that attracted the *Redressement Français* to America. Moreover, the *Redressement Français*' Americanophilia was far from uncritical, and it is a reasonable extrapolation from its ideologue Romier's writings to say that the elements of 1920s America that remain most repugnant today – that is, its racism and materialism – were also the elements the *Redressement Français* least wanted to imitate.

Rather, it was America's aura of stability and moderation that attracted the movement. To be sure, the reforms the *Redressement Français* demanded were not always explicitly explained as being inspired by the US, perhaps because of the aforementioned racism and materialism. Yet it is difficult to know how else one is to interpret, for example, the movement's opposition to the 1927 electoral reform on the grounds that what was needed was a system that reduced the

33 "Positions et données du problème financière," 1926?, Box 1, Series 485AP, AN.
34 "A propos de Redressement Français," 1926?, Box 1, Series 485AP, AN.

number of deputies to avoid "the parliamentary crowd," prolonged the deputies' mandates and had the chamber elected by half or third at a time "in order to tear the elected man, for a few years at least, from the obsession with reelection," and finally – this was listed as a separate point, even though it seems more like the expected consequence of the first two reforms – "an electoral regime whose effect is to contribute to political peace and not to excite divisions within the country."[35] It seems quite obvious that what the *Redressement Français* wanted was a system that would closely resemble the US Senate, which they apparently deemed to provide the stability France so badly needed. It is probably in the same light that we should view the movement's desire for a declaration of the rights of the citizen, mentioned earlier, which in addition to its obvious antecedent in the 1789 Declaration of the Rights of Man and of the Citizen also bore a close resemblance in conception to the US Bill of Rights, and which also was supposed to bring national reconciliation in its wake.

Given the nature of the *Redressement Français* and its reliance on the assumption that the base economy was healthier than the political system, one might assume that the Great Depression would have finished it. Indeed, its influence declined precipitously in the 1930s, as one might expect of a movement dedicated to free-market economics and predicated on the assumption that the country's underlying condition was good. At the same time, however, it is important to bear in mind that at no time was the *Redressement Français* a mass movement, nor was it intended to be. It was a group of thinkers, and, *qua* group of thinkers, its views changed surprisingly little in the course of the 1930s.

The Great Depression of 1929, which crippled the USA while initially sparing France, might have been expected to cure the movement of its Americanophilia, limited though it was. This, however, was not the case. In 1930, the movement's propaganda[36] was still advocating a Chamber elected on a staggered basis every two years for six-year terms – a sign that the American example still seemed compelling.

The movement's assessment of the class problem was basically unchanged, and was also heavily influenced by the American model. Its recipe for progress was still the disappearance of class barriers. Education was key: "Education of the masses: Enlighten them, guide them, associate them more and more with public affairs so as to make them understand their responsibilities, show them the means and throw open the ways by which they can accede to the elite."

35 "Un peu de philosophie dionysienne," 1927, Box 1, Series 485AP, AN.

36 "Situation politique et financière – le Redressement Français," 1930, Box 1, Series 485AP, AN.

The movement, however, still had no plans to accompany this effort to break down social barriers with policies designed to aid the situation of those who remained poor, for such policies were still deemed technically problematic or impossible; thus, for example, they wished to "use as the basis of taxes things and not persons," meaning that they would replace the income tax with a regressive consumption tax, deemed more technically viable.

None of this implied that the *Redressement Français* as a whole had begun to drift towards the notion of dictatorship (although, once again, their anti-partisan rhetoric meant that they had never excluded monarchists like Alibert). Neither, however, had their insistence on the hegemony of their ideas decreased. Besides the familiar but, as we have seen, far from anodyne reference to their appeal to "All Frenchmen of goodwill," their insistence on technocracy had acquired an even more pronounced antiparliamentary slant. "The laws are poorly made," stated the pamphlet. "They are the work of 900 people, the [Napoleonic] Civil Code is the work of 4 men. [It is necessary to] make the Council of State and the Court of Accounts responsible for their editing [*rédaction*]." In other words, the insistence on the transfer of power from the legislative to the judicial spheres had already begun – and even if France's judicial bodies were only to be responsible for the editing (*rédaction*) and not the issuance (*promulgation*) of laws, no one familiar with legal affairs could believe that the power to choose the way in which legislation was worded was a minor matter.

In 1930, France's decline into a state of near-partisan warfare followed by apathy had barely begun. As far as we can tell from the occasional communiqués the group continued to issue, however, the succession of catastrophes that rocked France in the 1930s only confirmed them in their diagnosis of France's ills. This is hardly surprising; they were neither the first nor the last individuals to demonstrate a tendency to assume that any developments in the sphere of public affairs proved them right, regardless of content.

As many historians have demonstrated, 1934 was a watershed in French history. By this point the Great Depression had begun to bite, but it was the Stavisky Affair, the mysterious death of a financier with ties to prominent Radical (that is, center-leftist) politicians, which seemed to demonstrate that French democracy had learned nothing since the days of the Panama and Crédit Mobilier scandals that had rocked the early Third Republic. The Affair seemed to confirm the radical right in its hatred of the parliamentary system, and on 6 February, in response to Prime Minister Daladier's effort to replace Paris's extremist right-wing chief of police, a massive demonstration which appeared directed at seizing power took place in Paris. If the movement was too fissiparous and uncertain of its own goals to achieve that end, it nonetheless succeeded in toppling the democratically chosen Daladier administration.

The events of 1934 prompted a final spurt of activity from the now almost moribund *Redressement Français*. It was significant for the future political orientation of many *Redressement* members that the movement's secretary, Cacaud, seemed more concerned about the Stavisky Affair than about the 6 February movement. Indeed, the depth and sincerity of his concern about the Stavisky revelations is apparent in the movement's records. In his own words:[37] "People talk right now of all sorts of new laws. The only law whose application I demand has no need for texts, it is written in human nature. It is falls under the competence of each of us: it is that of probity."

For moderate right-wingers for whom the Republic had hitherto been not an article of faith, perhaps, but certainly something that for the most part they accepted without question, the Stavisky Affair was probably more traumatic than for radical right-wingers who had never accepted the legitimacy of the system. If it did not create the *Redressement Français*' belief that there were profound problems with the French political system, it certainly confirmed it. Cacaud reasoned that the Stavisky Affair could never have happened if politicians had not taken over what should have been the preserve of the administration and the justice system: "[D]ecision-making power has been displaced from its official seat to move in reality to little secret offices, and, more and more, high administration, high justice, which have or should have authority and responsibility, lose it and can no longer either administrate or judge." The Republic, he concluded, was in danger: "What we must break is the habit of electors to see in their representatives only a distributor of favors, of dignities, of medals, etc... It is necessary to teach him again that the two great essential and durable guarantees are good administration and good justice, and that nothing can take their place."

What is particularly striking about this analysis is that it took a premise that would be repeated constantly at Vichy (that the Third Republic had transferred too much power from bureaucrats and judges) and applied to it a completely different conclusion (that it was necessary to rally around French democracy). Some of this may simply be the result of personal differences: by no means all of the *Redressement Français* members had ever been Republican, and by no means all of them would rally to Vichy. The document, however, also contains an important if perhaps unnecessary reminder that 1940 changed everything in France. It did not merely radicalize existing views or appear to point to an inherent weakness of the Republic; it displaced the entirety of the political landscape as if by an earthquake, and turned conclusions that even in 1934 were

37 "Situation politique," 1934, Box 1, Series 485AP, AN.

still relatively anodyne (that more decisions should be made by judges and bureaucrats) into an organized effort to prosecute the leaders of the fallen regime.

The *Redressement Français*, in 1934, still wanted a rallying around the Republic. We should not, however, confuse this with the kind of "no enemies to the left" rallying that a Léon Blum would have wanted. In fact, just as each grouping of unity-minded Republicans had their own notion of who the true heirs of the Revolution were, so these groupings possessed no consensus on what "unity" meant, which is of course why they found it so hard to achieve it. Thus, for example, Léon Blum's "unity" meant an alliance of Radical-Socialists, Blum's own *Section Française de l'Internationale Ouvrière* (French Section of the Workers' International) or SFIO, and the Communists, which necessarily precluded the allegiance of democratic-minded rightists (who could not reasonably have been expected to support a government dependent on the votes of Stalinists).

It should therefore be no surprise that the *Redressement Français*' definition of unity was equally inconsistent. Even as the movement called for a rallying around the Republic, it complained that parliamentary groupings that associated the center-left Radicals with the socialist SFIO and moderate republicans with conservatives and monarchists were illogical. (The second point, presumably included for the sake of a nominal symmetry which would allow the *Redressement* to preserve its apolitical self-image, would have destroyed the *Redressement Français* itself if its members had followed it.)

The events of 6 February made clearer what the movement meant by "unity." The *Redressement Français* saw the events of that day as a movement that was not antiparliamentary, but that could become antiparliamentary in the absence of reform[38] – a form of psychoanalysis that tempts one to believe that the author of the document had enough sympathy with the 6 February demonstrators to think that he understood their grievances. The subsequent governments of Gaston Doumergue and Pierre-Étienne Flandin, which obtained extraordinary powers from the parliament in an effort to combat the crisis, proved to be close to what the *Redressement Français* wanted – a broad coalition of the center and right that was capable of bypassing a sclerotic political establishment. When the Flandin government collapsed in 1936, the *Redressement Français* treated it as the end of an era, and issued their last major policy paper[39] in the form of an analysis of what had gone wrong.

---

38 "Les deux déterminants politiques," 1934, Box 1, Series 485AP, AN.
39 "Sur la situation politique," 1936, Box 1, Series 485AP, AN.

The *Redressement Français* admitted reluctantly that they had more or less obtained the coalition they wanted: the Doumergue-Flandin solution was "an excellent formula in itself," but had been vitiated by the fact that "the parties had not followed their leaders." It was with despair that the movement contemplated this problem of leaders and followers, which was to be so important to Pétain's image. A return to "the old politics of movable chairs" was out of the question, for the movement believed that French democracy, in its current incarnation, had already failed: parliament was "already absent" because it wanted to "neither fight nor oppose the government."

Such a situation was clearly untenable: "the government will thus find itself alone before the country, with full powers that remain part of the regular order of republican institutions, because they have been voted in a normal way by the Parliament, and constituted as appropriate for a short period." It had responsibility without power, in other words, while the parliament had power without responsibility. Clearly something had gone seriously wrong. Already, before the Popular Front had even come to power, the *Redressement Français*' line of reasoning was already excluding its future legal defense, the notion of the popular mandate, from consideration – for the cowardice of the deputies meant that France had ceased to have a system in which the leaders were responsible to the people, or, indeed, to anyone.

Rather wearily, the paper stated that the problem was not merely a few problematic individuals. While the deputies' higher duty might call for them to vote for unpopular ordinances, it was unreasonable to expect them to carry out that duty by voting for decrees made in their absence when they could reap the electoral benefits of irresponsibility by distancing themselves from the necessary deflationary measures. (We must once again ask here that the reader forget for a moment the Keynesian theory of sticky wages, which would undermine this economic analysis. All that matters for the moment is to accept that, in 1936, the *Redressement Français* was in excellent company in its economic errors; and John Maynard Keynes himself had not yet fully realized the theory that was to bear his name.) Deputies, the paper accepted, were only men, not heroes.

Yet the situation was dire, and in need of some sort of solution. The leagues – this was the blanket term for the crypto-Fascist groups that pullulated in 1930s France – wanted to "exploit the need for authority felt more and more by the country." The nation's youth, in particular (not that there was much of it during the *années creuses*, the hollow years of the mid-1930s caused by the lack of births in 1914–1918), were "more desirous of authority than of liberty." Matters were approaching a crisis.

Nonetheless, after all that has gone before, it should no longer surprise the reader that the *Redressement Français*' solutions had changed not at all. The key reform would be "the adoption of an electoral reform which would liberate the parties from the servitude of abnormal alliances, which would oblige the leagues to categorize and limit their activity within a less unjust and more reliable electoral system than the current one." This was to be buttressed by a "truce and union on economic matters" in order to ensure a stable government for the nation. *Plus ça change:* seven years after the Great Depression began in the USA, five after the collapse of the Austrian *Kreditanstalt* had precipitated the failure of the European banking system, and two after France had seen a democratic government overturned by crypto-Fascist mobs, the *Redressement Français*' solution was still a changed electoral system (apparently along the same American lines the movement had always advocated) and a national union against socialism.

The wheel, it seems, had come full circle; even as the *Redressement Français*' underlying ideas had changed not at all, the crisis of the 1930s had radicalized them to the point that they seemed to have lost faith in French democracy. One must, however, be clear. Nothing in the documents we have examined suggests a desire to try the movement's enemies for treason. On the contrary, we have seen that the movement accepted with resignation that deputies could not be expected to be "heroes," that is, to assume unpopular but necessary responsibilities. It would take the collapse of 1940 to make them believe that such deputies were not merely unheroic but treasonous.

4 Making Vichy's Trials

The complexity of the Vichy regime militates against generalizations. Most of those who shaped Vichy's trials had been more or less sincere Republicans before the defeat, like the members of the *Redressement Français* whom we have just examined. Not all, however, adhered to this consensus. The impact of the 1940 defeat did not merely turn democrats into authoritarians, but also enabled those who were already authoritarian in their beliefs to operate in an environment that gave greater scope to their preexisting inclinations.

One such individual was Raphaël Alibert, Vichy's first Justice Minister. Although a founding member of the *Redressement Français*, he was on the extreme right of that highly diverse group. He was a devout Catholic (which in French political terms tended to mean a conservative), as well as a convinced monarchist and anti-semite. He came to see Pétain, whom he hero-worshipped, as a proxy for the king he thought France needed. He was also a well-known legal scholar, and it was this aspect of his career that made him one of the main influences on Pétain in the early months of his government.

After the war, the tribunal assigned to try Alibert was unable to find hard evidence proving that he was responsible for the creation of the *Cour Suprême*,[1] but the circumstantial evidence is overwhelming. Certainly it was well known at the time that his voice was being heard at the very highest levels. "At Vichy, it is said that one of the most listened-to ministers is Mr. Alibert, Minister of Justice," one newspaper claimed in August 1940.[2] By October, another newspaper could be more specific: "Mr. Alibert has been charged with clearing the political terrain of all those considered to be divisive, who will be placed in preventive custody in light of their past actions."[3] In December, *La France au Travail* called him Pétain's "*éminence grise*" and claimed that "Marshal Pétain sees only through Mr. Alibert."[4] Henry du Moulin de Labarthète, Pétain *chef de cabinet*, would later recall in his memoirs Alibert's closeness to Pétain: "A familar presence from the first hour, he was the only minister who, by a notable privilege, was still invited, every morning, to the Marshal's table."[5] The pro-Vichy conservative

1 Garde des Sceaux to President de la Commission d'Instruction près la Haute Cour de Justice, 24 March 1945, Box 46, Series 3W, AN.
2 Unknown newspaper, 26 August 1940, Box 46, Series 3W, AN.
3 Unknown newspaper, 6 October 1940, Box 46, Series 3W, AN.
4 *La France au Travail*, 11 December 1940, Box 46, Series 3W, AN.
5 Henri du Moulin de Labarthète, *Le Temps des Illusions: Souvenirs (Juillet 1940–Avril 1942)* (Genève: Èditions du Cheval Ailé, 1946), 134–135.

https://doi.org/10.1515/9783110610161-004

Fernand Laurent even claimed after the war that Alibert had told him that his office was next to Pétain's at Bordeaux and that he determined who went in.[6] Pierre de Font Réaulx, Alibert's immediate subordinate, would testify that "Alibert loved greatly to edit (*rédiger*) the texts [of laws] himself. He edited the principal political laws emanating from the Ministry of Justice," including that which established the *Cour Suprême*.[7]

Alibert, then, had considerable influence over Pétain. It has generally been assumed that this influence was generally exerted in a highly conservative direction – certainly more conservative than, say, the legalistic *Redressement Français* view outlined in the previous chapter. This viewpoint, however, is not supported by the evidence. To be sure, Alibert was indeed an arch-conservative, a monarchist and a member of the monarchist *Action Française*. Yet it was the very essence of the *Redressement Français* that it did not allow such petty differences over the form of government to divert them from agreement over more important technical questions such as, for example, the position of magistrates. Moreover, Alibert was first and foremost a lawyer. He and his associates always defended him regarding his association with Vichy with the claim that what inspired him most were legal scruples over the position of magistrates. In his own words:

> The management of the Ministry of Justice in the course of the second semester of 1940 does not strike me as requiring any significant comments. Placed at the head of the Chancellery, I maintained what might be called "the current" following the existing habits and traditions, and conforming to the existing legislation. I do not in fact see any any legislative innovation worthy of note, either in civil or penal matters. I did, it is true, devote all my care to a reform of the statute of magistrates, but I did not have the time to complete it.
>
> I only want to make two essential remarks:
>
> 1. Never did I intervene in any manner in the administration of justice. Never did I give any order that might have impeded the freedom of the judges, never did I give advice or any indication of partiality, even in political matters. I set myself the duty of respecting scrupulously the independence of magistrates, and to this duty I remained faithful. My conversations with magistrates, including state prosecutors, concerned matters of a superior order: the general interest of Justice, the restoration of judicial power, the moral and material situation of the magistrates, reform proposals – never political subjects properly said, and never did these conversations take a turn implying pressure or threats.
> 2. The *Cour Suprême de Justice* created to judge those responsible for the defeat and for the lack of military preparation was instituted after a governmental deliberation.
>
> No influence weighed on its decisions, no decision to prosecute was the object of a governmental deliberation. I add that I did not personally designate any of the accused and that I

6 Testimony of Fernand Laurent, 31 May 1945, Box 46, Series 3W, AN.

7 Testimony of Font Réaulx, 13 May 1945, Box 46, Series 3W, AN.

> always abstained from any indication that could have altered the absolute independence of the magistrates who composed the Court.[8]

Of course Alibert would make such a claim in his own defense, especially after the fall of Vichy. There is however, every reason to think that he actually believed it. Gustave Cassagnau, the state prosecutor at Riom, would claim after the war that Alibert never instructed him to prosecute a given individual, and that he was entirely free to make such determinations himself.[9] Given that it would presumably have been to Cassagnau's advantage to claim that he was forced to do everything that he did under Vichy, it seems likely that he was telling the truth. There is also no reason to doubt Vichy Interior Minister Charles Pomaret's claim that it was Alibert's prewar legal experience of ministerial excess that warped his views of the Third Republic.[10]

Alibert, in other words, formed part of the *Redressement Français* consensus regarding the independence of magistrates (that is, regarding the necessity of abolishing or limiting "politics"). We shall see momentarily that the laws he drew up during the summer of 1940 were entirely consonant with the aims of a movement that admired the US Supreme Court and wanted to imitate it in France. Arch-conservative he may have been, but there is no reason to doubt the testimony of his immediate subordinate Font Réaulx that "I can add that regarding the Court of Riom, the goal pursued [by Alibert, presumably] was solely to investigate the causes of the lack of war preparation while carefully avoiding everything that could imply investigating the causes of the declaration of war."[11] In other words, Alibert's contribution to the trial seems to have been one that positioned itself strictly within the French debate on the causes of the defeat while ignoring the German demand to investigate the causes of the war. It was of a piece with the attitude that we discussed in the first chapter, as, indeed, one might expect from someone with Alibert's long prewar connection with the *Redressement Français.*

Certainly Alibert was in no mood for rapid and peremptory justice. The government waited until late July to establish the new *Cour Suprême*, until August to begin making arrests and until September to detain the most high-profile among the accused. As in so much else about Vichy, this process was a complicated mixture of continuity and change. By enacting a series of measures that were designed to put the leaders of the old regime in prison, the Vichy government

---

8 Alibert to *Garde des Sceaux*, 9 October 1944, Box 46, Series 3W, AN.
9 Testimony of Cassagnau, 11 June 1946, Box 46, Series 3W, AN.
10 Pomaret, "Bordeaux 40 ou Bazaine II." Box 46, Series 3W, AN.
11 Testimony of Font Réaulx, 13 May 1945, Box 46, Series 3W, AN.

did break with the Republican past, but there were important continuities even in the notion of arbitrary imprisonment: the edict used to imprison the fallen leaders of the Third Republic in September 1940 was a measure dating back to the Second Republic, but which Daladier had expanded considerably in November 1939.

This edict sheds important light on the nature of the continuities between Vichy and its immediate precursors.[12] In *La Déshonneur dans la République [Dishonor under the Republic]*, Anne Simonin has argued that the legal specificity of Vichy's arbitrary measures, the concept of the civilian state of siege, dated back to an attempt by Reynaud and Mandel to restrain the military in the closing days of the Third Republic.[13] In fact, this concept predates the emergency of May 1940 and was an extension of France's normal wartime functioning. In the law's original 1849 incarnation, the existence of a state of war automatically led to a state of siege in which extensive police powers were transferred to the military authorities. On 14 November 1939, Daladier had amended this law to transfer the power of administrative internment over to the prefects while adding the stipulation that detainment had to be reviewed by an independent commission. By the time of the invasion, around 1,000 persons had been detained under the modified legislation, including approximately 750 in the Paris region alone. There was thus a certain continuity between the prosecution of anti-war activists (mostly Communists) under the Republican regime, and the prosecution of Third Republic leaders under Vichy.

However, whereas Daladier's arrests of Communists targeted only those who had already largely been excluded from the political nation, Vichy's arrests were directed against individuals who had occupied positions at the height of power. On 3 September 1940, the Vichy government modified the law by removing the role of the independent commission – a rare example of the regime breaking with its love affair with independent technocrats. Within the next two weeks, all of our main protagonists – Jean Zay,[14] Pierre Mendès France, Vincent Auriol, Paul Reynaud, Georges Mandel, Léon Blum, Édouard Daladier and Maurice Gamelin – would be imprisoned under the new decree. The continuity of legal

---

12 For a discussion of the history of the law on administrative internment, see *Le Figaro*, 8 September 1945 (which blamed Daladier for the measure) and Pierre Mazé's response in *Le Gazette Provençale*, 13 October 1945 (which sought to exonerate him).

13 Anne Simonin, *Le Déshonneur dans la République* (Paris: Bernard Grasset, 2008), 366.

14 Zay had in fact been in prison since 16 August. Mendès France was arrested on 31 August. Mandel was imprisoned shortly after his arrival in Casablanca on the *Massilia*, but was released shortly thereafter with a personal apology from Pétain.

practice, then, belied a sharp shift in targets that exemplified an underlying shift in government intentions for the legal system.

The goal was the establishment of a series of trials designed to expose those who disagreed with the new order as not merely politically wrong but legally treasonous, within a context that would afford as much legal continuity as possible with existing practice. It was a remarkably ambitious effort, and one which was almost entirely without precedent either within or outside France. Alibert had the double task of ensuring that the right people were convicted while building a framework of legitimacy that was based on the promise of bringing an end to "politics" – a promise in which he himself may not even have believed, as he was a longstanding adherent of openly political movements like the *Action Française* in addition to the anti-political *Redressement Français*. Given the manifold contradictions involved, it is hardly surprising that the *Cour Suprême* took so long to establish, or that the vision behind it changed so much during the summer of 1940. The reason why the arrests and the law establishing the *Cour Suprême* were delayed was not because they were unimportant, but because they were problematic.

This ambition – in retrospect, over-ambition – sheds light on the reasons why the process of prosecution was so drawn-out. Alibert's various drafts of the laws that would eventually establish the *Cour Suprême* bear out this interpretation. What appears to be the earliest of the unnumbered and undated draft laws already refers to the act establishing the *Cour Suprême* by its ultimate designation, Constitutional Act N. 5, which hints that it was drawn up after as the other constitutional acts in early July.[15] The structure of prosecution established by these laws was so cumbersome that it would take two years to bring the government's main scapegoats to trial and would then fail to convict them.

This earliest draft of the law determining the organization, jurisdiction and procedure of the new court differed from the final draft in a number of different ways. The first was that the court was still to be called the *Haute Cour*, which was the name given to the Third Republic parliament when it sat as a court to try accused ministers. This reaffirms that the *Cour Suprême* was intended as a direct replacement for the former competence of the Parliament, and also that the choice of name was the product of a deliberate revision – although, unfortunately, it is impossible to determine who suggested it. Secondly, the court's jurisdiction, like its name, was substantially closer to its Republican forebear's. It was responsible for the following categories:

15 Draft of law establishing the *Cour Suprême*, marked "1ère version," undated, Box 1718, Series BB30, AN.

1. The Ministers or former Ministers guilty of having committed crimes, misdemeanors or errors in exercising or in the course of their functions.
2. The high military and civilian officials guilty of having committed the same infractions, as well as those of their subordinates whose responsibility is directly involved.
3. All persons guilty of having committed or prepared an attempt against the internal or external security of the state.[16]

This was a far more conventional definition than the one that Vichy would ultimately adopt, even if it had already started to diverge from the language of the constitutional law of 1875: "The Senate can sit as a court of justice to judge the President of the Republic or the ministers, and to have knowledge of attempts against the security of the State."[17] The Vichy law limited the circumstances under which ministers and former ministers could be judged, but in language that would presumably have been familiar to legal scholars; compare, for example, the equivalent section of the US Constitution, which lists "Treason, Bribery, or other high Crimes and Misdemeanors" as possible causes for impeachment.

This first draft also extended the new court's jurisdiction downwards to prominent civil servants and military leaders – a measure presumably directed against Gamelin, the commander-in-chief of the French forces during the German breakthrough. This question of whether the generals were as guilty as former ministers would continue to bedevil the trial. It is worth noting that the inclusion of military figures in the court's initial jurisdiction implies that Vichy never envisioned the kind of trial the Germans wanted, that is, one which would focus exclusively on war guilt; in that context, Gamelin could at most be accused of deceiving the government as to France's state of military preparedness.

The *Cour Suprême* would also have jurisdiction over crimes of high treason. The definition here differs from the Third Republic's only in the inclusion of the phrase "interior or exterior," which left the door open to prosecutions of bodies such as the Freemasons and the Communist Party (and possibly individuals like Mandel, who had just been accused of plotting to overthrow the government). This continued to be part of the *Cour Suprême*'s ambit, and at least some of the court's members took it very seriously: the *Cour Suprême* magistrate General André Wateau began a detailed but never completed investigation of the Communists and Freemasons.[18]

16 Draft of law establishing the *Cour Suprême*, undated, Box 1718, Series BB30, AN.
17 Jean-Pierre Maury, "Constitution de la IIIe République," Constitution de 1875, 3e République, 1998, accessed September 19, 2018, http://mjp.univ-perp.fr/france/co1875.htm#senat.
18 This investigation fills a good deal of Series 2W, AN. See, e.g., Box 54, Series 2W, AN.

Additionally, the draft law contained specifications on the court's composition. Unlike later versions, it does not specify whence the members of the court would be selected, merely noting that they would be named by the Council of Ministers and serve for life. Already, however, there is a concern for continuity with the Republic's highest non-political courts. The clerk of the court (*greffier*) was to be the same as that of the *Cour de Cassation* or of the *Cour d'Appel*, depending on where the court happened to be convoked.

At the same time, however, the government still envisaged keeping a tight control over the court. It could only be convoked, and the object of its session determined, by a decree in the Council of Ministers. Moreover, the draft law broke with centuries of civil law tradition by eliminating the barrier between the *juge d'instruction* (the judge responsible for the pretrial) and the final verdict; the new court would perform both duties. For the rest, the law did envision a few guarantees for the defendants; in particular, they were guaranteed legal representation, which would be found for them by the court if they could find none themselves. Moreover, the government attempted to avert the impression that the trial was directed at specific individuals by allowing the court to investigate events as far back as 1930 (which included Pétain's 1934 tenure of the Ministry of Defense).

This draft differs from the final one in substantial ways, but it already demonstrates the combination of a bizarrely specific concern for continuity with the preexisting legal system coupled with a complete unconcern for real justice that would characterize the promulgated version. Moreover, two clauses already appear in the first version that survived almost unchanged until the last. The first mandated that the new court's sessions be open to the public except when ordered by the court itself for reasons of public interest. This emphasizes that the purpose of the trials was a public one. More surprising, and, in the event, more controversial was the fact that the new court was limited to sentences envisioned in the first book of the already extant republican legal code, modified only by the specification that the law of 26 March 1891 (on suspended sentences) would not apply. This provision, furiously criticized in the radical right-wing press, almost certainly saved the life of several of the defendants, since the republican penal code had suspended the use of the death penalty in political trials.

The draft law went through several stages before its ultimate promulgation. The sections most frequently revisited were those concerning how the members of the new court would be chosen and what the specific terms of their jurisdiction would be. One version – undated, like all the others, but later than the one mentioned above – is written in pen rather than typed, and appears to be the product of someone (perhaps Alibert) brainstorming a possible phrasing for the new court's jurisdiction. Its spontaneity can be seen from the fact that it is full of crossed-out half-sentences. It offers two possible replacements for the reference to "attempt[s] against the security of the State" in the 1875 law, both of which contain the crucial phrase *trahison des devoirs de sa charge* [treason against the duties incumbent upon him].

As Daladier was to point out, this phrase was a neologism in French law. Unlike, for example, the use of the term "*Cour Suprême*," which was presumably inspired by the US Supreme Court whose example the *Redressement Français* had so admired, the phrase "*trahison des devoirs de sa charge*" had no meaning in the jurisprudence of other countries either. Its only previous appearance in French law had been during the trial of the prominent Radical and cabinet member Louis Malvy in 1918, during the previous era of national crisis and national union – and also, not coincidentally, the previous era of expanding definitions of treason. Then, however, Malvy had been acquitted of treason, although he was convicted of the more traditional charge of neglect of his duties. By replacing a phrase with a well-established past with one whose only occurrence in civil law had been a tendentious failure, the Vichy government transferred the burden to the new court to determine the phrase's meaning in terms of case law – a practice more familiar in common-law systems than in France.

This introduction of a new form of treason, therefore, was one full of consequences for the future. It is hard to be certain why the government chose the new language, but it is at any rate certain that it was a considered choice, since it was introduced as a revision. It also reveals that they were thinking of the trial in terms of First World War precedents. Tying the new trial to the Malvy affair meant appealing once again to the legacy of national unity left by Georges Clemenceau and to a more respectable effort to limit the boundaries of legitimate opposition. It thereby established the new regime within the continuity of "national" Republican governments. Moreover, since the *Haute Cour* had been unable to convict Malvy of treason according to the traditional definition, it also casts doubt on Barthélemy's later assertions that his was the only voice in the government that recognized in advance that the trial was going to be problematic. Clearly, the government was grappling from the beginning with the difficulty of finding a language to condemn individuals whose "treason" fell outside conventional categories such as *intelligence avec l'ennemi* (espionage) or attempts against the security of the State. The tortured language of treason-by-negligence that would ultimately be adopted by the *Cour Suprême* began not with magistrates, but with the government, which wanted to establish that the responsibilities of ministers represented an objective duty to the Nation rather than a subjective, political aim.

The question of how the members of the new court would be selected also bedeviled the drafters of the constitutional law. Early drafts merely specified that the magistrates would be selected by the government. In a later version, the government attempted to institutionalize the selection process. The president of the new court would be that of the criminal chamber of the *Cour de Cassation,* while the vice-president would be chosen from the members of the *Cour de Cassation.* Other members merely had to be current or former magistrates. A ligature connected this sentence with "soldiers from all branches of the Armed Forces, including reservists [i.e., in a country with universal conscription, virtually everyone – JDH] and the [wounded, crossed out] combattants of either 1914–1918 or 1939–1940" – which would have led to some difficulties if the Vichy government had lasted as long as its authors hoped. More importantly, it would also have meant that the new court would be a split military/civilian institution, composed partly of soldiers and partly of magistrates. A later draft elaborated on this military element, specifying that one member had to be a general, while four others had to meet other military qualifications. This restriction persisted in various forms through several drafts and was revised numerous times. In the end, it was watered down: the government could choose the members of the *Cour Suprême* (apart from the president and vice-president) from current and former magistrates, current and former members of the *corps constitués*, members of the council of the Legion of Honor, and officers. Even this effort to give a military aspect to the court was honored in the breach; in the event, all of the *Cour Suprême*'s members were current or former magistrates (although two, General Wateau and Admiral Octave Herr, had only been military magistrates).

Curiously enough, none of the drafts contains the final formulation of the court's jurisdiction, which was to be highly consequential for the development of the trial. This jurisdiction was to be limited to current and former magistrates and their immediate subordinates "accused of having committed crimes or misdemeanors in the exercise of their functions; or of having *trahi les devoirs de leur charge*, in the acts that contributed to the passage from a state of peace to a state of war prior to 4 September 1939, and in those that later aggravated the consequences of the situation thus created."[19] The crucial specification that the court's jurisdiction was specifically aimed at the events of 1939 was thus a last-minute addition. Prior to that point, the government appears to have been aiming at a statute for the court that would ignore direct references to current events as much as possible; this was, after all, intended to be a permanent body. The ad-

19 *Loi du 30 Juillet Rélative à l'Organisation, la Compétence et la Procedure de la Cour Suprême de Justice*, Box 1, Series 2W, AN.

dition of the new phrasing not only undermined the court's appearance of neutrality, but would also be frequently cited later as evidence that the government aimed at a war guilt trial rather than a trial of those responsible for the defeat. Neither element, however, formed part of the government's initial plans.

The evolution of the *Cour Suprême* shows how practical pressures forced the government to drift away from its original aim of a court that would superficially appear to adhere as closely as possible to Third Republic precedent. The first public calls for a trial of those guilty of the disaster had been made in the last session of the old Parliament, and it was certainly not beyond the government's power to hold a session of the *Haute Cour* that would exclude members likely to vote against a conviction. The need to show the government as being "above" parliamentary politics, however, ruled out not only this option but also (for another year, at least) the possibility of a non-judicial body holding an explicitly political trial. Instead, the government chose to rely on the bodies that were, from its exceedingly biased perspective, the least engaged in "politics" because they defined the boundaries of the political: the army and the magistrature. Vichy was to be the revenge of the experts.

This tendency was only to be reinforced as the trial progressed and the personnel behind it changed. By the time the trial was finally held in 1942, Alibert had long since vanished from the scene at Vichy. Rightly or wrongly, the Germans seem to have blamed him for helping to inspire the internal coup that removed Laval in December 1940, and Pétain promptly offered him up as a scapegoat. Alibert spent the rest of the Vichy years bitterly reproaching his former friend and leader for what he perceived to be his treachery. His role in the management of the *Cour Suprême* passed to two well-known centrists: Lucien Romier, whom we have previously encountered as the *Redressement Français*' chief ideologue, and Joseph Barthélemy, who replaced Alibert as Justice Minister.

Barthélemy, like Alibert, was also an outstanding legal scholar, but he was a far more moderate and conventional figure. Barthélemy has generally been characterized as an "Orleanist" – a conservative committed to modernization.[20] The Orleanists had absorbed some of the heritage of the French Revolution, especially its belief in progress; but they also conserved a certain distaste for the *hoi polloi*, whose political judgment was suspect. In general, they were archetypal classical liberals on the British model.

Barthélemy appears to have been an ineffectual hand-wringer rather than a driver of policy. He came to Vichy less out of any profound belief in its mission

---

20 Julian Jackson, *France: The Dark Years, 1940–1944* (Oxford: Oxford University Press, 2001), "The National Revolution: Sources."

than because of bitterness at his failure to parlay his legal expertise into a political career in the interwar years. His repeated electoral failures seemed to him to confirm that Republican politics could not understand the, to him, evident and apolitical correctness of the liberal economic notions he espoused.[21] Like so many others at Vichy, he continued to cling to office not because he sympathized with the government's objectives, but because he thought that his replacement would be worse. He visited Zay and others in prison to commiserate with them on their conditions, but did little to improve them. He eventually came to oppose the Riom trial due to a well-founded fear that it would turn into a public relations disaster, but was utterly unable to prevent it.

The man who overruled him was Lucien Romier. Prime Minister Darlan's correspondence with the sick Minister of National Education and Youth Jérôme Carcopino regarding the meetings of the cabinet in the crucial month of October 1941 show Romier having a furious argument with Barthélemy and Minister of the Interior Pierre Pucheu over the Riom trial.[22] In the case of Pucheu, who was well known for his Fascist sympathies, the debate may have entailed wider policy dimensions; but the central Barthélemy-Romier debate was probably strictly practical, since Barthélemy and Romier shared similar political inclinations both before the war.

In the end, Romier probably bore more responsibility than any other individual for the way the trial was handled. Indeed, Admiral William Leahy, the American ambassador, reported at the time that it was said at Vichy that the trial was the brainchild of Lucien Romier.[23] At Vichy, the former journalist and academic was popularly known as "Riomier."[24] Romier was almost certainly not at Vichy when the trial was conceived. He had followed the government in its retreat south as far as Bordeaux and had then returned to his native Beaujolais.[25] By 1941, however, his influence was beginning to be considerable.

As a personal friend and confidant of Pétain, Romier's role at Vichy was undefined but pervasive. Prominent he certainly was; at a 28 September 1941 ceremony for the Légion at Villefranche, photographs show him standing next to Pé-

---

21 Gilles Martinez, "Joseph Barthélemy et la Crise de la Démocratie Libérale," *Vingtième Siècle. Revue d'Histoire* 59 (1998).

22 Hervé Coutau-Bégarie and Claude Huan, *Darlan* (Paris: Fayard, 1989), 490.

23 Coordinator of Information, Western European Section, "Donovan Nuremberg Trials Collection," *French 'War-Guilt' Trial at Riom*, accessed September 20, 2018, http://lawcollections.library.cornell.edu/nuremberg/catalog/nur:00810, p. 4.

24 Henri, *Le Procès de Riom*, 30.

25 Christine Roussel, *Lucien Romier, 1885–1944: Historien, Économiste, Journaliste, Homme Politique* (Paris: France-Empire, 1979), 190–191.

tain and slightly ahead of Darlan[26] – which cannot have pleased that rank-obsessed admiral. Indeed, Romier's influence on Pétain was, for a time, second to none. The two men were friends – admittedly a rather lopsided friendship – and Romier enjoyed direct personal access to Pétain from his appointment as Minister without Portfolio in 1941 until his death in 1944. An article in the *Kölnische Zeitung* of 14 December 1941 suggested that he had become the third most important figure in the cabinet after Darlan and Pucheu, and presented him in positive terms as "The classical archetype of the conscientious councilor of a sovereign lord." His editorials, "a model of maturity and experience," "expressed a political opinion independent of parliamentary and partisan positions."[27]

Why would Romier deploy this considerable influence in favor of a public trial? It was abundantly obvious by this point that the magistrates were not likely to conduct the kind of trial Germany wanted. They might, however, still conduct the kind of trial that France wanted: that is, one which would ignore the question of war guilt but would pin responsibility for the defeat firmly on the shoulders of opposition parliamentarians. Public opinion mattered to Romier, who, as former editor of the *Figaro*, functioned naturally as a conduit between the regime and the people. As a man the *juste milieu* (middle ground) trusted, Romier was seen as an important propagandist who could help sell the National Revolution. Upon his appointment to the cabinet as Minister without Portfolio in 1941, he received many congratulatory letters, some from local notables expressing the hope that he could keep public opinion from rejecting the author's pet project. A man named La Mazelière, for example, hoped that he could sway opinion more forcefully against the Jews: "Already regarding the Jews, the public seems to consider them as victims of power rather than judging this reform [Vichy's discriminatory legislation] to be necessary."[28] (One can only imagine how Romier, who was not an anti-Semite, received the letter.)

Romier seems at least partially to have shared this opinion of his role as a link between regime and people. In one undated speech justifying the new *conseils départementaux* [departmental councils], he informed his audience that "It is nonsensical to believe that the majority of these changes will not have a permanent impact." He compared Vichy to a doctor healing the wounds of the French people, but added: "The sick man has at least the right to say what he feels and the doctor the duty to listen. Professor Leriche, if I remember correctly,

---

26 *L'Album de la Légion*, Box 1, Series 407AP, AN.

27 Summary of 14 December 1941 article in *Kölnische Zeitung*, Box 1, Series 407AP, AN.

28 La Mazelière to Romier, 6 September (evidently 1941), Box 1, Series 407AP, AN.

recommended to his students to listen to those they treated, lest they go against [their illness's] nature by mistake. Sirs, the departmental councils have been instituted in part to give you the opportunity to express in good faith what you feel."[29]

These statements shed a new light on Romier's support for holding the trial publicly. He was a believer in public opinion, and was not ashamed to present Vichy's face to the world. His stance in 1941 was not merely an error of judgment, but a reflection of a sincere belief that Vichy could win the war for the French spirit in a more or less equal combat with the Riom defendants. This belief was responsible for the central paradox with which this book began – a show trial that failed.

How could a man of Romier's intelligence, a respected scholar and journalist, sincerely hold adhere to such an absurd perspective?

* * *

> What I would like .... is not to impose a doctrine on you, but to try together with you to understand, to feel the mistakes which have been made, to see the results of these mistakes and also, if it is possible, to extract the truth that men of good will have always found when they wanted to look for it.
> – Lucien Romier[30]

Jean-Baptiste Lucien Romier was born in 1885 at Moiré in the Beaujolais. He received an intensely religious and Catholic education, including three years in Rome; but his religious views expressed the same eirenicism as his personality as a whole. By 1914, he was beginning to make a reputation as a historian of the French Wars of Religion, from which he sought to maintain a critical distance that was far from favorable to the Catholic side. His postwar magnum opus, *Catholiques et Huguenots à la Cour de Charles IX*,[31] is an exhaustively documented account of the origins of the French wars of religion whose explanatory weight rests heavily on personal weakness rather than on the malice of either party.

It was this assumption of a superficially neutral stance, based on a careful analysis of data – he investigated sources in twenty different cities for one of his

29 Undated speech, Box 1, Series 407AP, AN.
30 Lucien Romier, *Problèmes Économiques de l'Heure Présente; Conférences Données à l'École des Hautes Études Commerciales de Montréal, du 29 Septembre au 25 Octobre 1932* (Montreal: Albert L'Evesque, 1933), 18–19.
31 Lucien Romier, *Catholiques et Huguenots à la Cour de Charles IX* (Lagny: E. Grevin, 1924).

prewar books[32] – that was to mark his entire career. To be sure, this stance was common to the academic world at the time; we are still sixty years from the discursive revolution of the 1970s and its emphasis on points of view. Republican politicians, however, were rarely academics. Romier was to take into his political career the professional experience of a man who thought of himself as an academic, and whose major contribution to historiography was the diagnosis of a French civil war.

Even in later life, Romier never became a polemicist. He always remained friends with his political rivals, even after he had begun sending them to prison. Indeed, Blum even sent him an apparently coded message from prison, whose precise meaning is unclear, but whose tone of friendship is obvious (and which also makes it clear that Blum was well acquainted with Romier's status as a historian of early modern France).[33]

It was the impact of the First World War that started Romier on his indirect and crooked way towards the political world. Too sick to serve at the front, he sought instead to serve his country by analyzing France's industrial mobilization. It is an interesting coincidence, but probably nothing more, that the failures of France's industrial mobilization would furnish one of the key accusations at the Riom trial.[34]

Romier, unlike most men of his generation, never had the experience of serving at the front. However, the lessons he learned from the Great War – that industrial strength and modernity were the keys to national power, and that the way to achieve these goals was national unity – were typical of interwar reformers and admirers of Clemenceau. By the mid-1920s, Romier had largely abandoned his academic work in favor of articles and books about contemporary politics and economics, all of which were designed to drive this message home to a recalcitrant French public.

A conservative and a Republican in defiance of the traditional separation between those concepts, Romier retained important elements of traditional nineteenth-century liberalism, such as the belief in the advancement of human dignity as the only appropriate aim for a modern society,[35] but despised many liberal shibboleths such as the belief in progress (which continued to be dear to most of his allies in the *Redressement Français*). Thus, for example, in 1925: "To understand life, and above all to preserve it, man must banish from his calculations the illusion of progress. Continuous progress is absent from history as

---

32 Roussel, *Romier*, 69.

33 Blum to Romier, 22 January (no year), Box 1, Series 407AP, AN.

34 *Réquisitoire*, Box 2, Series 2W, AN.

35 Lucien Romier, *Explication de Notre Temps* (Paris: Grasset, 1925), 264.

it is from nature."[36] He was also less of an individualist than classical liberals had been. Like many moderate rightists of his era, Romier paid tribute to what he saw as the individualism of the traditional European economy, but he saw concentration and cartelisation as responsible for the prosperity of the 1920s.[37] Another element of his divergence from classical liberalism was his belief in the notion of aristocracy in the literal sense (that is, rule by the best men); indeed, one of his books quoted the neo-royalist Maurras to that effect.[38] His belief in the importance of soil and tradition is still more telling in placing him as much in the lineage of authoritarian conservatives like Maurras or Auguste-Maurice Barrès as in that of the great French liberals like Frédéric Bastiat or Jean-Baptiste Say. Finally, in the great quarrel of Catholics and secularizers that had dominated the history of republicanism in France, Romier came down very definitely on the side of the Catholics.

Yet Romier's Republicanism did impinge in certain important regards on his conservatism. He considered nationalism to be a deplorable excess of the modern world (even if, not very surprisingly, he found French nationalism a little less repellent than that of other countries – "deeper and more delicate, less summary, less brutal, less passionate.")[39] Romier was also not particularly racist for his time; he embraced a number of conventional stereotypes about Jews, including a section on them in a chapter on money, but he also viewed them as a religion rather than a race and concluded that "in a society that is otherwise solid, Jews play the role of yeast."[40] More convincingly, he also viewed it as absurd to believe that the West had a *mission civilizatrice* or that it was in any sense more civilized than the countries it had conquered, and he quoted the Indian poet Rabindranath Tagore approvingly regarding the West's spiritual flaws.[41] According to Romier, any superiority the West might have was purely technical, and therefore temporary; the rise of Japan had amply demonstrated that non-Westerners were no less capable of using Western techniques, and the age of imperialism was over. Europe had a culture of its own that deserved to be preserved from outsiders, but, being neither better nor worse, it also should not be imposed on them. To demonstrate that the USA did not share this culture, Romier thought it sufficient to point out that "they lynch black people."[42] To be sure, as

36 *Ibid*, 1.
37 Romier, *Problèmes Economiques*, 42.
38 *Ibid*, 241–242.
39 Romier, *Explication*, 158–159.
40 *Ibid*, 94–98.
41 *Ibid*, 263.
42 *Ibid*, 284.

the historian Elizabeth Ezra has pointed out,[43] the attempt to create a contrast between a "good" French racism and a "bad" American racism was the norm rather than the exception in interwar France; but the least that can be said for Romier was that, as the product of a racist time, his racism was rather moderate than otherwise.

If Romier situated himself a little to the left of reformist conservatives like Tardieu, he was still more remote from the Fascists-in-all-but-name who, according to many historians,[44] pullulated in the interwar period. He lacked the compulsive anglophobia that was typical of right-wing firebrands like Céline, as well as of the naval officers who staffed so many prominent posts under Darlan. Romier does not appear to have felt much fondness for the United Kingdom at the strictly emotional level, but he nonetheless viewed the British alliance as a basic necessity, not only for French self-interest, but for the future of Europe. As the only remaining European power capable of projecting force on a global scale, Britain found her destiny entwined with that of the continent, which would immediately lose what remained of its international preeminence if Britain crumbled.[45] This was not merely geopolitical calculation; Romier saw the Anglo-Saxon countries to be the world's best exemplars of successful democracy, because they had succeeded in taming it by means of a strong moral tradition.[46]

It is tempting simply to categorize Romier as a technocrat, or, in his own terms, a *jeune cycliste* – one of the individuals who, according to Robert Paxton's classic analysis, joined Vichy in an attempt to reform the moribund French economy. Many of Romier's proposals do resemble those later espoused by technocratic Vichyites like Jean Bichelonne. Although Romier was allergic to the word "plan," his proposals for handling the impact of the Depression[47] bear some resemblance to Vichy's efforts to rationalize the economy, which themselves prefigured Jean Monnet's after the war. The resemblance is strengthened by his insistence on the importance of inter-European economic cooperation,[48] even if this insistence was more in the mold of the French Radical Aristide Briand than that of the Nazi Albert Speer.

Romier, however, believed passionately that technical expertise alone was profoundly inadequate for the task of guiding nations, and even his early

---

43 Elizabeth Ezra, *The Colonial Unconscious: Race and Culture in Interwar France* (Ithaca, NY: Cornell University Press, 2000), 142.
44 See, for example, the previously cited works by Sternhell and Soucy.
45 Romier, *Explication*, 276.
46 *Ibid*, 167.
47 Romier, *Problèmes économiques*.
48 A leitmotif throughout his work.

works make clear his disdain for intelligence unguided by a higher ideal. Like many French conservatives in a nation dominated by the opposition of school and steeple, he despised what he called the "mandarinate"[49] of primary educators, whom he blamed for destroying French traditions (by which he presumably meant the hold of the Catholic Church). He even went out of his way to denounce "intellectualism," because "it takes for granted that intelligence and knowledge suffice to make the value of a man and to guarantee the success of his works."[50] Or again, "no technical teaching, however well-organized, will make young people into more than able imitators, if these young people lack the sense of the beautiful and the taste for perfection."[51] The real death-blow to the theory that Romier can be seen as a technocrat in the traditional sense, however, comes from his early writing, which is almost entirely on the theoretical level; his first major work, *Explication de notre temps* (from which most of the above citations derive), is all but devoid of concrete statistics.[52] Romier denigrated the purely technical even to audiences who applauded him as a great and influential economist.[53]

Romier, unlike his disciple Mercier, was not a businessman. He never managed any part of an enterprise. He was a historian with no academic training in economics. He was not a technocrat. Yet there was a technical element about the way he saw the world, and it stemmed from his vision of societal hierarchy.

The word "hierarchy" appears in a few places in Romier's work, but it is for the most part implicit, a thing taken for granted rather than a declared ideology. It can best be seen in his rather confused sociology. Romier expressed many times his belief in "aristocracy", a concept which should in this case be translated literally as government by the best men. Those naturally blessed, not merely with intellect – for intellect could be more a hindrance than a help in determining policy – but with a certain partly innate and partly learned gift of foresight would be the natural leaders of the community, and would determine its ultimate ends. (Like many greater French thinkers of the modern era – one thinks of Charles Baudelaire or Honoré de Balzac – Romier thought his society to be badly in need of an "ideal" to pursue, as he noted in one of his chapter headings: "Ideologies, for want of an ideal.")[54]

49 Romier, *Problèmes économiques*, 123.
50 *Ibid*, 170 – 171.
51 *Ibid*, 148.
52 *Ibid*, *passim*.
53 *Ibid*, 12.
54 Romier. *Explication*, 153.

Immediately beneath these individuals would be those we would conventionally describe as "technocrats" – that is, people of high intelligence, but without the extraordinary gifts required to lead. They might be *fonctionnaires* (bureaucrats) or army officers, but, in any case, they lacked the ability to think for themselves. Still lower was the *foule* or crowd, defined in terms that would have been extremely familiar to the French sociologist Gustave Le Bon, the inventor of crowd psychology and one of Mussolini's inspirations. If technocrats lacked the capacity to think for themselves, the *foule* was still further down on the scale. Romier maintained a knee-jerk commitment to universal suffrage. (This, incidentally, is not a misnomer in his case, as – like many moderately conservative Catholics[55] – he supported extending the vote to women, who were believed to be less secularized than men.) He also believed, however, that the *foule* – which he described, as Le Bon did, in conventionally misogynist terms – to be too easily led, too emotional, too "feminine" to lead. It could be easily manipulated by factors as trivial as the placement of an item within a newspaper.[56]

The factor separating these elements of society was not birth or wealth, although Romier had considerable respect for both. It was a quality he called *prévoyance*. The term was a leitmotiv throughout his work, although he never bothered to define it. From context, however, we can discern that *prévoyance,* literally "foresight," meant something similar to the colloquial term "savvy" in English – that is, a higher-than-rational capacity to discern the future beyond the boundaries of the literally foreseeable.

Prévoyance was the universal quality of the born leader, equally necessary for business and for government. In the former category, for example, he explained himself as follows:

> And here is a side of business that is perhaps the most subtle and the most importance: that of *prévoyance*. [...] A man may earn a great deal of money by playing the differences of fifteenths [i.e. by manipulating the stock market], who, thereafter, for lack of long-term *prévoyance*, for lack of being able to distance himself from his work, of having seen the evolution of the whole, of having seen that the long-term development of the economy was reaching a critical point, will find himself suddenly ruined. [...] Long-term *prévoyance* [...] is impossible without a certain general culture. To be a good businessman, it is necessary to possess two qualities which seem opposed, but which are absolutely complementary. The first is to know completely the technical aspects of his profession [...] As well, a

55 See, e.g., John Horne, 'Masculinity in politics and war in the age of nation-states and world wars, 1850 – 1950', in *Masculinities in Politics and War: Gendering modern history*, eds. Stefan Dudink, Karen Hagemann, and John Tosh (Manchester: Manchester University Press, 2004), 25.
56 Romier, *Explication*, 139.

> modern businessman cannot conduct his business unless he has an overarching view of the movements, not of his own profession, but of markets as a whole.[57]

Crucially, the existence of this *prévoyance* was dependent on the Rights of Man – specifically, of the right to free speech. Only public debate could guarantee *prévoyance* on a mass scale.[58] This concern for the category of rights, paradoxically enough, helps a great deal to explain why Romier would go on to serve as one of Vichy's spokesmen, and why he was so insistent that the Riom Trial be held in public. For a person who adhered to the liberal and Millite belief that good public policy was dependent on free speech, it was an entirely logical conclusion that what Romier saw as the correct policy should be exposed to the light of day, where it could best triumph in a free competition with competing beliefs. In other words, it was *because* of Romier's liberal belief in rights that his contribution to Vichy was what it was. Like the *Redressement Français* as a whole, Romier was not a born authoritarian; 1940 made him one. Prior to that point, he thought that the rule of men of *prévoyance* was perfectly compatible with democracy.

America, he felt, could lead the way – an opinion that he enunciated, in a typically cautious and roundabout way, in a 1927 work (around the same time that the *Redressement Français* was beginning to voice its support for a French version of the American electoral and judicial systems). The book's title, *Qui Sera le Maître, Europe ou Amérique?* [Who will be master, Europe or America?] would lead one to suppose that it was a polemical attack on an overseas rival. In fact Romier profoundly admired many aspects of American society, which he believed to have a vitalizing effect on all those who encountered it: "The same Chinese man whom you would have taken, in Beijing, to be a ghost of dead centuries, you will find him, in San Francisco or Boston, full of vigour. The poor Jew, who set out, with the marks of premature age upon him, from a sordid little village of the Orient, will astound you with his cleanliness and his verve on the banks of the Hudson or the Mississippi ... What a great lesson of the American example, the ease with which the so-called old races rediscover their youth upon contact with a new life, and what a powerful reason to be optimistic for all of humanity!"[59]

America, in Romier's view, had solved the problem of the new mass society. He felt certain that liberal and socialist explanations of politics were both wrong,

---

57 Romier, *Problèmes économiques*, 278–280.
58 Lucien Romier, *Qui Sera le Maître, Europe ou Amérique* (Paris: Hachette, 1927), 61.
59 *Ibid*, 126.

the former because they failed to take into account this mass society, the latter because it provided an incorrect account of the divisions within it. America, Romier believed, had disproved socialism – or rather had espoused a certain highly practical version of socialism – by uniting cadres (that is, technicians) with workers. In a land where Jack was as good as his master, where no social boundaries separated boss and worker, the truth of industrial society could be seen. The reality of the modern order was unity. America, Romier argued, had no politics: it was "a society rather than a political body"[60] and "owes nothing essential to politics."[61] Only by this abolition of politics could individual rights be secured in a way that did not challenge mass society, but embraced it.

Romier thought that the United States had not merely restricted the boundaries of the political, as political scientists like Claude Lefort have argued that all modern societies do; he thought that they had abolished politics altogether, even in the form of the mere jostling of interests at the center. The contemporary notion of the separation of "the political" and "politics" does not really apply to Romier. At the core of his thought was not debate but silence; and this was the product of the fact that Romier, who lived in the era of Hitler and Stalin, was experiencing a fundamentally different political reality from that of philosophers like Lefort, for whom the great experience of modern times was the *failure* of totalitarianism. Unity to French republicans in the 1930s was not a mere delineation of the sphere of legitimate disagreement; it had the concrete, immediate sense of unity against dictatorship. In this sense, Romier and his rivals (and future victims) in the left-wing Popular Front did not merely espouse similar ideas of legitimate politics; they also had a common political goal – the maintenance of non-totalitarian politics in France. It seemed, at that moment in French history, that resistance to absolute politics could be accomplished only by the elimination of politics, by the reduction of the political sphere to zero.

It was that reduction-to-zero that Romier thought that the United States had accomplished. In a society without politics, but with strong guarantees for freedom of speech, the men of *prévoyance* could direct policy without smothering the wishes of the people. Romier believed that any given problem of policy had a single correct solution, which, in the post-political society that was the USA, the men of *prévoyance* could find at their leisure.

Romier, however, was not an uncritical admirer of the United States. He thought, to be sure, that the US was a reasonable approximation of a perfect materialist society; and he also thought that settling the issue of material wealth

60 *Ibid*, 118.
61 *Ibid*, 114.

was crucial for national life to cease to be disrupted by "politics." A lack of "politics," however, was not enough; society also needed positive ideals.

* * *

Let us stand back for a moment. Romier was seeking to restrict the political sphere, indeed to abolish it, in the name of a higher good – the pursuit of individual rights. To a modern political scientist, this goal is very familiar; it is in fact the goal of any attempt to formulate human rights, which are by definition a limitation on the political. Romier went farther – he wanted to abolish politics, not merely limit them. His views differ from the classical paradigm of the creation of human rights in another way.

Most liberal views of the origins of human rights require something similar to Rousseau's "divine legislator"[62] – a stance outside politics from which rights can be enunciated. (Compare, for example, John Rawls' veil of ignorance.[63]) In the conventional view, these rights are to modern society what religion was to premodern society – an unquestionable limit, universally acknowledged, that could therefore be imposed on the political sphere without much debate. Indeed, Romier almost never discussed his Catholic beliefs in his published work. (It is, in fact, all but impossible to determine whether he was lapsed, so eager was he to eliminate all devotional bias from his work.) One might be forgiven for assuming that human rights had indeed displaced religion as the foundation of his thought.

In fact Romier's religion was everywhere precisely because it was nowhere. He espoused not a political theology (in Carl Schmitt's phrase) but a theological theology. A union of the masses on the US model would be good in itself, but Romier's concerns were not purely political. Europe needed to be restored on the American model precisely because the preservation of Europe was important, because it was the home of a particular kind of civilization – civilization defined in religious terms. His aim was therefore the union of masses behind their interests, on the US model, but such a union had to take place in Europe and under the direction of those with *prévoyance*. *Prévoyance* in turn came not from the bourgeoisie but from what we would call academia.

The foresight of the academics was in turn based on goals dictated by the peasant tradition, the conscience of the nation. The historian Jean-Louis Clément, who sees Romier's thought as being a basically neo-Saint-Simonian effort

---

62 Jean-Jacques Rousseau, "The Social Contract," in Jean-Jacques Rousseau, *Rousseau's Political Writings: New Translations, Interpretive Notes, Backgrounds, Commentaries*, ed. Alan Ritter and Julia Conaway Bondanella, trans. Julia Conaway Bondanella (New York: Norton, 1988), 108.
63 John Rawls, *A Theory of Justice* (Cambridge: Belknap, 1971).

to modernize France through the principle of association, dismisses his praise of the agrarian life as "a tactic of a missionary of 'modernity' to convince a naturally conservative bourgeois public;"[64] but such an interpretation requires that we ignore virtually everything that Romier published about his ideas. Romier saw the peasantry as the basis for true patriotism and true religion – for the instinctive understanding of the "civilization" of a group. As he put it, "Under a hundred successive regimes, the *fellah* has preserved the conscience of Egypt." Romier placed this group in explicit opposition to the "public bourgeois" Clément takes to be his audience: "It is not the *businessman*, it's the *farmer* and his more enterprising brother, the "pioneer," who created American society."[65] In other words, Romier was not – or was not only – a Saint-Simonian modernizer in disguise, but a sincere member of the large movement in interwar Europe that sought to reform society on the basis of peasant values.

This fact helps explain Romier's close friendship with Pétain, so proud of his peasant background. It is easy to see how Romier's views of the 1920s translated into an interpretation of French politics under Vichy in which French goals flowed from Pétain – the victor, the peasant, and the ultimate Frenchman – through Romier, the academic, and into public discourse via the Riom Trial.

Finally, individual rights – specifically, freedom of speech – provided the only guarantee that the *prévoyance* of the academics, inspired by the peasantry, could be heard. Only thus could the nightmare of a religious or doctrinal war be avoided. It is in this light that we can understand why Romier ultimately devoted his life to enlightening the public by means of his journalism, why he saw his role at Vichy as that of a link to the public, and why he ultimately insisted that the Riom Trial be public. He was merely implementing the views on the nature of public discourse that he had first enunciated in the 1920s.

Romier's emphasis on freedom of thought was, paradoxically, anti-pluralistic. Modeled on freedom of religion, and with a consequent scorn for those who clung to issues of "doctrine" (that is, of agonistic politics in Chantal Mouffe's sense[66]), it was poorly adapted to the toleration of competing doctrines. Romier's religion was precisely composed of the opposition to "religion" in the sense of the Wars of Religion, of which, as we have seen, he was one of the major historians. That is, it was composed of an opposition to "doctrine;" it was, to borrow an appropriate theological expression, eirenicist. This supposed destruction of

64 Jean-Louis Clément, "La Hiérarchie Catholique et les Principes de la Révolution Nationale," *Guerres Mondiales et Conflits Contemporains* 218, no. 2 (2005).
65 Romier, *Qui sera le Maître*, 55–56. Terms in italics are in English in the original.
66 Chantal Mouffe, "Deliberative Democracy or Agonistic Pluralism?," *Social Research* 66, no. 3 (Fall 1999).

doctrine, in the religious as well as the political sphere, was what he admired most about the USA. Religion itself, however – and not only religion, but Catholicism – survived the destruction.

Catholicism was the unstated reason why Romier's Americanophilism always remained qualified, why he saw America as a different civilization from Europe, and presumably also why he chose such a polemical title for his book on the United States. We have seen his enormous admiration for the religion denuded of doctrine that he saw as characterizing the United States. Yet this non-doctrinal religion's counterparts, the "standard" (i. e. the uniformity of the masses) and "making money" (both terms that he chose to leave in English in the original text), could not quite provide adequate spiritual consolation.

Romier believed that social values were preserved by a society's peasantry, once incarnated in America by the pioneers. Urban America, however, increasingly lacked such a peasant group to reaffirm its moral core, and, for that reason, America's high moral standards on the individual level could not prevent the moral decay of American civilization on the collective – and, specifically, the familial – level. Catholicism alone could defend the family from the terrifying American divorce rate. It was in this way that Romier, too opposed to doctrinalism to support Catholicism overtly, nonetheless snuck the Roman Church in through the back door.

Romier's opposition to doctrine, which was the basis of his religion, and his opposition to politics, which was the basis of his technocratism, were one and the same. For him, as for the *Redressement Français* he inspired, opposition to his ideas was factually incorrect, morally illegitimate, and, indeed, un-Republican. Prior to 1940, he could express these beliefs while still remaining on friendly terms with his opponents; but the defeat, for Romier as for so many others, changed error into treason.

5 Riom as National Revolution

Ability, intrigue, contrivances, "politics" in the worst sense of the term, were substituted to merit, which was never taken into account.[1]
– *Jacques Bainville on democracy*

Six individuals were ultimately selected to be tried at Riom. Two of them, Blum and Daladier, were prominent Popular Frontists whose selection came as no surprise. Blum had been Prime Minister of that government, and was also the leader of the SFIO (French Section of the Workers' International), a socialist party that had suffered a split from the Communists in 1920 over the latter's obedience to Moscow and had since become much more successful than the younger branch. It was a Marxist party, therefore, but considerably more moderate than the word connotes to American audiences today, and more interested (at least in the medium term) in peaceful parliamentary activity than in violent revolution. Blum had led those who insisted on, in his words, "remaining in the old house."[2] He was a progressive, but also a moderate, and had helped to mastermind the Popular Front – a broad coalition of all of France's leftist parties (notably the centrist Radical Socialists, the left-wing SFIO, and the Communist Party) designed to protect French democracy. It was the *Rassemblement Français*' unitary dream in left-wing guise.

In 1936, this alignment won the national elections. As the SFIO was now the largest party within the Popular Front, it was generally expected that Blum would become the new Prime Minister. This triggered protests from right-wingers like Xavier Vallat, later to become Vichy's Commissioner General for Jewish Questions, who already hated Blum for his ethnicity (he was Jewish), his writings on sex before marriage (he was in favor of it), and, of course, his leadership of the SFIO itself (he was to be France's first socialist Prime Minister).

Vallat and his comrades were soon to have further reasons for their hatred. The news of the electoral results spurred a wave of strikes and factory occupations in France, which Blum settled, even before formally assuming office, by the Matignon Accords – primarily a set of wage increases. Once he was formally in office, these were to be followed by other legislation designed to improve the lot of the French working class: paid vacations, the 40-hour week, and a series of nationalizations (including, most importantly for our purposes, that of the arms industry).

1 Jacques Bainville, *Two Histories Face to Face: France versus Germany*, trans. Paul Lefaivre (Paris: Nouvelle Librairie Nationale, 1919), 53.
2 David Frapet, *Le Socialisme selon Léon Blum* (Nonette: Créer, 2003), 50.

https://doi.org/10.1515/9783110610161-005

Blum, while a moderate in his own party, was therefore the most leftist Prime Minister the Third Republic had had. This leftism, however, did not entail a pacifistic defense policy. Although Blum continued to advocate for disarmament well into 1936, taking power forced him to confront the reality of a worsening diplomatic situation (Germany had reoccupied the Rhineland earlier that year), and he presided over a massive increase in defense spending.

This increase – which included a bill enabling 14 billion francs of new military expenditure – did not protect him from prosecution at Riom. Blum was perhaps the French right's most hated man, and it was probably inevitable that he would be indicted; but the court did its best to tie its indictment to the nominal subject of the trial, that of responsibility for the defeat. It did not mention Blum's ethnicity or condemn his reforms *en bloc*, and even described Blum's paid vacations as "a principle that can only be approved." At the same time, however, it objected to the implementation of such measures in defense-related industries, and complained that Blum's behavior towards striking workers had undermined national discipline. As always, this objection was couched in language that implied a nonexistent universality of support, at least from all right-thinking individuals: Blum's imputed policy errors were "contrary to the wishes of the Nation."[3]

Blum's defense minister, and his successor as Prime Minister in 1938, was Édouard Daladier. A lawyer by profession, Daladier was known for the vehemence of his rhetoric, which had earned him the moniker of the "Bull of Vaucluse" (his native region). Equally skilled as a public speaker and as a legalist, he was the worst possible target for prosecution in a public trial. He was, however, also the civilian most responsible for defense policy in the period from 1936 to 1940, and he was also hated even more broadly if less deeply than Blum. A reformer and Clemenciste of the center-left, Daladier had inherited Clemenceau's willingness to break strikes when the national interest demanded it – a willingness which he implemented in November 1938. He was consequently as hated by sections of the French Left as he was by sections of the French Right, a fact which underlines the extent to which Riom represented a quarrel between two branches of the national reformist consensus. Daladier was one of several Frenchmen who saw himself as a Clemenceau-like leader capable of unifying the nation, a fact that another of the accused's lawyers was to underline at the trial by exclaiming after one of his speeches that he was using the language

3 *Réquisitoire*, especially pp. 85–95, Box 2, Series 2W, AN.

of a real leader.[4] In Daladier, therefore, the court faced not just a defendant but a rival for the regime's own self-definition of legitimacy. It did its best to discredit the inevitable comparisons with Pétain by emphasizing Daladier's supposed failure to listen to the advice of the Supreme War Council, whose primary theorist was Pétain, and by alleging that Daladier "had not been a Leader."[5] Daladier was also accused of having lied to the nation about the extent of France's material preparations.

Blum's Minister of Aviation had been Pierre Cot, who had fled to the United States after the defeat and had wisely decided not to return. He was consequently tried *in absentia*. Cot was an ardent advocate of an alliance with the USSR, to the point that it has even been claimed that he was a Soviet spy.[6] Indeed, the court's indictment against him was the only one to imply that he had committed deliberate treason – that is, treason under the old definition of that word, rather than the novel treason-by-negligence so often invoked at Riom. The court had no concrete evidence that Cot had consciously committed treason, however, so it focused instead on his supposed politicization of the Air Force and willingness to tolerate strikes and indiscipline in aircraft-producing factories.[7]

In addition to Cot's political leanings, his former ministerial position was also a reason to indict him. France had once been a world leader in aviation, but she had struggled with the shift to mass production. While most of the supposed defects in France's material preparation for war have been revealed by later research to be imaginary – she had as many tanks as Germany, for example – her deficiency in aviation was very real, and the Stuka dive-bombers had played a significant in damaging the morale of the French troops during the crucial days of May 1940. Émile Dewoitine, the manufacturer of one of France's most famous military airplanes, was briefly imprisoned as part of the September 1940 roundup, but released a few months later. Instead, the court chose to indict Guy La Chambre, Cot's successor at the aviation ministry. La Chambre was an inoffensive figure, unhated and indeed mostly unknown, except perhaps for the extent of his inherited wealth. Like Cot, he had fled to the USA after the defeat; unlike Cot, he returned to France to face trial, believing that it was his duty to do so.

4 Riom Trial transcript, 13 March 1942, Box 25, Series GE, Archives d'Histoire Contemporaine des Sciences Po, Paris (henceforth AdHC).

5 *Réquisitoire*, especially p. 108, Box 2, Series 2W, AN.

6 G. Edward White, *Alger Hiss's Looking-glass Wars: The Covert Life of a Soviet Spy* (New York: Oxford University Press, 2004), 222.

7 *Réquisitoire*, especially pp. 161–174, Box 2, Series 2W, AN.

Blum, Daladier, Cot and La Chambre were political figures, in accordance with the Vichyite belief that the problem with interwar France was excessive politics. The two remaining figures, however, were in technical roles, and therefore demand additional explanation. Maurice Gamelin had been commander-in-chief of the French troops during the German breakthrough, and also had the reputation of being a political general with a sympathy for the Republic that was rare in the generally conservative officer corps. These facts explain why he was the only military figure indicted for the defeat. The *réquisitoire* or list of accusations against the defendants asserted that "All of Gamelin's errors noted in the course of the pretrial involve the conception that he seems to have had of his functions." Rather than presenting Gamelin as a merely misguided or even incompetent general, Vichy asserted that Gamelin's failure was a failure of leadership. He had, according to the *réquisitoire*, arbitrated between his subordinates rather than controlling them. His behavior was contrasted with the new principle of responsibility to the state that the trial was meant to inaugurate: he "did not want to be generalissimo, at least as far as responsibility was concerned." Extraordinarily, the official accusations against Gamelin did not mention his conduct in May 1940 – that is, during the actual events of the German military breakthrough – at all, preferring to focus on these supposed character flaws.[8]

The last of the six, and the only civil servant to stand trial, was Pierre Jacomet, the Chief Financial Accountant (*Contrôleur Général*) of the French Army and former General Secretary of the Ministry of War. Jacomet was a career bureaucrat who had had wide-ranging responsibilities in supervising the implementation of the relevant ministers' decisions. (He had, for example, played a prominent role in the Popular Front's nationalization of France's armaments industry.) His inclusion in the trial seems to have been an afterthought; he was indicted nine months after the other accused individuals (on 14 June 1941).[9] Moreover, he was accused specifically of having had political ambitions – namely, a desire to become, or to wield the powers of, a Minister of Armaments – which he was supposed to have prized over his duties as a bureaucrat. He served as the trial's representative of the type of civil servant Romier and the *Redressement Français* had attacked during the interwar period for having chosen political intrigue as a path to career advancement.

* * *

8 *Réquisitoire* (especially pp. 147–148), Box 2, Series 2W, AN.

9 *Information* against Jacomet, Box 1, Series 2W, AN.

These, then, were the six individuals the *Cour Suprême* could agree to indict. Their indictment reflected a complicated pattern of interlocking beliefs. We have seen that Vichy's notion of the causes of the defeat centered on a preexisting notion of the nature of the political, a diagnosis of error that the events of 1940 reified into treason. The present chapter, by examining the attitude of the witnesses and prosecutors at the Riom Trial, will explain how the attitudes of men like Alibert and Romier at the top were more or less independently echoed by what might be called Vichy's "middle management" – the cadres of civil servants, magistrates, engineers, and soldiers who testified in droves before the *Cour Suprême*, and without whom the system could not have functioned.

French trials, like those in other civil-law systems (as opposed to the common-law regimes of the Anglo-American world), are divided into two parts: the *instruction* or pretrial, during which evidence is assembled, and the trial proper. The Riom *instruction* was remarkably long, and reveals many elements that cannot be seen from a mere examination of the trial itself, at which only a score of witnesses testified. In contrast, during the eighteen months of the *instruction,* nine hundred witnesses, including some of the most influential of Vichy's supporters, filed before the *Cour Suprême* to give their account of what the old regime had done wrong (and, implicitly, what the new regime would have to change). In 1945, Maurice Ribet, one of Daladier's lawyers, described the process:

> The sides of the *dossier d'instruction* grew fat with a mass of depositions, some serious, others fantastical or childish; political passions sometimes made them grotesque. Soldiers, who were a majority, some malcontented or frightened politicians, prominent bureaucrats looking for salvage buoys, great industrial magnates sating sometimes some personal vendetta against army engineers. A whole court hastening to show itself in the alleys of Vichy awaited a summons from the judge charged with finding witnesses.
>
> Coming back from giving testimony at the Riom *instruction* became a consecration, equivalent to an oath of allegiance.[10]

Ribet's was a somewhat oversimplified view of the witnesses. There is, for example, no space in his account for the court's sometimes bizarrely sincere efforts to uncover the truth of the defeat, which frequently resulted in calling witnesses of a purely technical character. It is certainly the case that among the witnesses who for a year and a half paraded before the *cabinet d'instruction* were some of the most prominent men of Vichy. Vichy's Defense Minister Maxime Weygand testified, as did the commander-in-chief of the land forces, Charles Huntziger, and many others. Most witnesses, however, were considerably less prominent.

---

10 Maurice Ribet, *Le Procès de Riom* (Paris: Flammarion, 1945), 18–19.

Joseph Casademon, a mere customs official called to the court to help answer the question of whether the Popular Front had secretly delivered arms to Spain, was one such individual. Anxious to assure the court that he had never knowingly let war materiel pass his checkpoint, he nonetheless admitted that "I know and I have seen, like everyone else, that from 1936 to 1939 big trucks loaded with heavy boxes were sent from France to Spain accompanied by customs officials, but I never saw the nature of the transported merchandise. In every case I was never called to proceed to a customs examination." It is evident that the right-wing propaganda with which "everyone" was familiar did not make the court's work any easier, but Casademon's own primary concern was for his own reputation. He seems to have taken the question as a personal attack, as he hastened to add that he had received praise for his management of his checkpoint.[11]

The court's extensive reliance on minor technical witnesses, sometimes of low social status, is particularly intriguing because it reveals the court's view of its mission and the considerable leeway it possessed to determine the nature of the charges. Riom was not a political trial in the conventional sense of the term. Its witnesses and prosecutors deemed themselves to be as independent as the government claimed that they were. In execution as well as in conception, Riom was a technical phenomenon, designed to operate in strict opposition to "politics."

At the same time, however, the Riom testimonies can be seen as a form of lobbying – Vichy's supporters telling the court what they disliked about the previous regime. For the most part, the attitudes of Vichy's "middle management" regarding politics mirrored the attitudes of those at the top. They also demonstrate, however, how Vichy's attitudes regarding the political sphere related to other Vichy attitudes that are by now well-established in the historiographical literature, notably Vichy's obsession with concepts such as hierarchy, discipline, and responsibility. These concepts formed the core of the National Revolution that was supposed to transform French society by restoring respect for proper bourgeois values. They were therefore, in our eyes, political notions. Most Riom witnesses, however, saw no conflict between attacking the Riom defendants for being excessively "political" and attacking them for their failure to support these (actual or supposedly) traditional values. On the contrary, in their view, the one led to the other via the notion of a "miasma of indiscipline" created by left-wing politics.

11 Joseph Casademon's testimony, Box 38, Series 496AP, AN.

The Evils of the Political

Much as the notion that "politics" were what was wrong with the interwar system was common in almost all political parties except for the extreme left, the Riom *instruction* reveals that the condemnation of politics was a theme common among prosecutors and witnesses alike. Those closest to the political middle ground were most likely to share Vichy's interpretation of the Third Republic's failings as coming from overly "political" actions.

Raoul Dautry's testimony is particularly interesting in this regard, as Dautry was far from being a stereotypical Vichy supporter. Indeed, this former armaments minister under Daladier and Reynaud was prudent enough to withdraw from public life for the duration of the occupation, a decision from which he benefited after the Liberation, when de Gaulle appointed him Minister for Reconstruction and Town Planning. Like Romier and Alibert, Dautry had been a member of *Redressement Français* before the war, but his conduct under the Occupation was quite the opposite of theirs.[12]

Although Dautry agreed to testify before the *Cour Suprême*, he informed it openly that he considered himself to hold advanced social views. Yet he also denounced the forty-hour law, calling it "profoundly harmful for the economic life and morale of the country" – the word "morale," as always, being a veiled indication that he shared Vichy's concern that the Popular Front had played politics with the nation's spirit. Still more explicitly, he denounced the nationalizations as having a "political character."[13] It is evident that even such a middle-of-the-road figure as Dautry could still believe that the problem was one of excessive "politics" to the point that he was willing to denounce the Popular Front even to such a dubious audience as the *Cour Suprême*.

There were exceptions to Dautry's opposition to politics. Pierre Claudel, an officer of the air force charged with surveying factories for signs of sabotage, was highly unusual in attacking the administration of the factories for being *too* technical and insufficiently concerned with the national interest. More honest than some of his colleagues, Claudel admitted that the solution he proposed was a political one rather than the imposition of a technocratic solution: he alluded to "the impossibility that confronted the Air Ministry of changing the climate of its factories without a different political attitude."[14] The use of the term "politics" was not universally reviled; and one might be permitted to speculate

12 On Dautry's anti-Vichy stance, see Remi Baudouï, "Raoul Dautry, La Conscience du Social," *Vingtième Siècle. Revue d'Histoire*, no. 15 (1987).

13 Testimony of Raoul Dautry, Box 38, Series 496AP, AN.

14 Testimony of Pierre Claudel, Box 38, Series 496AP, AN.

as to whether Claudel had read the collaborationist journals in which it was sometimes a positive term.

From Politics to Indiscipline

Most Riom witnesses, however, hated "politics." They saw politics as leading to an equally important concept – indiscipline. Indiscipline was a poorly defined concept whose looseness allowed it to encompass, and thereby suggest a causal connection between, the strikes of 1936 and the military collapse of 1940. This had two important consequences. The first was to enable an instinctive alliance between military and bureaucratic testimonies, both of which deplored indiscipline among their subordinates. The second was to push blame down the chain of command. If indiscipline was the cause of France's long-term economic and short-term military problems, then those at the top of the bureaucratic and military hierarchies could safely claim innocence. This, however, created a problem: the French working class, in either of its manifestations as armaments workers or as private soldiers, was not on trial, and those who were on trial were unquestionably fellow members of the elite. This was where the condemnation of "politics" by Vichy and its supporters came into its own. It created a conceptual category with which to explain how the French masses could be corrupted by a carefully selected subsection of the elite – *fauteurs d'indiscipline* (supporters of indiscipline) – while still remaining pure at heart.

None of this chain of reasoning was explicit or imposed from above. It was a spontaneous phenomenon whose elements reappear in various forms in the testimonies themselves. The Vichy elite repeatedly developed the concept of *indiscipline* and its associate category of *fauteurs d'indiscipline* independently, as a product of their personal experiences of the 1936–1940 period. Thus, for example, for Émile Jeansen, an engineer, it was nationalization and the attendant *indiscipline* that caused France's dire shortage of planes:

> I had the opportunity to note in particular, that at the Bougenais factory, near Nantes, a nationalized factory, no workers showed up on certain Sundays, even though work had been planned for those days. There were also in this factory organized cells that gave orders to the workers. It was anarchy. The same thing happened in many other locations.[15]

Most other witnesses, however, avoided attacking the concept of nationalization directly and instead claimed that it was merely the implementation of national-

15 Deposition of Emile Jeansen, Box 39, Series 496AP, AN.

ization that was at fault. The implication, however, was always the same – that the Popular Front, by encouraging disorder and undermining established hierarchies, had retarded France's defense preparation and reduced her citizens' capacity to be soldiers. In this regard, the testimony of Jean Lachenaud, Director-General of Supervisory Operations (*contrôle*) for the army, was more typical than Jeansen's. He summed up his remarks on nationalization with the comment that "Nationalization is not, either from the point of view of production or from that of finances, an operation that should be condemned in itself. After a certain lapse of time, it is even possible that the new State Factories might have been able to produce more than under private ownership and to produce as cheaply." Yet his conclusion was nonetheless that the timing was unfortunate: "What we can say is that the experiment of 1936, at a moment when it was urgent to make an immense effort in arms manufacturing, was inopportune."[16]

The *réquisitoire* or list of accusations written by the state prosecutor, Cassagnau, in 1941 would consequently hold the nationalization against Blum. He was accused of having undertaken the nationalization with the aim of making it easier for a prospective disarmament agreement to be enforced. Cassagnau also claimed that the nationalizations were expensive, diminished the incentive to innovate and reduced the production of nationalized factories, but, once again, it was the Popular Front's supposed predilection for intruding "politics" into technical matters that formed the crown of the accusations. What mattered most to Cassagnau was that Blum had made the decision "towards a political end, while letting it be incorrectly claimed that it could be useful to National Defense."[17]

If there was some room for ambiguity in the discussion of nationalizations, the basic principle behind which many witnesses were reluctant to criticize, there was no such room for ambiguity in the discussion of the Popular Front's other social innovations. Here the supposed link between *indiscipline* and moral collapse surfaced even more clearly. The forty-hour work week, the *congés payés* (paid vacations) and the strikes were all assimilated into an atmosphere of indiscipline encouraged from above. For example, Jean Volpert, an aeronautics engineer, described the effect of the Popular Front's innovations on production as follows:

> The application of the social laws, imposing the 40 hour [week], reduced by about a third the yield of the workforce. The quality of this workforce was itself reduced by the atmosphere of agitation that reigned at this time.

16 Testimony of Jean Lachenaud, Box 39, Series 496AP, AN.
17 *Réquisitoire*, pp. 90–93, Box 2, Series 2W, AN.

> The loss of authority of the foremen and of the factory directors led, in many cases, to an indiscipline, to an anarchy incompatible with the proper conduct of the factories. As an example, I will cite a meeting held in the office of the Air Minister, M. Pierre Cot, at the start of the month of June 1936, during which the Minister harshly reprimanded the bosses of the occupied aeronautics factories in front of the workers' representatives.[18]

One can almost feel Volpert's indignation wafting from the page. Cot had no right to undermine the sacred authority of the *patron* (boss), and to do so in front of the workers was unconscionable. There was a social principle at stake that went far beyond the mere matter of the specific concessions the workers demanded. Politically-induced indiscipline ran the risk of undermining the national hierarchy.

Once again, the category of indiscipline was one that the witnesses shared with the government. Thus, Cassagnau's *réquisitoire* gave ample space to the witnesses' concerns about indiscipline and politicism. In the *réquisitoire* against Léon Blum, the term "indiscipline" was almost a litany. Communist agitation had contributed to "shake the authority of the bosses and of the foremen, and to propagate the spirit of indiscipline and nonchalance," wrote Cassagnau; "[t]his indiscipline, the Government of M. Blum did nothing to master." On the very next page, he complained of "indiscipline, agitation, hindering of production."[19]

Like many of the witnesses, Cassagnau attributed the *indiscipline* that caused the defeat to an inchoate atmosphere created by the Popular Front's insults against hierarchy. There was no space in his ideology for the idea that Blum might have had a legitimate choice of options regarding the 1936 strikers. Instead, Blum's policy choices appeared as "Weakness of the government of M. Léon Blum with regard to the strikes, factory occupations and antinational propaganda in factories working for the National Defense." Still worse, Blum had "perhaps more seriously weakened our country's production and morale and material strength to resist by tolerating or favoring, by his policies, worker agitation and revolutionary propaganda in all industries," especially defense industries. In the end, though, Blum's main crime was being "systematically passive;" even after the Matignon accords ended the 1936 wave of strikes, Blum and his ministers "did not want to show their authority." There followed the usual connection from failure of leadership to indiscipline: "From the point of view of morale, indiscipline and the spirit of rebellion could only be favored. The authority

18 Testimony of Jean Volpert, Box 41, Series 496AP, AN.
19 *Réquisitoire*, pp. 95–96, Box 2, Series 2W, AN.

of the bosses was greatly shaken. The foremen were worried, hesitant and could no longer make themselves obeyed."[20]

From Indiscipline to Hierarchy

Technical staff played an important and even predominant role in the *instruction*, one second only to that of the military. Any attack on any part of the social hierarchy was an attack on the whole, which was why Volpert, like many other witnesses, displayed a concern for the social status of the *maîtrise* (foremen). (This concern was shared by the court, whose *commission rogatoire* (investigative commission) of 6 May 1941 listed the condition of the *maîtrise* among the essential questions to be decided in the new case against Jacomet.)[21] If the chain of command was threatened, the result would be anarchy. There was, however, something else at stake as well. Volpert did not explicitly contrast his status as a technocrat with the uneducated workers whose unrest he feared; and nor did most of the other witnesses. Yet the very fact that the court relied so heavily on the testimony of *fonctionnaires* (bureaucrats) suggests a shared respect for technical expertise. For Vichy, the opposite of indiscipline was technocratic rule, just as the opposite of politics was justice.

Hierarchy was not merely an abstract principle for the Vichy regime. It took the concrete form of an expected deference, not only to those who were one's superiors now, but also to any individual to whom one owed a previous promotion. As we shall see, this principle went beyond Vichy and could be a cardinal virtue even for unimpeachably Republican politicians.

Deference, in turn, was defined as the opposite of backbiting. In the clientelist world of the late Third Republic, one could not benefit from a patron's graces at one moment and criticize them the next – although, of course, the whiplash of political allegiances in 1940 meant that this rule was distressingly frequently "more honored in the breach than the observance." For example, the testimony of Daladier's former Foreign Minister Georges Bonnet (who himself had by this time turned violently against Daladier) contains a violent critique over 100 pages long of Léon Noël, a former French ambassador to Poland, who in turn had publicly criticized the foreign policy of the Daladier government which he had once served. To be sure, Bonnet criticized Noël's analysis on substantive grounds, but first he denounced Noël's breach of the invisible laws of patronal

20 *Ibid*, 93–94.
21 Commission rogatoire, 6 May 1941, Box 47, Series 496AP, AN.

deference. Noël had been "severe against his former bosses," he wrote, and "aside from himself, he spares no one, not even the ministers to whom he owes his entire diplomatic career."[22]

Perhaps this is only the pique of a rather self-absorbed man, intensely concerned about his reputation (he later wrote a five-volume set of memoirs in an attempt to vindicate his foreign policy), who found himself betrayed by a protegée. Yet Bonnet's willingness to criticize his own superior while attacking Noël for criticizing his suggests that what mattered to him was that Noël was his client. A client, defined loosely as an individual promoted by a patron, did not have the right subsequently to criticize that patron.

In this sense, then, Vichy's preoccupation with hierarchy was not an innovation but an extension of Third Republic clientelism – or, rather, it was an example of the way in which Vichy grew from the Republic. It is therefore unsurprising that concerns about hierarchy and discipline both in and outside the factory appear repeatedly in the depositions, among both bureaucrats and army officers. On this point, they often sound very similar to industrialists like Maurice Goudard, president of the *Chambre Syndicale des Fabricants d'Accessoires pour Automobiles, Cycles, et Aviation,* who claimed that "The factory occupations ruined authority and discipline, discouraged the leaders of business, sapped the morale of the country."[23] Another such example among many can be seen in the testimony of Pierre Claudel, whom we have already encountered. Obsessed with the danger of communist subversion, Claudel claimed to have helped dissuade Reynaud from implementing a plan to form security teams of workers against sabotage with the argument that such an approach might lead to communist workers acquiring arms. In his view, the rot in the French air industry began with Pierre Cot, who had turned French factories into "experimental grounds for communist methods." The result – his terminology here is identical to Volpert's – was "anarchy." Claudel also displayed a similar concern for the authority of the *maîtrise*, which he claimed "does not command."

From Hierarchy to Irresponsibility

Such, then, was Vichy's image of the causes of the defeat. The Third Republic, by introducing "politics" into technical matters of armaments production and military preparation, had provoked indiscipline among the lower orders. Having lost

22 Bonnet testimony annexe, Box 37, Series 496AP, AN.
23 Testimony of Maurice Goudard, Box 39, Series 496AP, AN.

their respect for the natural hierarchy, the masses became unruly and unproductive, incapable of standing up to the German challenge. In general, though (there were exceptions, especially when the much-despised Pierre Cot was the subject of discussion), the witnesses did not presume to claim that this atmosphere of indiscipline had been created deliberately. Indeed, even after the disaster, it was unconscionable for respectable, centrist men to adopt the tactics of the communists or the ultra-collaborationists and accuse a French prime minister – any prime minister, even the much-maligned Blum – of deliberate treason.

Rather, most witnesses' explanation for the perceived failures of the 1936–1940 period hinged on another crucial Vichyite concept: irresponsibility. Echoing Romier's prewar critique of the Third Republic as a talking shop where politicians looked to their own careers rather than the national interest, these witnesses explained the disaster as the product of a combination of egotism and a system that failed to hold leaders accountable for failure.

This definition of responsibility was at best inchoate, for it contained no element of responsibility *to* anything. That was the fatal imprecision in the political thought of Vichy and its supporters that led to the bizarre phrase *trahison des devoirs de sa charge* (treason against the duties incumbent upon him). The concept of criminal negligence requires a breach of an obvious responsibility that any reasonable person could tell exists; but there was no politically neutral "reasonable person" who could define the *devoirs de la charge* of a prime minister in 1936–1940. This was a point that the defendants, and particularly Blum, would raise at the trial itself, arguing that the *devoirs de leur charge* were to the people who had elected them.[24]

It was therefore not incidental but crucial to the Vichy definition of responsibility that it was antidemocratic. The entire purpose of the concept was to supplant a democratic conception of the leader as responsible to his constituents and replace it with a conception of the leader as responsible to the "national interest" as defined by those now in power. Because the "national interest" was above politics and above debate, it enabled Vichy to present different conceptions of national interest as the work of politicians determined to salvage their own careers at the expense of the commonweal. Vichy was engaging in the German political philosopher Carl Schmitt's antipluralistic move of prejudging differing conceptions of political morality as the work of scoundrels bent on manipulating the political world for their own benefit.

Thus, for example, many witnesses accused the one civil servant among the accused, Jacomet, of a reckless careerism. Subordinating the interests of the state

24 Riom Trial transcript, 10 March 1942, Box 25, Series GE, AdHC.

to those of his personal ambition, Jacomet was supposed to have betrayed his duty as a neutral *fonctionnaire* by helping Blum to rationalize the politically-inspired nationalization of armaments factories, and by otherwise assisting the Popular Front in its antinational policies. Indeed, this perceived betrayal helps explain Jacomet's last-minute inclusion in the trial in June 1941. It also explains why a trial of Third Republic political leaders included a bureaucrat among the accused.

Thus, for example, the engineer Arsène Vallat remembered with bitterness an interview with Jacomet in 1937. Jacomet listened with "a very distracted air" and paid little attention to Vallat's complaints, offering only a loan which Vallat's company did not need. Vallat supposed that Jacomet was "much too occupied by politics and by his desire to be named Minister of Armaments."[25] Vallat may merely have suffered from a bruised ego, but he was wise enough to see that the court would look with a kindly eye on accusations of careerism and excessively "political" attitudes.

Another example of the way the accusations against Jacomet interacted with the concepts of politics, hierarchy and indiscipline can be seen in Georges Guerard's testimony. Guerard, an armaments engineer for the *Établissements Laffly*, offered the standard denunciation of the 1936 strikes, which he believed to be the consequence of the actions of a small number of professional agitators. One such agitator was supposed to be Raymond Colin, a communist and CGT official, who was supposed to be involved in organizing the strikes, but who, more importantly, had undermined the hierarchy of the factory: "He showed an arrogance full of violence and disrespect towards his hierarchical leaders and the factory directors."[26] It was this individual whom Jacomet was said to have protected, and whose rehiring Jacomet was supposed to have forced after Colin was fired for his political activities.[27] Auguste Vialles, an engineer at Laffly, backed up Guerard's story. According to him, Colin spent most of his time conducting political propaganda and had insulted his foreman. It was for this insult to the chain of command that he was fired, a decision with which Vialles agreed categorically: "The rehiring of Colin, in the *Établissements Laffly*, would have been harmful to its proper functioning and to the authority of the foremen. His firing was a relief for all the healthy elements of our workshops."[28]

25 Arsène Vallat testimony, Box 41, Series 496AP, AN.
26 Georges Guerard testimony, Box 41, Series 496AP, AN.
27 Georges Guerard testimony, Box 39, Series 496AP, AN.
28 August Vialles testimony, Box 41, Series 496AP, AN.

That the court took these accusations seriously can be seen from the fact that it was evidently deemed worthwhile to follow up on them. In addition to Vialles and Guerard, Louis Butor, another engineer at a different factory, was interviewed regarding the question of whether he had seen workers rehired due to government pressure. He was aware of only one case in which the factory manager's desire to keep a troublesome worker out of the factory was overruled.[29] Butor did not offer a comment on the merits of this decision.

From Irresponsibility Back to Politics

In spite of the fact that Jacomet was a *fonctionnaire*, therefore, the accusations against him support the notion that Vichy's supporters shared Romier's diagnosis of the ills of the Third Republic as stemming from excessive politics. They echo Romier and the *Redressement Français*' interwar complaint that bureaucrats had come to realize that the road to promotion was not technical competence but political activity. Cassagnau's final *réquisitoire* against Jacomet supports this conclusion. Cassagnau, too, emphasized Jacomet's careerism and asserted that his role had gradually expanded from being purely fiscal and administrative to surveying the execution of policy. He was said to have opposed the creation of an armaments ministry because it would have restricted his own powers. In addition to the charge of negligence (*impéritie*) that was made against every defendant, Cassagnau attached equal importance to the charge that Jacomet's actions had been determined by "the desire [...] to serve a *politique* at the expense of the *devoirs de sa charge.*" Jacomet, according to Cassagnau, had possessed the powers of an armaments minister without the responsibility, and to have used these powers with a "lack of impulse and spirit of *parti-pris* regarding armaments factories."[30]

Indeed, the *réquisitoire* could hardly have been more explicit in its indications that Cassagnau considered Jacomet's guilt to reside primarily in his attachment to "politics." For Cassagnau, the surest sign of Jacomet's attachment to politics (and careerism) lay in his implementation of Popular Front policies and his rehiring of workers fired for provoking strikes. Cassagnau denounced the "submission of M. Jacomet's actions and decisions to political preoccupations and plans," which could be seen in "the complaisance with which he greeted political recommendations and the influence that they had on his decisions; the tol-

29 Louis Butor testimony, Box 37, Series 496AP, AN.
30 *Réquisitoire*, pp. 122–128, Box 2, Series 2W, AN.

erance he accorded to illegal unions; his weakness with regard to employees or workers who had lacked discipline or even caused disturbances; finally, the manner in which he applied the nationalization law."[31]

By failing to reprimand indiscipline, Jacomet had allowed politics to enter into the technical sphere of armaments production. Therein lay his, and the Third Republic's, responsibility for the defeat. The same preoccupations with discipline, hierarchy and politics are repeated like a litany through the rest of the allegations. As head of a very large staff, Cassagnau explained, Jacomet "had the strict duty to firmly maintain discipline." He had betrayed this duty by inciting his subordinates to "weakness by his [political] attachments and his political preoccupations."[32] Rehiring of strikers was a criminal act because "such a weakness made a major contribution to the relaxation of discipline."

Jacomet understood perfectly the thrust of the accusations: the anti-political language of Vichy, as we have seen, was not so far from the mainstream that we should expect it to incomprehensible to any individual involved in French government. Cassagnau acknowledged that Jacomet "defends himself with energy against the charge of being a politician."[33] His protests, however, were in vain. Cassagnau insisted repeatedly that "M. Jacomet allowed himself to be guided by the desire to please or to avoid displeasing a certain politics."[34] To reintegrate strikers into the workforce in the name of a social policy was demagoguery, and "this demagogic attitude was inadmissible coming from a leader."[35]

An Overarching Category: Leadership

This appeal to the concept of the *chef*, or leader, was a key component of the indiscipline/hierarchy/politics nexus. If politics led to indiscipline and to the breakdown of hierarchy, it was the absence of leadership that led to politics in the Third Republic sense – that is, a situation in which a bureaucrat could supposedly seek to further his own career by advancing a sectarian agenda at the expense of the commonweal. No true *chef* would ever behave in such a way. A true *chef* was by definition above party, able to prioritize the national interest above his own personal benefit – able, in short, to make the "gift of his person" to the nation, as Pétain claimed that he had. In other words, a true *chef* was "re-

31 *Ibid*, 132.
32 *Ibid*, 135.
33 *Ibid*, 132.
34 *Ibid*, 136.
35 *Ibid*, 136.

sponsible," using the amorphous Vichy definition of responsibility that has already been discussed.

The government lost no opportunity to make it clear that the trial was about the nature of the *chef*, and that the defendants had failed to demonstrate true leadership. At the beginning of 1941, for example, as the trial preparations approached the six-month mark, Pétain arrogated to himself via Constitutional Act N. 7 the right to condemn those he deemed guilty of *trahison des devoirs de leur charge* (the same language as was used in the constitutional act establishing the *Cour Suprême*). He did so by making "former ministers, high dignitaries and high bureaucrats who had exercised their responsibilities (*charge*) for less than ten years"[36] personally responsible to himself. That the term "responsible" was not merely a verbal coincidence, but a deliberate attempt to create a contrast between republican irresponsibility and the responsibility of true (that is, authoritarian) leadership, can be seen in the reception of the new act by the moderate press. *Le Temps*, presumably with government encouragement, greeted the act under the heading of "Return to Political Logic":

> It could happen that naïve but upright persons could exclaim, "This didn't exist until now?"
>
> In fact, the exercise of public authority, in France, entailed virtually no responsibility. Public life offered the abnormal spectacle of which we saw the outcome in the form of the catastrophe of last June, and it was more or less agreed that mistakes committed against the nation brought with them neither punishment nor penalty.
>
> And it even seemed that certain responsibilities, dignities and honors attached themselves to some of those who had possessed them, and were accorded to them with the inviolability of an annuity.[37]

Le Temps proceeded to explain that this disgraceful time of unrestrained careerism had now been replaced by a culture of responsibility: "From now on, 'Secretaries of State, high dignitaries and high state functionaries' will owe loyalty to the person of the head of state, before whom they are personally responsible. Having promised to 'exercise their responsibilities for the good of the State, according to the laws of honor and probity,' they thus assume a responsibility that 'involves their person and their goods.'"[38] *Le Temps* was less explicit than many more radical papers in its references to the sins of the past, but the implication

---

36 Jean-Pierre Maury, "Le Gouvernement de Vichy," Acte Constitutionnel N° 7 du 27 Janvier 1941, accessed September 21, 2018, http://mjp.univ-perp.fr/france/co1940.htm#7.
37 "Retour à la Logique Politique," *Le Temps*, Box 26, Series 71AP, AN.
38 *Ibid.*

was clear: the France of the Stavisky Affair was over. From now on, the inadequate concept of responsibility to the people would be replaced with the more effective concept of responsibility to the nation – that is, to the hierarchical leadership.

Leadership and the Army

Leadership, then, was a crucial category of legitimation in Vichy France. Nonetheless, the category of leadership, and the definition of a good leader, was contested. We have seen the close relationship between the concept of leadership and the politically ambiguous heritage of Clemenceau. Clemencisme could be coopted by individuals of all political persuasions; and the Riom trial, from the government's point of view, constituted such an attempt to coopt a widely diffused but contested concept. For many of the individuals Vichy itself trusted to govern had formed part of the old, supposedly irresponsible leadership that the nation blamed for the defeat. In particular, Vichy was overwhelmingly populated by individuals who had been prominent in the military prior to 1940. Thus, when Pétain and his military colleagues referred to "the honor of the Army" that the trial was supposed to defend, what they meant was the honor of the professional officer corps, and especially of its most senior members. Pétain himself had been responsible more than any other individual for the prewar doctrine of the French army, even apart from his 1934 tenure of the Ministry of War, and it was therefore essential for the government to demonstrate the absurd conclusion that "politics" had prevented the government from listening to his sage advice. The primary debate revolved around the Supreme War Council, the most important advisory body of the army, of which Pétain was the senior member. The court sought to show that Daladier had ignored this body and had summoned it as rarely as possible. (It is difficult to believe that anyone was taken in by this effort to show that the nation's highest military body was not responsible for its military doctrine.) The Riom trial was therefore supposed to show that the military had had "good leaders," while politicians were, by definition, "bad leaders."

The key to demonstrating that military figures were good leaders was to place them in the "technical" rather than the "political" category. This accorded well with the army's preexisting view of itself. If the Vichy stereotype of the Third Republic parliamentarian was of a person who spoke too much and knew too little, the self-stereotype of the French Army was that it was *la Grande Muette* – the great mute – condemned to remain forever silent for reasons of honor. It was not a coincidence that Pétain and Gamelin adopted the same legal strategy at their respective trials. Both claimed to remain silent to defend the honor of the army and their subordinates, while nonetheless providing the court with immense volumes of written commentary in an effort to exculpate themselves. Gamelin, in spite of his initial disclaimer, also spoke on occasion when he felt he had something to contribute (for example, he denied that General Louis Keller had told him about tank shortages).[39] It was a strategy that made little sense from the perspective of logic – if speaking about the subject matter of the trial was offensive to honor, then so surely should have been writing about it – but that played well to the army's image. Writing represented an indisputable statement; speaking was perilously close to mere argument.

Gamelin, then, had made his choice. He would side with the military against the Republic. Gamelin was widely believed to be a relatively pro-Republican general, as generals went; and the fact that he betrayed the civilian leaders who had put their trust in him suggests how deeply appealing the cult of *La Grand Muette* must have been. That his silence was indeed a betrayal cannot be doubted. Certainly his former allies felt that way at the time; Blum reprimanded him gently at the trial,[40] and Daladier reproached him rather less gently in his diary, describing his reaction to the court's chief magistrate Pierre Caous's failed efforts to persuade the disgraced general to talk as "dolorous, painful, almost nauseating."[41] In both cases, once Gamelin announced his decision not to speak, all was said. Both Blum and Daladier evidently understood the topos that politicians talked and generals were silent; if Gamelin was silent, then he was siding with the generals and with the prosecution, rather than with the parliamentarians and the defense.

Indeed, Gamelin, as the only general to be tried, was an anomaly at the Riom trials. The first (and, due to the suspension of the trial, only) witnesses who spoke at the trial proper were all officers. A handful were civilians speaking in their capacity as reserve officers, but the vast majority were career soldiers, usually generals. Just as the drafts of the constitutional act establishing the *Cour Suprême* would suggest, Riom was the product of an alliance between the military and the magistrates, both of them self-defined as "technicians" and therefore good leaders.

We have already noted, however, that leadership at Vichy, for all its omnipresence, was a contested category and not a universal one. It could be contested from the perspective of alternative sources of leadership, but it also contained

---

39 Riom Trial transcript, 31 March, Box 25, Series GE, AdHC.
40 *Ibid.*
41 Édouard Daladier, *Prison Journal, 1940–1945*, ed. Jean Daladier, trans. Arthur Greenspan (Boulder: Westview Press, 1995), 133.

in itself major self-contradictions. Its replacement of responsibility-to-the-people with responsibility *tout court* left the leader unable to share responsibility with anyone, including his subordinates. In other words, either generals or ordinary soldiers could be responsible for the defeat, but not both.

This presented an immediate problem. The French Army of 1940 was a conscription force based on the principle of universal military service, which meant that the vast majority of French males had served in the military and had cause to identify with its rank and file. This meant that the prosecution was placed in the awkward position of siding with the professional military staff against their subordinates while implicitly appealing for the support of these same subordinates in their guise as members of the public. The obvious solution was to throw the blame onto the civilian political leadership by insisting on the problem of shortages, which, indeed, was the key component of the prosecution's case and was raised in some form by almost every witness. This was, however, only a partial solution, because, as have already seen, the explanation of Vichy's supporters for the supposed shortages was poor morale among workers caused by the prewar regime's demagogic policies.

We have already seen that in their depositions, discussed above, most witnesses tended to present the question as one of a "miasma" of malaise caused by rabble-rousing on the factory floor that went unhindered by the government. These *instruction* witnesses, however, did not face the challenge of cross-examination by the Riom defendants, many of whom were highly able in legal terms. In the very different conditions of the courtroom, therefore, the "miasma" explanation proved incomplete because the military witnesses, unable to comment directly on the question of the impact of 1936 on the workforce, could not restrain themselves from translating the question of morale among workers into a question about morale in general. This enabled them to condemn the Popular Front for undermining them in their key sphere of technocratic competence – the conduct of military operations – but it had the unintended side effect of altering the condemnation of the prewar regime's governing class into a condemnation of ordinary soldiers and civilian reserve officers.

This was a serious handicap in a trial that was aimed at convincing a population that had overwhelming cause to sympathize with ordinary soldiers. Not only were the witnesses insulting the government's own potential supporters, but they also afforded defendants the government wished to prove antinational the opportunity to drape themselves in the flag. This importance of this factor should not be overstated. Most French people were almost certainly not aware of the trial transcripts, and the mainstream newspapers carried only summaries that drifted from the first page as the trial progressed. Most of the damage to the government's cause was done in the early days of the trial, when Daladier and

Blum had their chance to speak, and not in the later weeks of remorselessly chipping away at the government's case. Nonetheless, this factor is significant inasmuch as it exposes the inherent contradictions of the government's position.

How it worked in practice can be seen in the court transcripts. The first witness to appear after the opening statements (which had lasted four weeks) was General Auguste Besson, who terminated his remarks on the state of the army in 1940 with a complaint about morale. In his view, the French no longer believed themselves to be a great nation. The French soldiers of 1940 had been preoccupied with material interests and had been educated in a way that predisposed them to resist military authority. Besson scrupulously avoided a direct attack on the Popular Front, dating the decline in education to 1930 rather than 1936.[42] His testimony was typical of the mainstream professional officer at the trial, who did not *faire la politique* (engage in politics), but who were nonetheless convinced – as many French people were, on both sides of the political spectrum – that something was wrong with the nation, more than with the military.

Besson's discussion of morale was much milder and less prejudiced than that of many other witnesses during the trial. Daladier, however, was evidently spoiling for a fight. The ensuing cross-examination was considerably more devastating than contemporary newspapers indicated. Daladier (who was far more thorough in the course of the cross-examinations than Blum, even if the latter's rousing rhetoric captured more of the headlines) mercilessly hammered home the point that the failure to guard the Ardennes adequately was a purely military failing that could in no way be blamed on the civilian leadership, and one, moreover, that could be directly traced back to Pétain's influence and his tenure of the Ministry of War in 1934. Moreover, Daladier seized the opportunity Besson had handed him to praise the patriotic spirit of the French nation:

> ...I cannot let pass without some protest the picture that has been drawn up of the French nation at different times, according to which France was not interested in her destiny, nor in that of Europe, that she had in short lost all moral value. I believe in the first place that that is not the truth and that it is of a nature to encourage campaigns of denigration and calumny that France can incidentally disdain, but that it would be strange to see develop themselves in the course of this trial and in favor of this trial.[43]

At this point Caous interrupted, but the damage had been done. Daladier's attack was not entirely fair. Any discussion of the defeat that mentioned the obviously relevant matter of national morale, which included essentially all of the

42 Riom Trial transcript, 17 March 1942, Box 25, Series GE, AdHC.
43 *Ibid.*

books written on the subject in the aftermath of the defeat regardless of the political complexion of their author, would have been open to the same criticism. Nonetheless, the attack exposes the internal flaws of the government's legal strategy. It was impossible to deflect the blame from senior military officials altogether without casting aspersions on the nation as a whole. It is difficult not to admire the artifice with which Daladier, in the space of two sentences, managed to turn this narrow foothold into an assault on the court itself.

Subsequent witnesses learned little from Besson's discomfiture. General after general approached the tribunal to list a national deficiency of morale as one of the causes of the defeat. General Henri Préaud, for example, described the attitude of his troops as one of resignation rather than enthusiasm. Similarly, General Alfred Conquet denounced the "decline of public spirit in France." He blamed matériel shortages and the presence of Communist agitators in the army for this sorry state of affairs.[44]

If one purpose of the trial was to protect the upper echelons of the military from blame for the defeat, it was clear that the government needed an alternative mechanism to suggest instead of an absence of national spirit in France. Instead, the government's case focused on an argument that should by now be familiar. The miasma of politics had tainted not only the factory floor (thus resulting in the matériel shortages about which nearly every witness was questioned) but also the nation as a whole, and, therefore, the army. As a technocratic branch, the army could not be subject to political interference, and Cassagnau was therefore eager to investigate every possibility of government intervention that might have a political motivation behind it. For example, he cross-examined General Paul Gérodias, who had been dismissed by Daladier after the general circulated a document regarding measures that could prevent a communist putsch in Spain. Gérodias himself saw this event as a misunderstanding rather than a deliberate act of political interference, and even Caous was skeptical (although he ultimately allowed the line of questioning), but Cassagnau was determined to follow up every suggestion that the army had been administered politically.[45]

It is important to remember in reading these sometimes rather dry documents that France was still a country of moderates, and that these moderates were still very much open to persuasion regarding the role of the military. We have seen that the question of prosecuting military leaders was one that interested public opinion from the very beginning, and that not all of those who wanted a trial were pleased with Vichy's decision to defend the officer corps. It is in this

44 Riom Trial transcript, 26 March 1942, Box 25, Series GE, AdHC.
45 Riom Trial transcript, 25 March 1942, Box 25, Series GE, AdHC.

light that we should view an April 1942 letter from, of all people, Armand Goeau-Brissonière, Mandel's lawyer, commenting that

> The court sessions seemed to me odious, especially when the nonplussed generals adopted a most unfortunate tactic and started to incriminate the morale of the army, to 'fire on their own men.'
>
> A probable compromise: by a law that shines with the desire to cast a penetrating and full light on events, the Marshal will extend to military operations the competence of the Court. How then to proceed without opening a second *instruction*, this time relating to the aforementioned operations? The debates will thus be interrupted, not from fear but from love of the truth.

Goeau-Brissonière went on to speak hopefully of the potential of the American air force.[46] France in 1942 was a complicated place.

A Case Study: The Cunin Report

The court-ordered report on the causes of the defeat by Cunin, the *contrôleur général* of the army, is an excellent example of how Vichy's middle management interpreted the interlocking concepts of politics, indiscipline, hierarchy and leadership. In Cunin's view, the failure of the Third Republic was a failure of leadership: "The function of the *Chef* is to foresee, to set principles and *hold to them*,"[47] he wrote, whereas the leadership of the late Third Republic (Cunin had the intellectual honesty to date the problem to 1933 rather than 1936) had spent too much time in the vain pursuit of disarmament. This "drift in the thought of the leaders"[48] led to a failure to determine what the true goals of French policy should be. Cunin continued: "Now, the role of the *Chef* is to accumulate advice, to choose, accepting the responsibility, to give orders, to demand and monitor their execution."[49]

We are a long way away here from the polemical tone of Cassagnau's *réquisitoire*. Indeed, much of Cunin's critique is entirely innocuous – no one could seriously quarrel with the notion that a good leader should check to ensure that her orders are properly carried out. Moreover, Cunin associated the cult of the leader with a philosophical voluntarism reminiscent of Henri Bergson that was

46 Goeau-Brissonière to Mandel, 11 April 1942, Box 74, Series 544AP, AN.
47 Cunin report, p. 94, Box 41, Series 496AP, AN.
48 *Ibid.*
49 *Ibid*, 95.

not present, or at least not stressed, in most other sources. As he put it, "Defeat is only the lot of the weak because they *did not want*, truly want, to be strong."[50] Yet the need to discuss policy failures in terms of grand conceptions of leadership (which carries with it an unspoken presupposition that others – that is, the defendants and their supporters – might have a different conception of leadership), as well as the insistence on the recurring figure of the Responsible Leader who is not responsible to anything in particular, places Cunin in the same camp as Cassagnau. For him, too, there was a massive void at the center of his thought where the Republic had placed the concept of pluralism.

Given this general similarity of thought, it should not surprise us to find that the notion of the *chef* was of a piece with the rest of Vichyite thought, and that Cunin shared with Cassagnau and most of the witnesses the exaltation of apolitical discipline. After contrasting the fruits of the Popular Front – "the idleness, the factory occupations, the hatred" – with the "discipline of production" found in Nazi Germany at the same period, Cunin waxed eloquent on the familiar Vichy topic of the dignity of work:

> It is not sufficient to open the treasury's vaults to transform public funds into cannons, into rifles, into munitions; an intermediary imposes itself, *WORK*, Work in *ORDER*, Work accepted joyfully, not as a punishment, but as a law of health, Work that makes the dignity of Man.
>
> They wanted to avoid EFFORT and they encountered MISFORTUNE.[51]

This cult of work is too familiar a theme for the historian of Vichy to concern us here, except to note that the discipline hierarchy politics nexus of concepts was firmly anchored in Vichy's cult of order.

Incidentally, this contrast of German discipline with French indiscipline was a common theme with Cunin. In another report for the court, he commented that "Germany through intense work, through iron discipline, forged the redoubtable army that gave her victory; France, the prey of a mystique that dissolved public spirit, did not succeed in obtaining from the masses a discipline of work, freely given, that in the absence of constraint would have permitted her to affront difficult circumstances with less risk."[52] As always, the logic of the incitement to indiscipline, expressed here as a "dissolving mystique", furnished a convenient means of suggesting responsibility without proving deliberate malfeasance. Cu-

50 *Ibid*, 99, emphasis in original.
51 Cunin report, pp. 49–50 (note that this is a different report by the same individual), emphasis in original, Box 41, Series 496AP, AN.
52 *Ibid*, 119.

nin's conclusion reiterated that what mattered was the role of the *chef*, and that the late Third Republic had failed to produce such a leader: "a Man was lacking, who, deciding, would have carried everyone with him." He sneered at the Popular Front's armaments record as a litany of words serving instead of deeds, summing up the failures of the prewar era with the comment that *on a parlementé*.[53] This was not, as a literal translation might suggest, a direct attack on parliamentarism, but rather a suggestion that the Third Republic's leaders had debated instead of acting. Still, it is difficult to avoid the impression that Cunin believed that parliamentary pluralism led inescapably to verbiage and a cowardly refusal to act or to accept the possibility of blame.

There was a wide gap between Cunin and Cassagnau, and there was a wide gap between Cassagnau and many of the trial testimonies. Cunin's overt voluntarism is reminiscent of prewar crypto-fascists like Colonel François de La Rocque and his Croix de Feu, while many of the witnesses clearly thought of themselves as technocrats (and, in the case of Dautry, have been portrayed in that light in the subsequent historiography). Yet, for all of their differences of tone and sometimes of meaning, the witnesses and officials of Riom had more in common than separated them. Even the defendants could sometimes successfully coopt parts of the Vichy consensus to their own benefit without thereby compromising their commitment to democracy. The politics-indiscipline-hierarchy-leadership nexus was a societal topos that had been radicalized by the defeat and that the government used to create a dictatorship. Dictatorship, however, was not the only possible outcome from it. Those who interpreted the defeat in a different light could adopt parts of the Vichy consensus without necessarily adopting Vichy's conclusions.

53 *Ibid*, 126.

6 Reynaud, Mandel, Auriol: The Limits of Legalistic Apoliticism

The Riom pretrial was extraordinarily long, lasting eighteen months from start to finish (31 July 1940 to 19 February 1942). Moreover, it rapidly became apparent that even if the trial itself proved to be a success, it would not fulfill all of the government's goals. Vichy had important reasons of its own to express its investigation of the causes of the defeat in juridical form; but, meanwhile, the radical Parisian right and – much more importantly – the Germans were pressing for an investigation of France's supposed responsibility for the causes of the war. This translated to a demand to indict Paul Reynaud and Georges Mandel, who had been among the most prominent of the Frenchmen who had demanded a firmer stance towards Germany, and whom the *Cour Suprême* at Riom refused even to indict.

Vichy attempted on several occasions to remedy these problems, but it was trapped on each occasion by the internal contradiction between its goals. First, taking advantage of the murky Leca-Devaux Affair (in which two members of Reynaud's personal circle were caught after leaving France with government money, as well as funds and gems belonging to Reynaud's mistress), the government attempted to force the *Cour Suprême* to try Reynaud and Mandel by expanding the court's remit to include peculation. This approach failed to persuade the *Cour Suprême* to indict the two men, but it had other flaws: Mandel was not involved in the Leca-Devaux affair (although the government opened a separate, equally unsuccessful investigation of his finances), and, more importantly, even if Reynaud and Mandel had been condemned for peculation, this would not have satisfied the German demand to condemn them for causing the war.

By the summer of 1941, therefore, Vichy in desperation had adopted another strategy. It formed the *Conseil de Justice Politique*, a heterogeneous body of Vichy's supporters tasked with judging the six Riom defendants along with Reynaud and Mandel. The Conseil was openly political even in its name, had little constitutional justification even under Vichy's own constitutional acts,[1] never scrutinized any of the *Cour Suprême*'s voluminous documentation except for

1 Unlike the *Cour Suprême*, it is not mentioned by name in any of these acts. Richard Weisberg, in Richard H. Weisberg, *Vichy Law and the Holocaust in France* (New York: New York University Press, 1996), 20, asserts that its constitutional basis was Act N. 7, which did not mention the (as-yet-unconceived) *Conseil* specifically, but which made French ministers and their immediate subordinates directly responsible to Pétain himself. If so, this was an even more flagrant violation than usual of the principle of non-retroactivity of laws.

https://doi.org/10.1515/9783110610161-006

the state prosecutor's official indictment against the accused, and was composed of individuals who had no particular qualifications except their supposed allegiance to Vichy. (Even this was in doubt, as one member would go on to join the Resistance).

The *Conseil* duly handed down the expected sentences of life imprisonment in a military fortress for the more important defendants, but it was an outcome that was obviously illegitimate and satisfied no one – not even the Germans, who still had not gotten their trial of the causes of the war. The defendants remained imprisoned, but the government had not obtained its legal justification for imprisoning them, much less any credible source of authority for its claim that politicians had cost France the war. The Riom magistrates were furious at being preempted, but continued to work towards the actual trial in February 1942. The only practical effect of the *Conseil*'s "verdict" was to give Blum further ammunition for the trial itself, where he pointed out to the Riom magistrates that the outcome of the trial had already been determined.

The *Conseil* is generally presented as an integral if incongruous part of the government's Riom policy, reflecting the government's supposed failure to offer a consistent constitutional principle separating the branches of government.[2] Yet it should already be apparent that a *Conseil de Justice Politique* could only very awkwardly be associated with a policy that was designed to show that Vichy stood above politics. Moreover, the fact that Vichy waited almost a year before forming the *Conseil* reveals the extent to which it was an expediency, designed to conciliate the Germans and provide a stopgap for the *Cour Suprême*'s interminable deliberations. This chapter will support that conclusion, demonstrating Vichy's growing frustrations in 1940–1942 as its effort to adhere to a legalistic policy while still conciliating German demands crumbled under the weight of its own contradictions.

Mandel and Reynaud

Reynaud and Mandel were almost invariably associated after 1940, in both the right-wing press and the accusations of the government. Unlike the defendants at the Riom Trial proper, both were resolutely right-wing. Their political positions were similar to those of Winston Churchill in Britain: solidly for the national interest and the Empire (Mandel had indeed been Minister for the Colonies), and, for that very reason, anti-German. Moreover, unlike many anti-German French

---

2 See, for example, Bancaud, *Exception Ordinaire*, 104.

nationalists who came to support Vichy (including, most notably, the monarchist Charles Maurras), Reynaud and Mandel never gave any signs of being willing to accommodate themselves to the occupation. Hated by the Germans and the arch-collaborationists, devoted to the cause of French resistance, and with a far better claim to political legitimacy (if they had ever exercised it) than that of the unelected, prickly and profoundly idiosyncratic Charles de Gaulle in London, they represented a perpetual if unrealized threat to the Vichy government.

This being the case, the fact that the *Cour Suprême* at Riom did not execute what the government clearly considered to be its duty of indicting these dangerous figures is the most striking and surprising indication that its political independence was, at least to some extent, real. If the Riom magistrates could refuse to prosecute the two men the Germans most wanted prosecuted, then it is difficult to believe that the government could force the magistrates to do anything they did not wish to do.

Moreover, there is no question that the wishes of the government were more or less aligned with those of the Germans on this issue. To be sure, Pétain made an initial effort to coopt Reynaud, who was known to be well liked in the United States, by assigning him to the Washington embassy. Being posted to the US was an obvious way to reward prominent Republicans for rallying to the regime, and, indeed, the well-known Radical and former Prime Minister Camille Chautemps would ultimately be dispatched there on an ill-defined mission. The American government, however, spoiled this plan by responding with a letter expressing shock that Reynaud would be considered for a post representing a government with which he clearly had strong disagreements.[3] That was the end of the matter. From that point on, it was clear that Reynaud would be *persona non grata* at Vichy.

The fact that Reynaud was even considered for the post, however, suggests that the government had not yet made up its mind as to how to treat him. His activities for the next few weeks are somewhat obscure. After entrusting valuables belonging to the government and the Countess Hélène de Portes, his mistress, to friends in order to get them out of France (of which more below), Reynaud retired from public life for the moment. On 28th June, he was involved in a car accident in which de Portes was killed and Reynaud was seriously injured. Under the circumstances, the accident could only be considered suspicious. The *Cour Suprême* evidently thought so, as they conducted an investigation, but they were unable to discover any evidence that the crash was caused by mal-

3 Note by Paul Reynaud, 13 July 1940, Box 72, Series 2W, AN.

feasance.[4] In the absence of data to the contrary, there is no reason not to allow this conclusion to stand, especially since Reynaud's most powerful enemies had no need to arrange an "accident" if they wanted him dead. In any case, after being discharged from hospital, Reynaud was promptly imprisoned by the government, which had by this point evidently made up its mind as to his fate: he was to be tried by the *Cour Suprême* alongside the other *responsables de la défaîte.*

Mandel experienced a somewhat similar trajectory; he was arrested almost immediately on charges of seeking to connive with the British to overthrow the government in order to replace it with one bent on resistance in North Africa, but was then quickly released with a personal letter of apology from Pétain. "I have acquired the conviction that this denunciation [for treason] had no basis in fact and was a manoeuver or provocation to disorder," wrote the Marshal.[5] In other words, Mandel's accusers were being tarred with the brush of "politics," which, for Vichy, was the deadliest of the mortal sins.

Mandel was soon arrested again, however, and was brought up on similar charges before the military tribunal of Meknès in Algeria. When the military *juge d'instruction*, Colonel Henri Loireau, returned a verdict of *non-lieu* (that is, of insufficient evidence to proceed to trial), the government suspended the jurisdiction of the Meknès tribunal and transferred it to the *Cour Suprême* at Riom, which was evidently expected to prosecute Mandel as one of the authors of the war. By September 1940, therefore, the Vichy government had clearly made up its mind that Reynaud and Mandel were to be prosecuted.

The government's motivations, however, were fundamentally different in the case of Reynaud and Mandel than in those of the other defendants. We have seen that there was near-universal public support for the notion of a trial, but that the identity of the putative culprits varied widely according to one's priorities and political complexion. For the Riom trial as a whole, therefore, what mattered was that predominantly civilian representatives of the defunct regime should be shown to be responsible for the defeat in a manner that would set up a contrast between ineffective Republican and effective Vichyite systems of responsibility. In the case of Reynaud and Mandel, however, the relevance of the individuals involved went beyond their republicanism. Reynaud and Mandel had to be prosecuted because they were so hated by the Germans and the ultra-collaborationist right (and Laval, who seems to have tried to direct the trial against Rey-

---

4 Investigation by Cassagnau, 22 August 1940, Box 72, Series 2W, AN.
5 Pétain to Mandel, 17 June 1940, Box 72, Series 544AP, AN.

naud from its very inception[6]), but, at the same time, it was difficult if not impossible to present any convincing case that either was responsible for the long-term causes of the defeat. This meant that the regime was in the unpleasant position of being forced to invent an increasingly obvious series of trumped-up reasons to imprison the two former leaders. Worse still, it also meant that their imprisonment could not convincingly be presented as part of a project of national restoration, but was clearly imposed from abroad. Moreover, Reynaud and Mandel were right-wingers and could not credibly be presented as *fauteurs d'indiscipline* in the sense of the Riom indictments.

It is impossible to say for certain why the Riom magistrates refused to classify Mandel and Reynaud along with Daladier and Blum, but the reasons were almost certainly among the three listed above. Whatever reasons the magistrates gave themselves at the time, the fact that Reynaud and Mandel were not *fauteurs d'indiscipline* surely weighed particularly heavily upon them. After all, neither obvious violations of legal norms nor the risk of appearing to describe France's entrance into the Second World War as criminal were barriers to indictment at Riom. Alain Bancaud has persuasively argued that the Riom court cared about legal principles only to the extent that they did not run counter to the government's explicitly expressed intentions,[7] a suggestion that seems undeniable in light of the fact that the court displayed no concern for the retroactive nature of the laws it was tasked to enforce.

Similarly and crucially, we will show in the following chapter that the court was initially willing to contemplate indicting Daladier for declaring war illegally (without a parliamentary vote on the matter), thereby conceding the principle that the trial could be about the causes of the war rather than those of the defeat. Since this point in fact constituted the entirety of the distinction between an "internal" trial and a "collaborationist" trial, the court had yielded the intellectual terrain and was now quibbling only about the personalities involved. The distinction between trying Daladier for starting an illegal war and trying Reynaud for advocating an unwinnable war was not one about French patriotism versus German impositions. It was about the fact that Daladier, in his capacity as Defense Minister under the Popular Front, had supported an agenda that many moderate right-wingers believed to have weakened the moral fiber of the nation by undermining established hierarchies. The court understood this as an "apolitical" accusation and was therefore willing to entertain it, whereas it understood collaborationist claims that Reynaud had caused the war as "political" and therefore

6 Note by Reynaud, undated, Box 24, Series 74AP, AN.

7 Bancaud, "Le procès de Riom: service et renversement de la justice."

unworthy of discussion before a court that confined itself to a strictly technocratic sphere of competence.

The way this worked in practice can be seen in the way in which the court reacted to the government's second effort to prosecute Reynaud. By the early autumn of 1940, it had become apparent that the court was not about to behave as the government wished, but a further set of allegations against Reynaud had meanwhile become current in the right-wing press. By this time, the fact that Reynaud had sent valuables out of the country in June had become known, which gave rise to wild speculation among right-wing radical journalists who were only too willing to believe that all Third Republic politicians were venal and corrupt. The government needed Reynaud prosecuted, but it does not particularly appear to have cared about the object of accusation (in contrast with the Riom trial proper, for which it was crucial that the question of responsibility for the defeat be settled). In some ways, the possibility of accusing Reynaud of a *crime de droit commun* (a criminal offense) was even better; it obviated the question of *ex post facto* legislation and accorded well with a narrative in which careerist and egotistic politicians had sold out the nation. Reynaud was therefore initially sent to be tried, not by the Riom court, but by the military tribunal of Clermont-Ferrand.

Historiographical representations of the Riom magistrates have varied from misguided but occasionally patriotic (Michel) to hidebound and overly insistent on the limits of their responsibility as interpreting the words of the legislator (Bancaud).[8] In the case of the Clermont-Ferrand military tribunal, however, there can be absolutely no question that it was the tool of the regime. Its leader, Jean Perré, was a devotee of the extreme right who would be condemned to twenty years' imprisonment after the war for his prosecution of resistance leaders. As for the *juge d'instruction*, Colonel Leprêtre, we shall meet him in a subsequent chapter as the man primarily responsible for the condemnations of the Popular Frontists Mendès-France and Zay. He escaped prosecution after the war primarily because he had already been shot by members of the Resistance and partially paralyzed. We shall examine in the following chapter some specimens of their bias and vitriol against their victims. No one could seriously present such individuals as closet Republicans.

Yet the government was entirely unsuccessful in persuading Leprêtre to convict Reynaud, an infinitely more important figure than either Mendès-France or Zay, of peculation. Reynaud later claimed that Leprêtre's attitude after the trial

8 Michel, *Procès de Riom*, 84; Bancaud, *Exception ordinaire, passim.*

made it clear that he "considered his [Reynaud's] good faith as clear."[9] A disparity this striking between Leprêtre's known predilections and his behavior craves explanation.

The Leca-Devaux Affair[10]

21 March. Paul Reynaud becomes Prime Minister and Minister for Foreign Affairs.
Sometime in May. Paul Reynaud converts 5 million francs to dollars to use for pro-Allied propaganda in the USA.
24 May. First decree of quitus from President Lebrun covers Reynaud's use of secret funds.
16 June. Reynaud and cabinet resign.
17 June. Reynaud is offered Washington embassy.
18 June. Reynaud visits Pétain to discuss this. Leca gives back (part of?) the secret funds to Font Réaulx.
19 June. Leca and Devaux named to Washington Embassy and given diplomatic passports.
20 June. Lebrun signs second decree of quitus and backdates it to 16th. Leca and Devaux decide to head to Lisbon via Spain.
21 June. Leca and Devaux leave for St Sebastien.
22 June. Leca and Devaux arrive in Madrid. They are arrested and their suitcases, containing money, papers and jewels, seized.
23 June. Leca and Devaux allowed to leave and go to French embassy in Madrid.
24 June. Reynaud informed of Roosevelt's attitude and decides to refuse embassy. Leca and Devaux return to St Sebastien to find their families and write to Paul Reynaud to tell him of arrest and seizure.
25 June. Leca and Devaux leave for Lisbon. Paul Reynaud hears of their Madrid arrest on the German radio.
26 June. Baudouin visits Paul Reynaud twice. On second visit, de Portes admits to him that she gave her fortune to Leca. Paul Reynaud writes his account of the matter to Baudouin, removing two lines concerning amount at Le Roy Ladurie's suggestion.
28 June. Car accident. Leca and Devaux arrive in Lisbon, where they are informed of disciplinary measures against them the next day.
30 June. Leca and Devaux write to Baudouin to justify themselves.
5 July. Laffon visits Paul Reynaud and tells him of Leca's Madrid statements.
13 July. Paul Reynaud meets Leca's sister and writes justificatory letter to Baudouin.
24 July. Leca and Devaux flee Lisbon.

Dominique Leca and Gilbert Devaux had served in Reynaud's ministerial cabinet – in other words, they were leading civil servants – and were considered to be under his protection. Reynaud denied that they were also his friends.[11] The cor-

9 Note by Reynaud, 8 November 1940, Box 24, Series 74AP, AN.
10 Unsigned timeline, undated, Box 24, Series 74AP, AN.
11 *Ibid.*

respondence between Leca and Reynaud after the Liberation, however, does seem to be friendlier than a mere professional acquaintance would suggest. Probably it was one of those relationships intermediate between friendship and mere mutual respect that so frequently flourish in work environments.

When Reynaud resigned as Prime Minister, Leca and Devaux immediately began making preparations to leave the country via Spain and Portugal with the USA as their destination. They claimed that their objective was to travel ahead of Reynaud to the French Embassy in Washington, where they expected Reynaud to be appointed ambassador. When Leprêtre questioned him regarding this incident, Reynaud claimed that he had pleaded with the two men not to leave the country, but they ignored him.[12] They took with them some of Reynaud's personal papers, large quantities of state money in the form of gold bars, and some jewelry and gold belonging to Mme de Portes, who had entrusted her fortune to them in the apparent hope of avoiding spoliation by the advancing Germans. They successfully crossed the Spanish border, but, upon their arrival in Madrid, their bags were opened by the Spanish police, the goods contained therein impounded, and the incident reported to the French government. Leca and Devaux themselves successfully escaped abroad and eventually found themselves in London.

The reader may well wonder why we have tarried so long in details of this apparently unremarkable incident. The misadventures of two venal or misunderstood bureaucrats are not generally conceived to be the stuff of history, except perhaps in a microhistorical sense. The Leca-Devaux affair, however, is a far more complicated and interesting matter than appears at first glance. It reveals two extremely important elements of how the transition from French Republic to French State operated at the level of political culture: firstly, the persistence of personal networks between Republicans and Vichyites, and, secondly, how the concepts of honor and money were categorized for French right-wingers in 1940.

* * *

The trajectory of Leca and Devaux – their rapid flight out of the country immediately after it became apparent that the French government was about to seek an armistice, their close personal association with Reynaud, and their eagerness to reach the Anglo-Saxon world – might lead the reader to the assumption that they were would-be Gaullists. Nothing could be further from the truth. They associated with Gaullism only because their first choice – collaboration – was for-

12 *Information*, 19 August 1940, Box 72, Series 2W, AN.

cibly closed to them. On 30 June, the pair sent a letter[13] addressed to Vichy's Ministers of Foreign Affairs and of Finances (that is, to their old associates Paul Baudouin and Yves Bouthillier respectively, whom they also cited as character witnesses) that read in part:

> Does anyone doubt our political attitude? There too, you know better than anyone in the world how we have judged events in France over the previous few years. You know how we thought, how we acted. We rowed with you against the current, but at the moment and the place where the current was most rapid.

In other words, they were claiming to be supporters of Vichy *avant la lettre*, a conclusion they drove home by stating that "a certain past must disappear. You have the duty to burn it out if necessary. But do you consider us to belong to that past?" Hinting that they were willing to turn on Reynaud, the two fugitives asserted that friendships did not matter in the face of the necessity for "new sap," and that the *République des camarades* (Republic of friends, a derogatory term for Third Republic clientelism) must end. "France, for us," they explained, "is above all the respect of a certain number of Frenchmen in whom we believe." In other words, the letter was a plea for mercy that could hardly have been more craven. In other circumstances, it is clear that Leca and Devaux could easily have followed in the steps of the ministers to whom they were writing – old friends and protegés of Reynaud who went on to become prominent ministers under Vichy.

In fact, these two ministers (both of whom then rose to ministerial office in the early days of the new regime, and who were both closely involved in the efforts to prosecute Reynaud) were close analogues to Leca and Devaux in their prewar careers. Both Baudouin and Bouthillier had risen to prominence as civil servants under Reynaud. Baudouin in particular, like Leca and Devaux, had had his political start as a member of a ministerial cabinet. The list of Republican politicians who trusted his judgment is impressive. He had been *chef de cabinet* of Joseph Caillaux, a prominent and formerly leftist Radical (who had turned admittedly somewhat to the right in his declining years). Moreover, none other than Blum had appointed him, along with the unimpeachable economist Charles Rist, to the leadership of the Foreign Exchange Committee. After the war, in spite of his obvious and justifiable bitterness, Reynaud testified to his prewar loyalty: "Responsible to both George Mandel, Minister of Colonies, and myself, Minister of Finance, he defended my fiscal policy in quarters

13 Leca and Devaux to Ministry of Foreign Affairs and Finance Ministry, 30 June 1940, Box 72, Series 2W, AN.

where my campaign for devaluation had hurt me." This willingness to defend Reynaud's policy earned Baudouin a further promotion to the position of secretary of the War Cabinet (after de Gaulle refused the post). It is evident that Baudouin was a rising man in the Republican ranks, who had turned his technical skills as a civil servant and his willingness to serve his political masters into a very promising career. Reynaud later claimed that "Not being a member of parliament, he had no influence on the ministers," but the fact that he was promoted yet again to Undersecretary of State for Foreign Affairs suggests that Baudouin was on the verge, if not of greatness, at least of launching a respectable political career under Reynaud's auspices.[14]

Baudouin had already given hints of radical right-wing sympathies prior to his appointment as Vichy's first Foreign Minister. He was one of the earliest supporters of an armistice and was said to be *persona grata* in Fascist Italy (to which sympathies he owed his final pre-Vichy appointment).[15] His trajectory, however, suggests that he would have done quite well for himself under a Republican government; indeed, he had already done so, although ministerial rank was a considerable promotion for him. Moreover, while it is difficult to detect hypocrisy in person and even more so at a distance of seventy years, Baudouin's attachment to Reynaud seems to have been reasonably sincere. Immediately after Reynaud resigned, Baudouin wrote to him stating "how proud I am of the hours I spent at your side ... how I admire your willpower and your courage. You saw me, yesterday morning, trying with all my strength to persuade you to continue to lend to the government all your strength, all your magnificent qualities of leadership."[16] Even if we cannot take Baudouin's words too literally, it is at any rate certain that Reynaud was not yet in bad odor at Vichy.

Baudouin's past association with Reynaud and his steady rise under Reynaud's auspices make it all the more surprising that Baudouin was in the vanguard of the charge against his former master. This could have been the mere treachery of a careerist; but Baudouin continued to correspond with Reynaud on a tone of friendship even after the investigation against Reynaud had begun, and, indeed, even after Reynaud had clearly fallen out of favor. On 4 July, Baudouin wrote to express his hope that Reynaud was recovering well from his car crash and to regret the fact that "the appearances [in the Leca-Devaux case] are turning against you."[17] Everything suggests that both parties at

14 Note by Paul Reynaud for Paul Baudouin's trial, 1947?, Box 25, Series 74AP, AN.

15 *Ibid.*

16 Cited in a note by Paul Reynaud, 8 November 1940, Box 24, Series 74AP, AN. The same box also contains the original letter, 17 June 1940.

17 Baudouin to Reynaud, 4 July (1940?), Box 24, Series 74AP, AN.

this stage still thought of each other as friends. When Reynaud wrote to Baudouin to express his anger that the latter had chosen to conduct the Leca-Devaux affair through official channels instead of contacting him personally (an anger which only makes sense in the light of a close personal relationship between the two men), Baudouin responded that his hand was forced by the enquiry in Madrid.[18]

A misunderstanding so profound suggests that a clash of worldviews. Reynaud, a veteran of the *République des camarades*, naturally assumed that his friend and protegé would not hand him over to the tender mercies of the courts without first satisfying himself of his guilt. For Baudouin, on the other hand, once Spanish Minister of the Interior Serrano Suñer had informed him of the recovery of Leca and Devaux's luggage, the matter was beyond his control. The Vichyite vision of justice was of a mechanical, impersonal process. The magnitude of the disaster of 1940 was needed to exhibit the rift between the two men. Under the old dispensation, a disagreement on a foreign policy question would not have prevented personal friendships between Third Republic leaders; but that world was now gone for good. As with most revolutions, the transition was incomplete – Reynaud would still benefit somewhat from his connections at Vichy, and Vichy itself was rife with personal intrigue – but Baudouin's emphasis on impersonalism was of a piece with the theory, if not always the practice, of the new order.

* * *

Clearly, Reynaud was ill-advised in his choice of friends. It is, however, also clear that he did have many friends in the new regime – and not merely among those who had worked with him, but also among individuals who knew him only by reputation. Among these was the investigating magistrate at Clermont-Ferrand, Leprêtre, who – as we will see in a subsequent chapter – was a devout acolyte of Vichy, but who also seems to have conserved considerable esteem for the fallen premier.

Reynaud's interrogation by Leprêtre on 19 August 1940 is illuminating of the degree of the magistrate's support for the fallen Prime Minister, although it gives us fewer ideas as to its causes. At every stage, Leprêtre's questioning was remarkably gentle, especially compared to his conduct in the Mendès France and Zay cases. Concerning Leca and Devaux's departure for Spain, for example, he commented that they "seem to have been transferred in a somewhat premature fash-

18 Baudouin to Reynaud, 17 August 1940, Box 24, Series 74AP, AN.

ion to the Embassy of France at Washington (Financial Division)."[19] At a time when the radical right-wing press was making wild accusations of embezzlement and treason on a vast scale, "a little premature" was the kindest wording for the flight of Leca and Devaux that Leprêtre could possibly have used.

In the end the government had to transfer the case away from Leprêtre and to the *Cour Suprême* – a remarkable admission of the regime's inability to control its magistrates. Matters only continued to deteriorate from there. The cornerstone of the Leca-Devaux Affair, as we have seen, was the accusation that Reynaud had misused secret funds. Under French law, to prosecute an official for the misuse of official funds, it was necessary for the department concerned (in this case, the finance ministry) to make an official statement of the missing amount. Because the funds in question were secret, however (and hence discretionary), it was not normal for the finance ministry to maintain a strict accounting of them. The problem was further complicated by the fact that Lebrun, the outgoing President of the Republic and the only person to whom Reynaud was accountable for the use of the funds in question, had given him a *quittance* or receipt to cover his use of them.

Vichy's response to this issue amply demonstrated that its concern for legality was far from consistent, especially where there was no popular oversight. Finance Minister Bouthillier, himself one of the cadre of *Polytechnicien* technocrats of *X-Crise* promoted by Reynaud (along with Baudouin and Leca), sent the justice ministry a *note officieuse* or unofficial memo advising them to proceed with the trial without a specific account of the sum that was supposedly missing. Not only was this procedure highly abnormal in itself, but the *note officieuse* was withheld from the official dossier of the investigation. Yet these breaches of due process were in vain: the *note officieuse* did not prevent the case from falling into stasis, and, by 1942, the government seems to have been trying to revisit its own judicial errors in an effort to suspend a case that had become an embarrassment.[20]

These technical problems confirm what the Riom trial indicated – that judicial procedures, however abused, have their own logic. Once the government had decided that the basis of the accusation would be financial misconduct, it immediately encountered technical problems it had not foreseen. It seems, however, unlikely that this was the primary reason why Vichy was so unsuccessful in prosecuting its prime suspect. Rather, the regime had once again fallen into the

19 Reynaud testimony, 19 August 1940, Box 72, Series 2W, AN.
20 There is considerable detail on these complicated twists and turns in the various legal briefs submitted to the court on Reynaud's behalf, which can be found in Box 24, Series 74AP, AN.

Riom dilemma – it could not simultaneously base its claim to legitimacy on the transfer of power to civil servants and then ignore what these civil servants had to say. If the French magistrature had so much difficulty finding grounds to prosecute Blum, it was certainly not about to indict Reynaud.

Then there was was the question of personal contacts. The persistence of personal ties between prominent members of the Vichy regime and those it imprisoned was by no means limited to Reynaud, although he was certainly an extreme case. The French political classes fragmented in 1940 along lines that appear largely haphazard. Neither one's position on the right/left spectrum (consider Gaston Bergery) nor one's apparent devotion to the Republic (consider Laval) were infallible predictors of one's stance with regard to Vichy.

This, as far as it goes, is all well understood and well attested in the historiography of Vichy France. What was not been as well documented is the fact that the way this fragmentation cut across preexisting lines of political entanglement and personal friendship meant that, although imprisoned, prosecuted and occasionally (Mandel, in 1944) killed, Vichy's most prominent political prisoners enjoyed a highly unusual degree of political access. The culture of the *République des camarades*, under which the embittered opponent of yesterday could easily become the cabinet colleague of tomorrow, was precisely what Vichy was trying to kill; but it died hard. Imprisoned, but not isolated, the prisoners of Chazeron or Bourrasol called upon mutual friends through which pleas for justice, occasionally heard or at least acknowledged, filtered up through the ranks of the political system.

Consider the bizarre case of Michel Clemenceau, the son of the great Clemenceau whose legacy Vichy and its opponents disputed. Michel Clemenceau maintained ties with both sides, visiting Mandel and Reynaud before dining with Pétain. He evidently felt this situation to be morally impossible; as he told Pétain, he could not eat at two mangers.[21] This was the harbinger of the new language of polarization that Vichy had done so much to create; but, in fact, Clemenceau's situation was far from anomalous. Consider this letter from Émile Cartayrade to Auriol in 1942: "Edouard[22] asked me to tell you that the Doctor who is a mutual friend of Pierre Laval and of you has intervened with the 'Premier' for his liberation. He did not hide from the latter the ties of friendship that unite Edouard and you. P.L. hastened to take the requested steps and it

21 Pétain trial transcript, Box 49, Series 496AP, AN.

22 I have been unable to determine the identity of this "Edouard." The obvious candidates, Edouard Daladier and Edouard Herriot, were not released at this time. Probably we are speaking of smaller fry.

seems that it is to these steps that we owe the rapid liberation of Edouard. For Cus, it is Cathala who intervened."[23]

Events like this, in which personal ties of friendship provided imprisoned politicians with unusual levels of access, rarely ended so happily as in these instances; but they were nonetheless characteristic of the Vichy system. In few other dictatorships can there have been such strong connections between dissidents and the regime's own leaders. It was the norm rather than the exception for the lawyers of prominent imprisoned individuals to be able to seek personal contact with the leading members of the regime. Thus, for example, Mandel's lawyer Joseph Besselère wrote to him in November 1942[24] regarding a journey to Vichy he had undertaken with the objective of persuading the regime to take action regarding the German seizure of Mandel in the course of their invasion of the unoccupied zone.

As in the previous instance, Besselère's contacts at Vichy had been indirect but prominent. He had immediately sought to contact the well-known (but non-Vichy-affiliated) conservatives Louis Marin and Joseph Laniel, but discovered that they had already sought to intervene on Mandel's behalf. Laniel, who was later to serve as Prime Minister himself and would be remembered for presiding over the defeat at Dien Bien Phu, had sought an interview with Laval, but succeeded only in meeting his *chef de cabinet,* to whom he explained his concern ("his anguish," as the letter put it). He later returned and succeeded this time in meeting Laval, a signal achievement at a time when the prime minister must have been inundated with requests. Laval assured him that "I will answer for the security of your friends: be without worry, their life is not and will not be in danger." Besselère, who seems to have been a personal friend of Mandel and who evidently understood exactly how much this assurance was worth, prevailed upon Laniel to return and see Laval again. Laval reiterated that "no matter what may happen, your [Mandel's] security and that of Mister Reynaud, will be entirely assured *under my personal responsibility.*"

Meanwhile, André Le Troquer, Blum's lawyer, had also been seeking an interview with Laval. Laval admitted that he had been surprised by the German entry into the Unoccupied Zone, but stated that he had reached an agreement with the Germans that would ensure that the policing of that zone would remain a French responsibility. It is clear that Laval was very much on the defensive in all of these conversations, even with a relatively unimportant (and left-wing) individual such as Le Troquer. Le Troquer, indeed, even dared to suggest that the

23 Cartayrade to Auriol, 19 May 1942, Box 30, Series 552AP, AN.
24 Besselère to Mandel, 14 November 1942, Box 74, Series 544AP, AN.

French police should collaborate in an escape attempt. Unsurprisingly, Laval was adamantly opposed – "That under no circumstances, for all of France would pay for it" – but the fact that such a suggestion could even be made is an indication of the dynamic of the interview.

Meanwhile, Mandel's other prominent friends had not ignored his plight. Laniel and Marin, as well as Auguste Champetier de Ribes (a devoted Catholic and early supporter of De Gaulle), had decided to stagger the dates of their appeals to Laval in order to avoid offering the appearance of a united faction. This, too, is significant in its implications: personal appeals on behalf of imprisoned opponents of Vichy were safe enough, but anything that smacked of the Third Republic's party politics was not.

Due to this problem of timing, Besselère did not know at the time of the letter what Marin had done on Mandel's behalf. Champetier, however, had seen the Papal Nuncio, who promised that he would arrange for the Pope himself to send a personal letter to Laval indicating his concern for Mandel's safety. As for Besselère himself, he had been able to obtain a personal interview with Barthélemy, who had asked Laval (whom he intensely disliked) what was likely to become of the seized prisoners. Laval had reiterated to Barthélemy the assurances he had given to Laniel that he had "Avetz's" [sic] agreement that the treatment of the prisoners would remain a French concern. (He was presumably referring to the German Ambassador, Otto Abetz.) Besselère also succeeded in obtaining an interview with Pierre Cathala, one of Laval's personal associates. Cathala had in turn sought an interview with Laval, who reiterated his assurances that Mandel was safe and added that he knew that Mandel "was showing great courage." Finally, Besselère visited the Radical deputy Robert Surcouf, who in turn visited Jules Brévié, Vichy's Minister for Colonies. Brévié in his turn visited Laval, who reiterated his assurances of Mandel's safety.

Mandel's murder in 1944 showed how worthless these assurances were, except in the sense that Mandel's ultimate fate would indeed be decided by Frenchmen rather than Germans. One suspects that everyone concerned knew what these assurances were worth, given the sheer number of individuals Besselère prevailed upon to receive the same reassurances from Laval, as well as the fact that Mandel wisely composed a will in captivity.[25] Nonetheless, they retain a certain significance for two reasons. Firstly, the question that naturally poses itself in such a circumstance is why, given their obvious misgivings regarding his trustworthiness, Mandel and his supporters even bothered to pester Laval

25 Mandel's will, 1943, Box 74, 544AP, AN. Touchingly, Mandel requested that his ashes be brought back to Paris "after victory."

with their concerns. This suggests that, meaningless as Laval's assurances would ultimately prove, they were nonetheless seen as having a certain value at the time; and this value presumably came from the fact that the procession of individuals expressing concern with Mandel's fate demonstrated that there was, if not a party – we have seen that Mandel's supporters were very careful to avoid giving that impression – at least a group of prominent individuals within Vichy who would be upset if anything were to befall the imprisoned politician. In other words, Vichy's claims to have destroyed the party system were, like its claims to administer apolitical justice, both quite genuinely felt and less than meaningful to an outsider who did not adhere to Vichy's tendentious definitions of those terms. The party system had not survived, but factionalism certainly had, as had a broader sense of political affiliation that distinguished, for example, left from right. Herein, perhaps, lies the clue to Vichy's failure to prosecute Mandel and Reynaud; these individuals, even in their fallen state, simply retained too much sympathy on the French right to be railroaded in the manner that Blum and Daladier could be.

There is, moreover, a second and perhaps more important significance to the fact that Vichy's prisoners retained the capacity to lobby at the highest levels. It is impossible to imagine such scenes in Nazi Germany or Stalin's USSR; and they were the product of the fact that Vichy believed in rules – grotesque rules, certainly, with no relevance to the real burden of responsibility for the defeat, but rules nonetheless. There is, of course, a continuum of rules-based practice; not even the USSR rejected rules altogether, and Vichy was willing enough to bend them at times – but the general contrast is real enough. In this regard, the definitional feature of Vichy's judicial system – *pace* Alain Bancaud – was not that it was arbitrary, but that it was a good deal less arbitrary than the results of the system suggest.

The *Conseil de Justice Politique*

The *Conseil de Justice Politique* is usually presented as the height of Vichyite arbitrary rule, an example of the superficial nature of the judicial constraints on the regime. If, however, one accepts the interpretation proposed here that the Vichy regime sought to move through "apolitical" channels and despised the recourse to politics, then it becomes evident that the creation of an explicitly political council on the causes of the defeat cannot be seen as a victory for the regime, but rather as a setback for its conception of itself.

We know little directly about the origin of the *Conseil de Justice Politique*, but there is considerable circumstantial evidence regarding Vichy's probable motivations. Many historians have noted that the foundations of the regime began to crack in mid-1941. As the breach with the Republic became more and more overt, and as it became increasingly evident that the regime had badly miscalculated in its famous wager that Germany would "wring Britain's neck like a chicken," the hopes that wide sections of the population – even future resisters like Henri Frenay – had invested in Vichy began to wane.[26]

As the bases of the regime's support began to crumble, a mood of panic set in at Vichy. On 12 August 1941, Pétain gave his famous "*vent mauvais*" (ill wind) speech, in which he acknowledged that partisans of the old "politics" of party and faction had begun to raise their heads and called for unity under his leadership. Ominously, Pétain stated that it was necessary to "destroy their enterprises, by decimating their leaders."[27] The end of the speech fulfilled this promise by anouncing the creation of the *Conseil de Justice Politique.*

By this point, substantial sections of Vichy's supporters were gravely troubled by the *Cour Suprême*'s delays, to the point where it had become impossible to mention the court without excusing or attacking the slowness of its procedures. The *Conseil de Justice Politique* was an expedient designed to protect the regime from attacks of this nature. Pétain himself seems to have been highly frustrated by the slow pace of the trial, and to have forced through the measure over the objections of Barthélemy.[28] The formation of the *Conseil de Justice Politique* is therefore incomprehensible without an understanding of the fact that it was not an organized part of Vichy policy but a desperate resort to methods the regime had hoped to avoid.

Two other factors, however, need to be considered in relation to the government's decision, but these, too, came from outside the regime. Besides Vichy's domestic concerns, the regime still had to deal with the opinions of neutrals, particularly the US. Franklin Delano Roosevelt, who had followed the Riom trial with attention,[29] was even more interested in the fate of Mandel and Reynaud, presumably because of their known Americanophile and pro-resistance sentiments. He asked Leahy to tell Pétain that the USA was deeply interested in "respect for justice and human treatment" with regard to Vichy's political detainees, especially Mandel, Reynaud and La Chambre.[30] The odd combination of individ-

---

26 For the most comprehensive interpretation of the course of French public opinion during the Occupation, see Pierre Laborie, *L'Opinion Française sous Vichy.*

27 Bernard Durand, Jean-Pierre Le Crom, and Alessandro Somma, *Le Droit Sous Vichy* (Frankfurt Am Main: Klostermann, 2006), 285.

28 Weisberg, *Vichy Law,* 19.

29 Press clipping, 18 November 1950, Box 23, Series GE, AdHC.

30 Goeau-Brissonière to Mandel, 20 November 1941, Box 41, Series 544AP, AN.

uals may suggest that Vichy's lack of respect for justice was particularly obvious in the case of individuals who were not politically affiliated with the left.

Finally, of course, there were the Germans.

* * *

If the role of public opinion in Pétain's calculations is speculative, and the role of the Americans unclear, the role of the Germans is certain. It exploded into prominence in the spring of 1941, in the so-called *affaire des gardes territoriaux*. As war with the US appeared increasingly imminent, the German foreign ministry launched a desperate last-minute effort to sway American public opinion by trying to compel the French to hold a trial that would pin the blame for the war on the Allies. It is in this relation that the fact that Reynaud and Mandel were condemned by the *Conseil de Justice Politique* but never even indicted by the *Cour Suprême de Justice* becomes critical. Ever since Eberhard Jäckel and Robert Paxton's pathbreaking work on the Vichy regime, it has become increasingly obvious that Vichy was embarrassingly eager to volunteer every possible avenue of collaboration in an effort to secure a place in the new Europe, provided that this did not impinge on her "sovereignty" – that favorite Vichyite buzzword.[31] It is all the more surprising, therefore, and exposes the centrality of the stakes involved, that on this single issue – the formation of a kangaroo court that would find or forge evidence pinning war guilt on Reynaud and Mandel – Vichy was unwilling to yield.

It was Abetz who began the campaign to have Reynaud and Mandel executed. On 8 March 1941, he wrote to the German Foreign Ministry a letter that appealed to the well-known German obsession[32] with the *franc-tireur*, the unaffiliated sharpshooter who had bedeviled the German occupation of France in 1871. Abetz noted that there had been reports in 1940 of German parachutists being killed by Frenchmen belonging to civilian formations (*gardes territoriaux*) rather than the regular army. In his view, these Frenchmen were legally *francs-tireurs* and could be shot under the laws of war. (This was a rather tendentious interpretation of the Hague Convention, which had not banned partisan movements outright but only required them to wear identifying marks indicating their affiliation with a recognized army structure.) Many members of these civilian formations were now in German captivity, and Vichy, given its well-known sensitivity to

31 Espionage was one such reserved, "sovereign" area where Vichy was willing to resist. Simon Kitson, *Vichy et la Chasse aux Espions Nazis: 1940–1942: Complexités de la Politique de Collaboration* (Paris: Autrement, 2005), *passim.*

32 See, e.g., John N. Horne and Alan Kramer, *German Atrocities, 1914: A History of Denial* (New Haven: Yale University Press, 2001), 87–174.

the question of POWs, could certainly be expected to make every effort to save them from their fate. Since Reynaud as the head of the government and Mandel as Minister of the Interior had held ultimate responsibility for the actions of the civilian formations, Abetz suggested that the two imprisoned leaders be shot in place of those they had "turned away from the right path." "The execution of Reynaud and of Mandel would impact two of the primary French causers of the war and would represent a just expiation for the crimes committed against German airmen and parachutists," he suggested.[33]

The letter makes nonsense of the view, popular among the Resistance at the time, that the Germans were the *original* motive force behind the Riom trial. Abetz was clearly interested in having Reynaud and Mandel killed, but, even in early 1941 (when trial preparations had been ongoing for months), it is apparent that he still had little interest in making the French do the dirty work themselves, or in making use of the result for propaganda in France, since he still spoke in terms of extradition to Germany. Instead, a new German demand cut across lines of political debate regarding responsibility for the defeat that were already clearly established in France.

Indeed, from the perspective of Vichy, that was the problem. The regime had no difficulty with the idea of having Reynaud and Mandel executed, and, if the proposal had remained at the stage that Abetz suggested in March, the French government would doubtless have acceded to the request. The German foreign ministry, however, more attentive than Abetz to the international benefits to be gained from a trial of French leaders, stood his proposal on its head over the course of the following months. At first, events seemed to be unfolding along the lines foreseen by Abetz. Pétain wrote directly to Hitler to request mercy for the imprisoned *gardes territoriaux*, and Darlan agreed to extradite Reynaud and Mandel in return for the granting of this request. On 5 July 1941, however, Ribbentrop wrote to Abetz to inform him that the German demands were to be changed. Instead of having Reynaud and Mandel extradited to Germany and shot there, they were to be sentenced to life imprisonment by the French themselves:

> We will however make the relaxation of the sentence dependent on the condition that the French Government, for its part, inflict on Reynaud and on Mandel the penalty of life imprisonment and accept the strict responsibility of ensuring that the two former ministers will never escape and will never flee abroad. Moreover, we must demand that the French Government place at our disposal all the documentation that they have, and that casts light on the political collaboration of Reynaud and Mandel with the Government of the

33 Abetz to Foreign Ministry, 8 March 1941, Box 25, Series 74AP, AN.

> United States. We already have proof that the two former ministers worked in favor of war with Roosevelt and his entourage, notably with former Ambassador of the United States [William] Bullitt, but we value reinforcing our documentation on this matter by the evidence which is still in the French archives and which is very voluminous and convincing. It is of great interest for France, as for Germany, to expose the proceedings of those who advocated for war, because we would contribute in that way effectively to oppose the present advocates of war in the United States and to accelerate, in this way, a peace agreement.[34]

The French did their best to accommodate this request, in a manner that makes clear that Pétain and Darlan had no particular compunction as to its substance. On 8 August 1941, Abetz reported on a further meeting with Darlan as follows:

> As regards the captured members of the *gardes territoriaux*, whose amnesty the Reich Government has made conditional on the life imprisonment of Reynaud and Mandel by the French Government (*Drahterlass Nr. 3556 vom 6.7.41*), Darlan explained once again his readiness for such an outcome. Marshal Pétain intends to remove the current trial from the purely juridical remit of the *Cour Suprême* of Riom and have a political sentence handed down. This procedure will entail the life imprisonment of Reynaud and Mandel.[35]

This report represents the extreme point of the French strategy of conciliation. In response to German demands, Pétain had agreed to reverse the entire policy of his government by resorting to openly political means to condemn Reynaud and Mandel. It is quite clear that, whatever the concerns regarding legitimacy and legality Vichy may have had, they could never trump the regime's desperate eagerness to be treated as a partner by the Germans. Four days later came the *vent mauvais* speech.

The regime, however, was soon trying to find a way to weasel out of its promises. Reynaud and Mandel had to be condemned, but perhaps a more palatable means to do so could be found. By 18 August – only ten days after the meeting the earlier report described – Darlan had taken the first step back. He told Abetz that no documentation concerning Reynaud and Mandel's supposed plotting with Roosevelt and Bullitt could be found. The two men were still to be politically condemned on 15 October, along with the other defendants, but Darlan expressed a pious hope that the Riom trial would turn up documents that would meet the Germans' criteria.[36]

---

34 Ribbentrop to Abetz, 5 July 1941, Box 25, Series 74AP, AN.
35 Abetz to Ribbentrop, 8 August 1941, Box 25, Series 74AP, AN.
36 Abetz to Ribbentrop, 18 August 1941, Box 25, Series 74AP, AN.

As expected, the *Conseil de Justice Politique* sentenced Cot, Gamelin, Daladier, Blum, Reynaud and Mandel on schedule. (The other two defendants, Jacomet and La Chambre, were referred back to the *Cour Suprême* because the *Conseil de Justice Politique* was uncertain as to the degree of their guilt.) Nonetheless, Vichy proceeded with its plans to hold a strictly judicial trial, whose schedule was accordingly ramped up to January 1942. Minister without Portfolio Jacques Bénoist-Mechin explained the decision to Abetz as follows:

> It had been Marshal Pétain's intention to sentence MANDEL and REYNAUD on October 15, 1941 to life imprisonment for political reasons; after this decision had been taken so much more incriminating material against REYNAUD and MANDEL had been found that this sentence would be justifiable on a criminal basis, even a death penalty might be considered. Marshal Pétain preferred to sentence REYNAUD and MANDEL for criminal and not political reasons. The trials against REYNAUD and MANDEL could be completed at Riom by February 1942.[37]

It is difficult even to begin to enumerate all of the lies in this short paragraph. It goes without saying that no "incriminating" evidence in the Germans' sense – that is, evidence that Reynaud, Mandel, Roosevelt and Bullitt had planned the war among them – could have been discovered, since no such evidence existed. Moreover, if the Vichy government had had incriminating evidence of any kind, they certainly would have used it. The notion that the trials of Reynaud and Mandel could be "completed" by the *Cour Suprême* by February, when that court had consistently refused even to indict these individuals, was preposterous. Finally, the *Cour Suprême*, being limited by the prewar criminal code regarding political offenses, lacked the authority to pass capital sentences in any case. The maximum sentence it could pass was the sentence that the *Conseil de Justice Politique* had already passed: life imprisonment in a fortress.

It is not easy to explain why anyone at Vichy could possibly have thought that the Germans would be taken in indefinitely by this tissue of lies. To be sure, the Germans were unlikely to verify the French claims for themselves, but the 31 October message named a specific date (February) by which Reynaud and Mandel were to have been convicted. When February came and went without these hated figures being condemned or even indicted, the Germans were bound to be furious – which is, of course, exactly what happened.

One can only conclude that the Vichy regime was desperate. To allow the French POWs to be shot would have been contrary to the entire tenor of their pol-

37 Abetz to Foreign Ministry, 31 October 1941 (English translation in original), Box 25, Series 74AP, AN.

icy of conciliation, to which they were by now far too deeply committed to withdraw. At the same time, for the "apolitical" government to risk an openly political conviction would have been disastrous for public opinion and contrary to Vichy's own self-image.

* * *

So much, then, for the origins of the *Conseil de Justice Politique*. As for its deliberations, little direct evidence exists; it was a highly informal body that did not keep minutes and that based its deliberations entirely on the *réquisitoire* against the defendants. We do, however, possess some indirect evidence on the subject, most notably the testimony of Charles Vallin,[38] one of its members. Vallin wrote his testimony in December 1945, at the height of the postwar *épuration*, and was clearly concerned with explaining away what had become a highly inconvenient attachment. Although a member in good standing of Free France, which he had joined in 1942, he had nonetheless been judged ineligible for public office at the Liberation. It is therefore necessary to bear in mind that his testimony bears the mark of special pleading even more than is usual for personal retrospectives on events.

Vallin's later change of loyalties suggests that the choice of him for the *Conseil* was in itself a mark of the rather haphazard way in which it was constituted. His account of this selection bears out this interpretation. Vallin, a devout right-wing Catholic who had been a member of the far-right *Action Française* until it was condemned by the Pope and had then joined the quasi-Fascist[39] *Croix de Feu*, had long been a friend of Du Moulin de Labarthète, Pétain's *chef de cabinet*. Around August or September 1941, Du Moulin de Labarthète sought a personal meeting with Vallin and told him that "I thought of you because you are an unimpeachable fighter and have the right to speak." In other words, Vallin's name came up as the result of a last-minute nomination by a single prominent but not all-powerful individual, who justified that choice purely because of the candidate's military record. It is difficult to imagine a more different atmosphere from that which reigned over the selection of the judges of the *Cour Suprême*.

Vallin claimed that he initially treated the nomination with skepticism on a number of grounds, beginning with the statement that he did not understand

---

38 Charles Vallin, *Note sur ma participation au Conseil de Justice Politique*, 18 December 1945, Box 25, Series 74AP, AN.

39 The question of the *Croix de Feu*'s relationship with Fascism is highly controversial and arouses strong opinions. There is no consensus on this issue among historians, but Robert Soucy, in "French Fascism and the Croix De Feu: A Dissenting Interpretation," *Journal of Contemporary History* 26, no. 1 (January 1991), strongly suggests that the Croix de Feu was Fascist.

how Pétain could pass a sentence on the *inculpés* before their guilt had been determined by the court. This objection (which Vallin claimed was brushed aside by Du Moulin, who told him that he would have the right to come to whatever conclusion he chose) has the ring of postwar second-guessing about it, but his other grounds seem more plausible. He claimed that he had told Du Moulin "You know [...] that I have an opinion of the question of responsibility that is not very orthodox."

> I had had, in fact, a few months earlier, in the course of a conversation with Du Moulin, the opportunity to tell him that, if I could not erase the responsibility for the defeat, I could not allow that one should mix with this trial that of responsibility for the war, Germany being in my view the sole party responsible for the conflict. I then added to my interlocutor that the proceedings that they were talking about beginning against Paul Reynaud and Mandel because of their supposed "bellicism" [support for war] would to my eyes be a monstrosity.

On a similar note, Vallin objected to the inclusion on the *Conseil* of an individual who had committed himself publicly to blaming France for the defeat.

If this diverged, as Vallin claimed, from Vichy's "orthodoxy," the divergence is minimal and it is easy to see why Du Moulin was willing to overlook it. We have already seen that the difference between responsibility for the defeat and responsibility for the war was crucial in justifying French support for the trial, even among individuals who shared Vichy's diagnosis of the former. Reading between the lines, and knowing Vallin's prewar career, it is easy to see that Vallin fits into this category rather nicely. His explanation of his reasoning for his ultimate choice to accept the invitation to serve on the *Conseil de Justice Politique* is exemplary: "Having participated in the campaign of 39–40 as a first-line combattant, at the head of a company of light infantry, in conditions that earned me the Legion of Honor on the field of battle, I suffered cruelly, like all the combattants, from what we could observe during the course of this campaign, as regards the country's lack of preparation, the insufficient nature of her armaments and the disastrous conduct of operations." Many of the Riom witnesses lacked his combat experience, but the general notion of "the insufficient nature of her armaments" was an important component of the government's accusation against the Riom defendants. In fact, there was nothing about Vallin's statement that would have appeared out of place among those of the officers who testified at Riom.

In other words, Vallin's major concern in the matter of the *Conseil* concerned the by-now-familiar matter of the differentiation between the causes of the war and those of the defeat, which had by now been transformed into a personal differentiation between Blum, Daladier and Gamelin on the one hand, and Reynaud and Mandel on the other. Vallin's testimony did not proclaim this outright, which is understandable given his situation in 1945; but it is easy enough to read it between the lines. Thus, for example, he noted that Laniel had prevailed upon him to join the *Conseil* to act as a voice for Reynaud's interests, and he and the two other individuals on the *Conseil* who dissented from its ultimate verdict differed from it on two issues: firstly, that the penalties pronounced should be provisional pending the verdict of the court (a caveat that by now should not surprise us), and, secondly, that Reynaud and Mandel should not be convicted.

Vallin's testimony exposes the doomed nature of Vichy's partisan effort to overthrow partisanship. While it would be possible to say that the party system had reemerged by 1941, with right-wingers refusing to condemn one of their own, it would be more accurate to say that Vichy's blindness to the Schmittian question of sovereignty had come home to roost. Vichy had attempted to recategorize one kind of political behavior as illegitimate, while other kinds remained in the sphere of legitimate dissent. All political systems contain some such differentiation; but the attempt to recategorize this differentiation unilaterally, without even being aware that such a differentiation was occurring, was bound to raise the question of who was entitled to judge what was legitimate and what was not. By late 1941, this problem had become painfully obvious. The Vichy coalition was beginning to splinter.

Honor/Dishonor

If Reynaud may be said to have had a single defining character trait, it was his obsession with honor, both national and personal. Honor was his central motivation; he used it to explain, or at least to provide an excuse for, nearly all of his actions. While imprisoned, for example, he justified his conduct while in office, not with any practical claims regarding the United Kingdom's capacity to remain in the war (as De Gaulle did), but rather with the assertion that France was honor-bound to uphold her word that she would not conclude a separate peace. In 1941, responding to accusations in the Vichyite press that his opposition to an armistice led to a useless waste of life, he wrote to Pétain: "Having 'lost everything but honnor,' what would remain to our people, if we lost our honor?"[40]

It seems probable that Reynaud was seeking to speak a language that Pétain understood – after all, the signatory of the Armistice was unlikely to react well to suggestions that there were practicable alternatives. His concern for honor, how-

40 Reynaud to Pétain, 5 April 1941, Box 24, Series 74AP, AN.

ever, was very real. It surfaces most notably (as in the letter quoted above) in his reaction to the press campaigns against him. Reynaud was horrified by his inability to respond to these attacks; it is evident that honor, for him, was not something to cry of in the wilderness, but was distinctly related to reputation.

Thus, for example, Reynaud wrote a series of letters to Pétain over the course of the summer of 1940 complaining about attacks against him in the press. On 9 August, he remarked that *Gringoire* was publishing scurrilous accusations against him regarding his role in the Leca-Devaux affair.[41] On 6th September, it was the *Éclaireur de Nice* that had published an article claiming that Weygand had wanted an earlier peace.[42] These messages did not cease after Reynaud was imprisoned. On 17 January 1941, for example, he complained that Pierre Héricourt had called him a thief on national radio.[43]

There is nothing very surprising in the fact that Reynaud attentively monitored his reputation or that he was obsessed with justifying his policies. The pattern is common to politicians after they have left office. Rather, what is noteworthy is the approach Reynaud took to justifying himself. He complained that he was not allowed to respond to accusations, which we might expect; but he also complained that the press was allowed to make such accusations in the first place. Thus, for example, Charpentier wrote on Reynaud's behalf to Caous to complain that the censor had not stopped *Gringoire* from publishing lies about the former Prime Minister.[44] In other words, Reynaud believed that the government was responsible for preventing the press from defaming political figures.

Charles Walton has published a remarkable study of the concept of defamation during the French Revolution,[45] which suggests that the turmoil of 1789 led to an abrupt redefinition of the notion of free speech. The absence of a societal consensus regarding permitted speech was, in his view, a factor that contributed to the advent of the Terror. It is possible that a similar dynamic worked in the case of Vichy, and that the shock of 1940 redefined the limits of what was acceptable and what was defamation. After all, it was a very different matter to protest that a policy might lead to national ruin and to assert that it already had. It is in these terms that we should understand the nexus of honor and politics under the Occupation.

---

41 Reynaud to Pétain, 9 August 1940, Box 24, Series 74AP, AN.

42 Reynaud to Pétain, 6 September 1940, Box 24, Series 74AP, AN.

43 Reynaud to Peyrouton, Box 24, Series 74AP, AN.

44 Bétolaud to Reynaud, 12 October 1942, Box 24, Series 74AP, AN.

45 G. Charles Walton, *Policing Public Opinion in the French Revolution: The Culture of Calumny and the Problem of Free Speech* (Oxford: Oxford University Press, 2011).

At the same time, however, we should bear in mind that the dynamic worked both ways. Vichy was at least as concerned with dishonoring its opponents as they were with resisting the imputation of dishonor. Indeed, the use of "dishonoring" accusations, generally involving some suggestion of cupidity, was not particular to the Reynaud case but part of Vichy's general modus operandi. Because of the very long prehistory of Republican scandals, which had in 1934 been returned to the public eye by the Stavisky Affair, it was remarkably easy to taint Republican politicians with accusations of peculation. Such accusations also reinforced the stereotype, which we have encountered in previous chapters, of the Republic as a place where politicians felt no responsibility to the commonweal and where no scandal could ever keep a sufficiently well-connected individual down. Thus, for example, the suspicious death of Stavisky had led to Camille Chautemps' resignation and precipitated the most severe crisis in interwar French politics, but Chautemps continued to play an active role in government. It was therefore natural for Vichy to resort to this kind of accusation when it sought to prosecute Republican politicians.

In the light of what we have already seen in previous chapters, it is not difficult to adduce another reason why Vichy resorted repeatedly to dishonoring accusations against its enemies when accusations of treason had failed. Even if honor had been of less crucial significance to the French political culture of the time, the regime had few alternatives. Its reluctance to admit openly that it was prosecuting people for their views left it no choice. Only the radical right-wing press was willing to call for Auriol, Reynaud, and Mandel to be condemned in an openly political manner, and even they had qualms on the subject. Even the extremely collaborationist *Gringoire*, in the course of an article that accused Blum and Auriol of exporting arms to Republican Spain and stated that Auriol had stolen from the treasury, observed that such specific accusations would mean that "One can see that it is not at all, as some still claim to think, a matter of a trial of opinion or of a more or less debatable, because imprecise, responsibility, but on the contrary of a very clear accusation."[46]

Unfortunately, accusations of peculation had one aspect that was unfortunate for the regime. Their very specificity and concreteness could prove a drawback, as they could very easily be disproved by an analysis of the income of the person in question. A single accountant, Charles Mulquin, presided over most of Vichy's analyses of this kind. Mulquin was among the unsung heroes of Vichy's political cases, and for an eminently typical reason: he behaved as a good professional, and consequently produced reports indicating a complete absence of

46 *Gringoire*, 3 October 1940.

peculation. Once again, the procedure Vichy had started turned out to possess its own logic.

Mulquin was the key figure in the Mandel case. To be sure, unlike Reynaud, Mandel was accused of more serious offenses as well as peculation. He was indeed among the first political defendants to be arrested under Vichy, well before the regime's September sweep. As one of France's most prominent and most anti-German conservatives, Mandel was suspected of wanting to be the French Churchill, the incarnation of the national spirit of resistance. (He was also Jewish, although, as we will see, this did not make it easier for the government to prosecute him.) The regime therefore suspected him almost immediately of plotting with the British envoy Duff Cooper to form a government in Morocco, and arrested him.

This initial effort was unsurprising. Most dictatorships seek to incarcerate or at least monitor those they suspect of plotting to overthrow them, especially under circumstances as troubled as those of July 1940. There was, therefore, nothing very illuminating about the motivations behind the first *information* against Mandel, which seem to have been dominated by primarily practical concerns. The primary significance of this event, rather, is its relevance as an early indicator of Vichy's difficulties in controlling the judiciary. The *magistrat d'instruction* of the military tribunal of Meknès, Colonel Loireau, found no evidence that Mandel had in fact conspired against the security of the state. He therefore pronounced a verdict of *non-lieu*. There is no reason to see in this act, as Reynaud did,[47] an unusual personal will to resistance on Loireau's part. (This is not to question Loireau's personal courage; he was subjected to forced retirement because of his decision to defy the government.) Rather, he was merely doing his duty as a magistrate charged with investigating a specific indictment, precisely as the decidedly pro-Vichy Leprêtre did in the case of Reynaud.

As in Reynaud's case, after the initial indictment of Mandel had failed, the government sought energetically to discover evidence of financial malpractice on his part. Also as with Reynaud, they were largely unsuccessful. The accountant used in the Mandel case, Mulquin, was the same as the one used for Reynaud, and he came to similar conclusions. To be sure, he discovered lacunae in Mandel's fiscal past that could be deemed cause for concern, mostly connected to his tenure as Minister for Colonies. For example, Mandel had discussed a revaluation of the Indochinese Piaster with regard to the French Franc in 1938, which had led to much speculation before being abandoned. There was, however, no evidence that Mandel was directly involved in this speculation, and it seemed

47 Paul Reynaud, *Au Coeur de la Mêlée: 1930–1945* (Paris: Flammarion, 1951), 1012.

implausible that he would have abandoned the revaluation if he had been financially interested. Mulquin dutifully noted, however, that a "Dietholm et Cie" had bought 5.35 m francs of piasters, and that Mandel's *chef de cabinet* was called André Dietholm. Similarly, Mandel controlled the distribution of pro-colonial advertisements in French newspapers, which could theoretically have led to fraud, but there was no evidence that it did; and he had formed a *Comité d'Or* which engendered speculation, but there was no evidence of his personal involvement in this speculation.[48] Such were the profoundly unimpressive results of an investigation that took two and a half years to complete (from 21 December 1940 to 6 June 1943). Once again, the government's ambitions ran ashore on the anfractuous shoals of reality.

This was a common pattern at Vichy. Determined to adhere as closely as possible to legalism, the government repeatedly sought to accuse its opponents of fiscal irregularities, only to find out upon investigation that no such irregularities existed. Such problems could even hinder the government's efforts to convict individuals who, unlike Reynaud and Mandel, had adhered to the Popular Front.

An Unsuccessful Prosecution of a Leftist: The Strange Case of Vincent Auriol

The Vichy regime's prosecution of Vincent Auriol was doubly ineffective. Much as with Reynaud and Mandel, the regime attempted to indict him twice – firstly as one of those who caused the defeat, and secondly for peculation – and failed on both occasions.

Again as with Reynaud and Mandel, the "political" offense came first. Auriol was among those rounded up in September 1940 and placed under administrative internment by the regime. This initial round of internments was broad-based; the government had evidently not yet worked out the precise identities of those who were to take the blame for the defeat, or even whether they would (as eventually happened) limit the prosecution to politicians and government officials. Auriol thus found himself imprisoned in the rather bizarre company of Marcel Bloch (a major French armaments manufacturer), Dewoitine (another arms manufacturer, who had lent his name to one of France's best-known military airplanes), and several other less well-known financiers and industrialists.

---

48 Mulquin report, pp. 172–176, Box 69, Series 2W, AN.

In spite of the manifest injustice of this procedure and of his advanced age (born in 1884, he was of the generation of socialists that preceded that of his friend Blum), Auriol was a model prisoner who rarely sought to object to his treatment. Nonetheless, he was retained longer than most of those caught by the initial broad-spectrum roundup. The industrialists and financiers were all released in February 1941, a development that coincided with Darlan's ascension to power. Auriol, on the other hand, remained in prison until the next month, when the poor state of his health forced the government to allow him to seek medical treatment. (As with so many of Vichy's prisoners, a friend had interceded for him.) They did not bother to return him to prison, keeping him instead under house arrest.

Meanwhile, Auriol was being subjected to the now-familiar stream of accusations regarding his financial probity. The radical right-wing press maintained a constant barrage of insults against him, expressed in terms that referred back to the history of Republican scandals. "A politician never despairs. The history of the Third Republic murmurs it to him all through an uninterrupted chain of scandals," wrote *Gringoire* in 1941 in the course of an allegation that Auriol had stolen funds intended for armaments.[49] As usual, the radical Parisian right had little confidence in Vichy's willingness to prosecute those they deemed guilty.

Indeed, Vichy was unable to find any suggestion of improbity regarding Auriol's behavior on the national level that was convincing enough to bother to indict him. In February 1941, however, a denunciation from a certain M. Angles, described in the court records as an "industrialist," finally succeeded in providing Vichy with material to arraign Auriol before a local court.[50] It was, however, over a year between this denunciation and Auriol's eventual appearance before the *tribunal de première instance* of his hometown of Muret.

Unsurprisingly, the accusations concerned fiscal improbity, but regarding Auriol's local political activity as mayor of Muret (from which Vichy had recently persuaded an apparently reluctant town council to remove him). For this reason, the *Cour Suprême*, which was the government's first choice for investigating the matter (which reveals how much faith Vichy still had in the *Cour Suprême* at the beginning of 1942), decided to defer the matter to the Muret court for investigation[51] – a decision that doubtless benefited Auriol, given his considerable local

49 *Gringoire*, 8 August 1941.
50 *Accusations contre Vincent Auriol (1942)*, Box 31, Series 552AP, AN.
51 *Conclusions*, November 1942, Box 32, Series 552AP, AN.

popularity. They centered on a company called *Énergie Électrique de la Garonne* (EEHG), which supplied hydroelectrical power to Muret.

Angles had claimed that Auriol had received half a million francs from EEHG, but an initial inquiry suggested that the money had in fact gone to the town of Muret as compensation for EEHG's use of the city's waterfalls as power sources. Further investigation revealed that the matter was a little more complicated than had initially appeared. Auriol had indeed served as EEHG's lawyer at various times between 1931 and 1940, albeit not while holding ministerial office. More importantly – since this was the point on which the affair finally turned – he had indeed received a substantial sum from EEHG in 1931, when he sold part of his orchards to that company as part of its program of hydroelectrical generation. This was necessary because the land in question would be submerged by the dam that EEHG proposed to build.

At this point, the terrain of the case shifted. The prosecution now alleged that Auriol had taken advantage of his local standing to sell the land at a rate above market value. The matter was therefore handed over to that familiar figure of the Vichy (and, indeed, French) judicial landscape: the independent accountant and assessor, tellingly known as the *expert*. It was this expert's report, the *expertise*, that would decide Auriol's fate.

In fact, as has so often been the case in the course of this story, the notion of a perfectly disinterested technocrat proved fallacious. Auriol's case was finally addressed by a 27 September 1942 report[52] written by a man called Joseph Bize. It is impossible, at a distance of seventy years, to determine the rights and wrongs of the case; but Auriol's lawyers certainly believed that Bize was far from being a neutral party. He had in fact been quarreling with Auriol since 1929, giving rise to what a draft of the defense's November 1942 *conclusions* referred to as "lively incidents." This remark, together with another that described Bize as incompetent, is crossed out in the draft.[53] Auriol, like most of Vichy's political prisoners, preferred to keep his criticisms of the justice system to himself.

In any case, even Bize's personal animus (assuming that it existed) could not succeed in tainting the report sufficiently to indict Auriol. The property had been sold for 509,930 francs, and the Bize report valued it at 459,005 francs. (One admires, once again, the extreme punctiliousness of the French legal system even – or perhaps especially – under Vichyite conditions.) The 10 % difference was not the stuff that made or broke political careers. Already, on 14 May 1942, the police

---

52 Report of Joseph Bize, Box 32, Series 552AP, AN.

53 *Conclusions*, November 1942, Box 32, Series 552AP, AN.

commissioner involved with investigating the case, Pierre Fournera, had stated that he could find no evidence of misconduct on Auriol's part.[54] Almost a year later, on 12th May 1943, the *juge d'instruction* of the Muret court, André Reboul, finally delivered a verdict of *non-lieu.*

Meanwhile, the Riom trial proper had already come and gone.

54 Report of Pierre Fournera, 14 May 1942, Box 32, Series 552AP, AN.

7 Riom as Parliament

We have finally arrived at the trial itself – the first moment during which the government would actually have to confront the defendants' arguments directly. It was not up to the task. Blum was a masterful public speaker whose central accusation – that what was on trial was not a few individuals but the Republic – would invariably form the centerpiece of later accounts of Riom. Then and later, the joke that Blum had managed to put the government on trial was a common one. No less effective as a public speaker was Daladier, the "Bull of Vaucluse," whose turns of phrase during the trial were less memorable than Blum's, but whose pretrial preparation was impeccably comprehensive. He dazzled less than Blum during the early days of the trial, partly due to illness. (In yet another sign of Vichy's legalism, the trial was briefly adjourned when Daladier appeared too sick to continue.) In the subsequent months, however, he appeared far better briefed than Blum, who had largely abandoned his pretrial preparation well before the trial started because the interminable delays had convinced him that he would never be formally tried.[1] Daladier would wear down the government's arguments week after week, as the trial dragged on seemingly interminably (opening on 19 February, it would not conclude until 2 April, when the court adjourned for what was supposed to be a short recess but which was ultimately prolonged indefinitely).

More important than what happened, however, was what the French public heard – and, in the event, the French public heard almost everything. Stenographies of the trial circulated widely,[2] and detailed accounts also appeared in most of France's major newspapers and many foreign ones. Romier could not have more comprehensively won his argument concerning the public nature of the trial. Riom was to be a journalists' paradise.

In this it was the heir of the old Republic. Journalists at the trial would repeatedly compare and contrast the judicial *débats* (trial hearings) with parliamentary *débats* (debates on policy). By establishing responsibility to the State as the measure of good policy, and by assigning the assessment of that responsibility to the judicial system, Vichy had effectively replaced the legislature with the judiciary as the primary mechanism for assessing the validity of government policies. This helps explain how Blum's dazzling but less deeply informed parliamentary-style rhetoric could impress the public even more than Daladier's lawyer-like grasp of minutia. Both parliamentarians, however, were in their ele-

---

1 See Blum's correspondence with Auriol in Box 19, Series 570AP, AN.
2 Moch to Blum, Box 19, Series 570AP, AN.

https://doi.org/10.1515/9783110610161-007

ment. Turning Parliament into a court ultimately meant turning the Court into a parliament – a public debating space where oppositional voices could once again be heard. In the end, the government's desire for a Court-as-parliament was incompatible with its desire to control the narrative of the trial.

Yet the government had little choice. If the trial was to be performative, to demonstrate why Parliament had to be replaced by a court, then it had to appear to be an exemplar of the best judicial practices, and it had to be public. The regime was throwing its fate into the hands of journalists and magistrates.

The Newspapers and the Start of the Trial

The small village of Riom was not a propitious location for the trial of the century. Its proximity to Vichy was the only point in its favor. Unlike Vichy, it was not a tourist attraction; in fact, the government chose to situate the journalists' official lodgings in a village six kilometers away, Châtel Guyon, and to provide a bus to the trial (although many chose to find lodgings of their own in Riom or Clermont-Ferrand).[3] A memorandum explained the process: "Due to the almost [struck out] total absence of available places at Riom, it is necessary to make arrangements for lodging for the people called to that town by the trial, that is to say: magistrates, witnesses and journalists."[4] Journalists, in other words, were considered indispensable enough for the government to ensure them lodgings and convey them to the trial, yet the original location had been chosen with no regard for a mass influx of people. It was an apt metaphor for the trial as a whole.

Government passes[5] were necessary to attend the trial. In the event, a hundred and forty journalists received them. Of these, only fifty-seven wrote for French newspapers. The remaining came from across the world, demonstrating the trial's perceived international importance. Most of the Fascist and occupied countries were represented, from Hungary to Spain. There were also representatives of neutral countries, mainly South American, and even several journalists from United States newspapers, including the *New York Times* and the *Chicago Daily Press*. Finally, there was a large German contingent, sent to report on France's self-accusation, which rapidly dwindled along with the press contingent in general as it became apparent that the trial would not be as Germany had

3 Filippi to Sudry, 9 March 1942, Box 1718, Series BB30, AN.

4 *Logement des Magistrats, Témoins et Journalistes*, Box 1718, Series BB30, AN.

5 *Liste des Journalistes Étrangères Assistant au Procès de Riom*, Box 1718, Series BB30, AN.

hoped.[6] It is clear that Vichy ultimately did not shrink from publicity, in spite of the earlier debate between Romier and Barthélemy regarding the advisability of holding the trial in public.

The government had banked heavily on using the trials as propaganda by means of favorable newspaper coverage. They had no intention of leaving this coverage to chance. Minister of Information Paul Marion was entrusted with organizing press coverage of the trial and provided newspapers with a series of *Consignes Générales d'Orientation* (General Introductory Instructions) designed to provide a framework for their reports. This attempt backfired when the *Consignes* were leaked; they were notoriously widely available to the Riom public, a fact that was even mentioned at the trial itself.[7]

The *Consignes* confirmed, in an unusually bald form, the preoccupations of the Vichy government and what it hoped to gain from the trial. Firstly, the trial was to be defensive. There was to be no possibility of suggesting that Pétain was responsible for France's unpreparedness; nor, indeed, were any of his policies to be subject to criticism. This point apparently weighed so heavily on Marion – with reason, as it transpired – that he made almost the same point twice in different parts of the text. The journalists were ordered to "Remember that the object of the trial is limited to the failure to prepare for war, in France, from 1936 until May of 1940, for reasons that will emerge clearly [one cannot fault Marion's optimism] from the hearings."[8] Still more explicitly, a later point ordered newspapers to include official refutations of defense arguments, especially "if some day the proceedings touch on the person of the Marshal [Pétain] and his policies." The army was supposed to be equally above criticism: journalists were to "demonstrate that this trial cannot be that of the Army which, from followers to leaders, was forced to fight without possessing indispensable tools for conducting a modern war." In other words, Pétain and the army were sacrosanct, and the press coverage of the trial was to dispel any clouds of doubt that might still cover them.

Secondly, having adequately defended the incumbent regime, the press coverage of the trial was to legitimize it further by discrediting its precursors. Newspapers were to "explain whenever possible that the real trial is that of the state of affairs from which the catastrophe resulted, in order to permit the French people, thrown into misfortune, to judge clearly the methods of government of which it

---

6 For the dwindling attendance at the trial, see James de Coquet, *Le Procés de Riom* (Paris: A. Fayard, 1945), 18.

7 For the availability of the *consignes*, see Edouard Daladier and Léon Blum, *Les Grandes Journé es du Procés de Riom*, ed. Roger Genebrier and Pierre Mazé (Paris: La Jeune Parque, 1945), 21.

8 All citations from the *Consignes* are from *Ibid*, 14–15.

was the victim." Finally and most critically, they should "frequently reiterate the fact that the policy of the Marshal in every domain was inspired by the necessity that emerges from this obvious fact: France is condemned to construct a new regime or perish." Discrediting the previous regime was not merely an end in itself, but would shore up the foundations of the new by exposing the lack of alternatives.

No fewer than fifty new specific *consignes* were added to the general ones in the course of the trial. Amusingly enough, the very first stated that the press was not to provide an account of the speech by Le Troquer, Blum's lawyer, in which he revealed the existence and contents of the *Consignes Générales d'Orientation*. Even the existence of censorship was to be censored. This order was apparently so ineffective that the third *consigne* promptly countermanded the first, allowing brief mentions of the *consignes*. The eighteenth then stated that the *consignes* could only be mentioned as they became relevant to later debates. The fortieth, brief though it is, is eloquent as to the extent to which the government must have given up hope of winning the press battle: "Stop giving newspapers the *Consignes* on the Riom trial."

The other new *consignes*, like those issued before the trial, were heavily focused on forbidding press reports on the defense's attacks on Pétain's record as War Minister in 1934, on the generals, or on the armistice. These accounted for twenty-two of the fifty *consignes*. Others forbade the repetition of defense invocations of the name of General de Gaulle. ("*Interdiction rigoureuse*" [rigorous interdiction], the *consigne* notes, simultaneously dramatizing the importance of the issue – no other *consigne* used similar language – and admitting the government's inability to get its other orders enforced "rigorously.") The newspapers were instructed not to repeat speeches suggesting German responsibility for the war, revealing the real equality between France and Germany in many categories of materiel, or attacking the *Conseil de Justice Politique* that had already condemned the Riom defendants. One lonely *consigne* made a forlorn attempt to prevent the beleaguered state prosecutor Cassagnau from looking incompetent by ordering that newspapers should not mention a slip of his tongue (he had said 1940 instead of 1939).[9]

This, then, was what the government wanted from the newspaper coverage of the trial. The actual coverage was not entirely congruent, but nor was it as uniformly unfavorable as the weary tone of the censor might suggest. The drawn-out agony of the trial after its initial phase received little attention of any kind, as it was pushed from the headlines by news from the Eastern Front and by the

9 *Consignes Particulières de Presse*, Box 36, Series 496AP, AN.

Anglo-American bombing of the Renault factories at Boulogne-Billancourt in Paris. After the first few days, middle-of-the-road newspapers like *Le Figaro* and *Le Temps* continued to publish summaries of the debates, but largely refrained from commentary on either side. The major exception were the frequent articles that appeared in *Le Figaro* under the byline of James de Coquet, the colleague and immediate subordinate of Romier at that newspaper.

Coquet's postwar book about the trial[10] presented the defense in a positive light. During the trial itself, however, in his capacity as *Le Figaro*'s man on the spot, he adhered woodenly to the prescriptions set out in the government *consignes*. His summary of the *réquisitoire*, for example, emphasized its defense of Pétain's policy in 1934 and made the accusations against the defendants appear moderate, reasonable, and above all apolitical:

> It was in 1934, on the urgent request of the Marshal, that the military budget was increased to 14 billion, then to 64 billion for the following year. The hearings will demonstrate that at that point French industry could only absorb 4 billions' worth of armaments contracts. It would doubtless have willingly made an effort to equip itself to respond to the necessities of national defense and absorb this massive offer of military credits. The policies undertaken by the 1936 government paralyzed the efforts of industry, partly by the fears that they inspired and partly by the hindrances to production they produced. It is here that M. Léon Blum's responsibility is particularly relevant. The accusation against him turns, not on his policies in themselves, but the consequences that certain union-related measures have had on our [military] production.[11]

One has to admire the audacity of an article that claimed, on the one hand, that it was "the policies of the 1936 government" that caused the collapse and, on the other, that it was not "its policies in themselves" that were the basis of the accusation. Such were the difficulties of presenting a political trial as an attack on politics.

Coquet's postwar account of the trial placed great emphasis on the restrictions placed on the press. As we have seen, these were certainly extensive, even if most were honored in the breach. It is possible that, even at the time, Coquet considered his peculiar "moderate" reporting on the trial to be the best that could be done under the circumstances. To a 1942 audience, however, it must have appeared to vindicate Vichy's claim to the center ground. His articles constantly editorialized on the accusations against the defendants in ways that made them seem reasonable and even modest.

---

10 De Coquet, *Le Procès de Riom.*

11 James de Coquet, "La Première Audience du Procès de Riom," *Le Figaro*, 20 February 1942.

It is certainly the case that, whatever Coquet's views of Vichy, he was always full of praise for Vichy's courts and magistrates. Reacting to the common criticism that the trial had taken a ridiculous amount of time to begin, he turned its procrastination into a further proof of the court's desire to hew as closely as possible to an ideal standard of impartial justice:

> When one follows the hearings of this river-debate, one understands why the *instruction* lasted eighteen months and the verdict is not foreseen before the summer. Frequently one reproaches Justice for being slow. But who would want her to be snorting and tugging her bridle like a warhorse? The justice that takes place today before our eyes does not risk incurring later on the reproach of not having taken precautions. It is punctilious, and it is with circumspection that it lifts the veil of this recent past that led to an immense disaster.[12]

This claim that any delays were merely the result of excessive legalism (after the *Conseil de Justice Politique* had already passed sentence without a trial![13]) fit comfortably into the Vichy narrative, but it was not one explicitly prescribed in the *Consignes*. This eminently middle-of-the-road journalist had apparently invented it for himself. A sometimes excessive respect for the technical skill of magistrates was not the exclusive preserve of Vichy.

Coquet's reporting on the trial resembled the official version in other ways. He gave short shrift, for example, to Blum's claim that Riom was the trial of the Republic: "It would be more just to say that it is the trial of a certain idea of the Republic. It is not in doubt that the men who appear today before the Supreme Court have never in their arguments, or even perhaps in their spirits, sacrificed the country's interests. But they thought to defend it by talking about its defense; they thought it armed as soon as they had debated its armaments."[14] The spirit behind these words was indeed moderate compared to the collaborationist press, which did not hesitate to accuse the Riom defendants of the worst moral turpitude. It was, however, fundamentally the same as that of the *réquisitoire*, which, indeed, never claimed that the defendants were guilty of deliberate treason but only of gross negligence (*impéritie*). Moreover, Coquet's summary of the accusations as being about the defendants' tendency to prefer words to deeds was reminiscent of the common Vichy paradigm of the Third Republic as a talking shop. Even in this supposed moderate's coverage of the trial, therefore, the groundwork for the notion of a parallel between judicial *débats* and parliamentary *débats* had already been laid.

---

12 James de Coquet, "Le Procès de Riom," *Le Figaro*, 5 March 1942.
13 See *supra*, chap. 6.
14 James de Coquet, "Au Procès de Riom," *Le Figaro*, 21 February 1942.

Indeed, the condemnation of the defendants' speeches as being somehow "parliamentary" in nature was widespread in journalistic commentary on the trial, and not only in newspapers that needed to fear the censor. The Swiss but generally pro-Vichy *Journal de Genève*, which circulated widely in the Unoccupied Zone, introduced the defense attorneys' speeches with an advance condemnation of their form: "Mirabeau wrote somewhere that eloquence is a power of which one must be wary. One thought of these words while listening to [...] the defense attorneys."[15] The leaders of the Third Republic were politicians and hence incapable of authenticity or real feeling, as the mere fact that the defendants had not already confessed their guilt amply proved: "No one could say that these two people [Daladier and Blum] on whom so much responsibility weighs have at any time cried out sincerely from their hearts in a way that would demonstrate that behind the politician, behind the accused, there is a man, just a man, who appeared to think for a moment of the dead and the prisoners."[16] One wonders what words, if any, could possibly have swayed an opinion so evidently determined in advance. This, however, is perhaps the wrong way to interpret the article, since it was precisely the defendants' facility with words that proved their lack of authentic feeling. In a similar vein, even Pierre Scize, another journalist affected to the trial – but who had written for resistance journals since early in the war – described "a certain facility" with which Blum gestured, explaining to an audience presumed to be familiar with Blum's prewar political speeches that "you know his manner."[17]

Radical right-wing journals, as we shall see shortly, tended to have mixed views on the trial as a whole; but, precisely for this reason, they tended to be far more clairvoyant in observing and condemning the parallel between court and parliament, which they saw as a reversion to the bad old days. *L'Oeuvre*, Marcel Déat's newspaper, made explicit the connection between the speeches of the defense and parliamentary verbiage: "Having driven out the parliamentarian, he returns at a gallop ... And you will find, in the voice of the accused, well-known inflections, tremolos of the parliamentary tribune, when he defends himself – but solely by affirmation – against the accusation that he reduced the French Army's cadres by five thousand officers."[18] *Les Nouveaux Temps* accused the defendants of wanting to "bury reason under reasoning."[19] Yet another newspaper, meanwhile, said that Daladier spoke with "that art of oratory innate in the

15 "Au Procès de Riom," *Le Journal de Genève*, 24 February 1942.
16 *Ibid.*
17 Unknown newspaper, 11 March 1942, Box 26, Series GE, AdHC.
18 "Des canons? des munitions?" *L'Oeuvre*, 28 February 1942.
19 Guy Crouzet, "Passe d'Armes à Riom," *Le Nouveaux Temps*, 23 February 1942.

South,"[20] a phrase redolent of old quasi-racial stereotypes of Third Republic parliamentarians as Mediterranean blowhards from the *sud qui gouverne* (the south that governs) who existed to batten on the hard work of the more Germanic *nord qui travail* (the north that works). *Les Nouveaux Temps* described Blum and Daladier as "leaping on the adversary as in the most glorious days of their reign" and pleaded to its readership that "We must not allow, in order to permit this Riom Trial, the prestige and magnetism of parliamentary eloquence to reintroduce itself in our unhappy country."[21]

Thus the very success of the defense's reasoning could play into stereotypes of the parliamentarian as a cunning lawyer or southern blowhard, better at twisting words than at promoting positive change. This was a key element of the Vichy attack on the fallen regime, exemplified in Pétain's famous claim that "I hate the lies that did you so much harm," which the once-moderate but now ardently collaborationist newspaper *Le Petit Parisien* quoted verbatim in the headline of one of its articles on the trial.[22]

This connection between the juridical present and the parliamentary past, then, constituted a major theme of the press coverage. Even the trial's opponents used the parliamentary analogy – albeit to discredit the trial for being overly "political:" "The court sessions were more like a parliament than a judicial tribunal," wrote one Communist observer.[23] After two years of autocracy, France's journalists looked with astonishment on a hauntingly familiar spectacle.

The Newspapers and the Trial's Failure

As the trial progressed, it must have become increasingly obvious to those present at Riom that the government was failing to make its case against the defendants. To be sure, government reports initially underestimated the scope of the disaster; indeed, the reports sent to Pétain himself continued to dismiss Daladier as a mediocrity well after he had landed some of his shrewdest blows.[24] Even the most ardently pro-Vichy press, however, was beginning to see the writing on the

20 Unnamed newspaper, 3 March 1942, Box 26, Series GE, AdHC.
21 Guy Crouzet, "Passe d'Armes à Riom," *Le Nouveaux Temps*, 23 February 1942.
22 Geo.-Ch. Veran, "À Riom, les Accusés Répètent 'Les Mensonges qui Nous Ont Fait tant de Mal'," *Le Petit Parisien*, 23 February 1942.
23 Jean Van Heijenoort, "The Riom Trial: The Truth About French "Democracy"," *Marxists Internet Archive*, accessed September 23, 2018, https://www.marxists.org/history/etol/writers/heijen/works/riom.htm.
24 Trial report, Box 522, Series 2AG, AN.

wall. *Le Petit Parisien* continued to refer to Daladier and Blum as responsible for the defeat but, by the 25th of February, was already starting to attempt to distance Pétain from the outcome of the trial: "Sovereign, the Court pursues its work of justice. But the Marshal has other responsibilities. And they are those of a country eager, certainly, for truth, but on whom graver worries weigh than that of listening to ghosts ..."[25] The court, repository of the law, remained sovereign, as the French people had once been; but this phrase was now being used to *limit* the importance of the trial.

Curiously, it was the radical right-wing newspapers who, from the beginning (and, indeed, even before it began), were most critical of the government's conduct of the trial. The apparent paradox disappears when one realizes that, in contrast with the enthusiastic but inchoate encouragement that was typical of most ideas on the subject, the collaborationist press had always had its own concept of how the trials should be conducted. In general, collaborationist journalists had even less sympathy for the slow, legalistic process embraced by the government than most citizens did;[26] and some of them had a far more concrete idea of how to replace it.

Much of the collaborationist Paris press, to be sure, merely adhered to the widespread notion that there should be a trial, but that it should be conducted with haste. *Je Suis Partout*, for example, would argue in August 1941, with reference to the murder of the ex-Popular Frontist Marx Dormoy, that the alternatives were "Law unarmed or arms outside the law." Under this interpretation, a (successful) trial was the best possible outcome, but it is clear that there was little toleration for Vichy's legalism, which *Je Suis Partout* (along with much of the radical right-wing press) saw as an effort to keep cards in hand for a future alliance with the Anglo-Saxon powers.[27] In other words, the Paris collaborationists were certainly pressing for a trial, but it was a significantly different trial from the triumph of legalism for which Vichy hoped.

Other collaborationists would ultimately reject the idea of a trial altogether. Léon Bailby's Marseille-based *L'Alerte* welcomed the "Conseil de Justice *politique*," commenting that "We have said a hundred times that the responsibility for our reverses is above all *political*." Bailby, unlike many at Vichy, was clear-sighted enough to realize that attempts at judicial proceedings, "in the narrow and restricted sense of the word," against persons who were merely guilty of fail-

25 Geo.-Ch. Veran, "Daladier étant Souffrant l'Audience est Renvoyée à Vendredi," *Le Petit Parisien*, 25 February 1942.
26 For public criticism of the length and legalism of the trial, see *supra*, Chap. 2.
27 *Je Suis Partout*, 4 August 1941, Box 26, Series GE, AdHC.

ing to check spending or to exact enough assistance from the British, were bound to fail – but, he asked rhetorically, "how can we deny that their responsibility is nonetheless direct and appalling?"[28]

This discourse struck at the very heart of the Vichy consensus by attacking its key element: the condemnation of politics. Ultra-collaborationists saw the refusal to admit that the country was politically divided as the fraud that it was. By 1941 and especially by 1942, most of them must have felt this political divide in person, as their support for German victory and rabid opposition to the Anglo-Saxon powers, never popular, became ever more alienated from the mainstream of French political discourse.

While some collaborationist proposals could be presented as extreme versions of the National Revolution, their differing conception of Riom could not be explained away in these terms. We have seen that even strong supporters of the trial tended to oppose the notion of a war guilt trial; but a war guilt trial was precisely what the Germans wanted, and, necessarily, their allies along with them. This divergence increasingly forced collaborationists into open attacks on Vichy's handling of the trial. *Les Nouveaux Temps*, for example, greeted Hitler's speech attacking the Riom trial for its failure to admit French responsibility for the war (which *de facto* ended the trial) with an article headlined "L'Agonie de Vichy" [Vichy on its Deathbed]. Through its exegesis of Hitler's words, it declared the French government "MENTALLY IN CAHOOTS WITH THOSE WHO WISHED FOR WAR AGAINST GERMANY."[29]

There was, then, a clear difference of substance, tone and direction between the extreme right-wing press on the one hand and the government and its supporters on the other. The radicals wanted a trial, certainly, but not the trial that the government ultimately conducted. They did not understand the centrality of the government's concern for legalism or for respecting the technical knowledge of the magistrates, but they did realize that these concerns were bound to undermine the trial's success. *Les Nouveaux Temps* summed up the problem: "These magistrates, these generous attorneys, grown old in a peaceful line of work, run the risk of *not being up to the task*" (emphasis in original).[30]

One side-effect of the fact that the radical right-wing press was opposed to the trial as constituted by the government, and took advantage of every opportunity to demonstrate its weaknesses, was that a very wide audience became immediately aware of the trial's failings as it progressed. To be sure, resistance jour-

28 *L'Alerte*, 24 August 1941, Box 26, Series GE, AdHC.
29 *Les Nouveaux Temps*, Box 26, Series GE, AdHC.
30 *Les Nouveaux Temps*, 23 February 1942, Box 26, Series GE, AdHC.

nals like *Combat* covered the same flaws from an angle far more appealing to a modern audience; but the circulation of radical journals like *Gringoire* was enormous. With the moderate mainstream press either on Vichy's side or afraid to speak out, it is likely that the radical journals' coverage of the trial had a very different effect from the one intended. Their attitude helps explain how the public became aware of the inadequacies of the trial in spite of the censor.

It is only fair to note, however, that sometimes, if rarely, a newspaper would dare to offer outright support for the defendants. *L'Effort*, which represented those socialists who supported Vichy, quoted Blum and his attorney Samuel Spanien's speeches so extensively in the early days of the trial that their sympathies were obvious. They even cited Spanien's assertion that "in the verdict that you will deliver, History will one day look for the proof of your independence"[31] – a blatant suggestion that only a verdict of *non-lieu* would be perceived as being neutral. The origin of those who ultimately found themselves at Vichy was not irrelevant; when the lines were drawn, even Vichyite socialists displayed a clear partiality to their old leader.

The Magistrates

The radical right-wing attacks on the Riom Trial were in part predicated on the notion that the *Cour Suprême* was constituted of career magistrates. Indeed, the Riom magistrates were far from being the collection of politically chosen "national" (that is, right-wing) figures envisioned in the early drafts of the law establishing the court.[32] Instead, a February 1942 brief for Barthélemy[33] makes it clear that the magistrates were chosen according to the double criteria of patriotic fervor and legal respectability. The government did not even take advantage of the possibility it had given itself in the constitutional act establishing the court to fill half its posts with soldiers, choosing instead to focus exclusively on individuals with legal backgrounds.

In the extremely pro-administration atmosphere of Vichy, it is unsurprising that the Riom magistrates were routinely covered with praise. We have already seen that James de Coquet, the *Figaro*'s man on the spot, had nothing but praise for the magistrates of the *Cour Suprême*. Although, as we have seen, the radical

---

31 *L'Effort*, Box 26, Series GE, AdHC.

32 *Supra*, chap. 4.

33 *Notes biographiques*, 17 February 1942, Box 1718, Series BB30, AN. It is remarkable that Barthélemy had apparently waited until the trial itself to seek information on the background of the *Cour Suprême*'s magistrates!

right occasionally attacked the magistrates for excessive legalism, Coquet's admiration was typical of most of the journalistic coverage of the trial. *Le Mot d'Ordre* offered a typical impression of the presiding judge, Pierre Caous:

> Presiding Judge Caous follows the hearings with grave and sustained attention. He tilts his head slightly to the left and gazes directly into the eyes of the person addressing the court.
>
> When he speaks, his sensitive voice corresponds exactly to the expression of his soft blue eyes and rosy face. And yet the tone admits of no response.[34]

Indeed, many of the individuals selected for the trial ranked among France's most prestigious magistrates. To be sure, Caous was far from an apolitical figure. He had served as the state prosecutor in a number of politically charged cases, including the late Third Republic's greatest scandal, the Stavisky Affair.[35] At the same time, however, his lengthy career at the *Cour de Cassation* lent him gravitas. Similarly, Vice-President Henri Lagarde (who replaced Caous as President for much of the *instruction*) had served at the *Cour de Cassation* since 1929 and was a noted specialist in criminal law. Paul Tanon had been a magistrate since 1906 and had entered *the Cour de Cassation* in 1937. François Oliver-Martin had received his legal doctorate in 1901 and had enjoyed a long and distinguished career as a law professor, in the course of which he had received several honorary degrees from foreign universities and published numerous books on French legal history. René Baraveau had spent his life as a judge and, like Tanon, had entered the *Cour de Cassation* in 1937. Émile Lesueur, yet another veteran of the *Cour de Cassation*, had also received recognition for his work on French history. Maurice Lemaire had served as the First President of the Court of Montpellier.

Even André Wateau, although a soldier by profession, was far from a legal neophyte. A graduate of the prestigious Sciences Po, he had a doctorate in law and had been a lawyer in his youth. As an early advocate of aerial photography and the author of numerous articles on military aeronautics, he could also be convincingly presented as an expert on the subject matter of the trial itself.

If the magistrates of the *Cour Suprême* could all be conveniently presented as professionals, this was not their only qualification. The biographical notes sent to Barthélemy seemed to accord an equal priority to the magistrates' past military experience, which varied from the simple service in the First World War that should be expected of men of their generation (for they were for the most part men of mature years) to honors and distinctions above the call of duty.

34 *Mot d'Ordre*, 23 February 1942, Box 26, Series GE, AdHC.

35 *Notes biographiques*, 17 February 1942, Box 1718, Series BB30, AN. See this document for the biographical details listed in the following paragraphs.

Caous in particular had had a highly distinguished wartime record. It would be convenient for the purposes of the present work if this attention to military expertise could be assimilated to the magistrates' legal expertise as a further example of Vichy's cult of technocracy; but it seems likelier that the military record of the magistrates was considered relevant for the same reason that many of those who wrote letters to the *Cour Suprême*, discussed in the previous chapter, frequently mentioned their families' and their own military service regardless of its applicability to the current war. That is, service in the military was evidence of being a good citizen; it was proof of being truly French – and only truly French magistrates could preside over the trial of a French regime.

The magistrates, then, were hand-picked, but hand-picked from a pool of scholars and practicing magistrates with unimpeachable legal backgrounds. No fewer than five had served the Republic's highest court, the *Cour de Cassation*, before serving that of Vichy. It is therefore fair to present them as a microcosm of the best that the French magistrature had to offer.

Both during and after the war, the magistrates – Caous in particular – would present themselves as the victim of circumstance. The new Gaullist regime was not eager to call into question the loyalty of the magistrates that it itself relied upon to enforce its own judgments, a contradiction that the now-prosecuted collaborationists remarked upon with an understandable bitterness.[36] Thus, for example, Caous was even summoned to Pétain's trial as a witness, in which capacity he enunciated a highly unpersuasive defense of the French magistrature's obedience to questionable orders during the war which was nonetheless warmly received by the court.

Indeed, the court assembled to try Pétain could hardly have been more warmly disposed to Pétain's leading magistrate. Caous was present because he had requested the opportunity to defend himself against attacks in the press, particularly by the socialist newspaper *Le Populaire*, which was less than enthused by the magistrature's collective acquittal of themselves. The presiding judge of the Pétain trial, Paul Mongibeaux, had therefore chosen to use his discretionary power to give Caous a venue to justify himself and his profession, apparently in the hope that Caous would say what he, as an officially neutral party, could not. He could scarcely restrain himself from supporting Caous, however, interrupting him in the middle of his summary of *Le Populaire*'s attacks against him to add, "You could say [that the attacks were] against the whole magistrature!" Caous proceeded with a completely unapologetic testimonial, responding

36 Alice Kaplan, *The Collaborator: The Trial & Execution of Robert Brasillach* (Chicago: University of Chicago Press, 2000), 116.

to *Le Populaire*'s statement that his conduct was hardly worth of praise (*éloge*) with the stern rejoinder that "That is entirely my own opinion. A magistrate who simply does his duty does not merit any praise."[37] He pointed out triumphantly that, almost uniquely among France's magistrates, the judges of the *Cour Suprême* had never been asked to swear an oath to Pétain ("To the person of the Head of State," Mongibeaux corrected him). When the court was constituted, its magistrates were sworn in according to the old formula, and they were never called upon to retake the oath when it was changed. Of course, the fact that Vichy had so much faith in its choices that it saw a personal oath of allegiance as superfluous hardly speaks well for the republican spirit of the Riom magistrates.

In any case, the point was moot; Caous, alone of the Riom magistrates, had in fact taken the oath in any case in his quality as chief prosecutor of the *Cour de Cassation*. This bothered him not at all, since Caous seems to have been completely unaware of the notion that personal obedience to a head of state might be considered unusual for a supposedly neutral judge. (It is only fair to note that French magistrates were and are state employees and that their loyalty is always supposed to be to the state; but that is a different matter from a personal oath to a specific figure.) Indeed, so unabashed was Caous that he repeated part of his oath to Pétain before the court that was engaged in trying Pétain, lingering on the promise it contained to be a "worthy and loyal magistrate" and adding "What does it matter that they added that we should also swear an oath to the head of state. How does that change, how does it diminish the reach of the wording of the magistrates' oath?"[38] He proceeded to quote his own words at the beginning of the Riom trial that the court would ignore the condemnation pronounced by the *Conseil de Justice Politique* a few months earlier. This entirely innocuous statement, Caous believed, constituted proof that his oath to Pétain had not modified his conduct. As for his colleagues, Caous claimed, remarkably enough, that the magistrates had never discussed the trial between them – even after its suspension – because "we were magistrates and we knew that a magistrate, master of himself, keeps himself in check and does not formulate an opinion until the end of the judicial hearings."

It is evident that Caous' opinion of his profession was extraordinarily high and had in no way been compromised by the events of the war. In his view, the magistrates were perfectly neutral and had done no more than their duty in prosecuting the leaders of the old regime after they had already been sen-

37 Pétain trial records, p. 101, Box 49, Series 496AP, AN.
38 Pétain trial records, p. 101, Box 49, Series 496AP, AN.

tenced to prison terms without trial by the leader of the new regime. The magistrate who had proudly commented during the Riom trial that he did not read any newspapers because he did not need to know what public opinion thought of him or of his court[39] thus remained perfectly consistent.

Whether Caous truly was as neutral as he claimed, and probably believed, is another question. After the war, Blum and *Le Populaire* were unwilling to forgive and forget, and reproached the Riom magistrates for their willingness to participate in such a fraud. At Pétain's trial, Blum stopped short of describing the Riom magistrates as traitors but bitterly reproached them for this willingness. Indeed, Blum had hammered home this point even before the Riom trial itself. "You have been judged as well as me,"[40] he had thundered to the magistrates, in what was probably the most famous phrase of the trial. This attitude, however, seems to have been limited to a restricted section of the French left. Even Daladier, who had as much cause as Blum to hate the Riom magistrates, appears after the war to have been rather grateful to them for their failure to arraign him on war guilt charges. Indeed, he extended the same praise even to the state prosecutor Gustave Cassagnau, and seems to have believed that the cause of the 15 April suspension of the trial was that Cassagnau was about to recommend a verdict of *non-lieu* (case dismissed) which the court would have accepted.[41]

It was this interpretation, with its patriotic magistrates gallantly defying the German-inspired notion of a war guilt trial, that appealed most to the imagination of postwar France. Henri Michel, too savvy a historian to adopt the idea at face value, nonetheless paid tribute to the magistrates' unwillingness to accept the notion of a war guilt trial, which he believed to have been the only factor that saved Reynaud and Mandel.[42] We have seen that a war guilt trial would have been extraordinarily unpopular even in the large section of French public opinion that accepted that the Third Republic was responsible for the defeat.[43] Opposition to such a trial positioned the magistrates in the company of the mainstream of Vichy's supporters. It is virtually impossible to tell if the government ever really intended to force through such a matter; in any case, it can hardly have been the magistrates who prevented them, since they not only chose to interview witnesses regarding the legality of the war, but were still doing so in early 1941.

---

39 Riom Trial transcript, 1 April 1942, Box 25, Series GE, AdHC.

40 Blum to *Cour Suprême*, 20 October 1941, Box 1, Series 2W, AN.

41 Pétain trial records, p. 43, Box 49, Series 496AP, AN.

42 Michel, *Le Procès de Riom*, 61.

43 See *supra*, chap. 2.

Indeed, the nature of the questions the court posed to witnesses leaves no doubt that the Riom magistrates were seriously investigating this issue. The key problem concerned the nature of the 2 September 1939 vote of war credits, which the Daladier government had interpreted as constituting authorization to go to war the next day. The radical right in France had always insisted that this decision violated the Parliament's constitutional right to decide matters of war and peace. It is evident that the magistrates took this question very seriously in the early months of the trial. On 4 December 1940, for example, the court called Sabinus Valière, the President of the Finance Commission of the Chamber of Deputies, to testify. Lagarde asked Valière if Daladier's response to a question posed by one of the members of the Finance Commission "could permit the members of the Commission to think that the vote of credits did not imply authorizing the Government to declare war?"[44]

The Riom magistrates, then, were more than willing to adopt extreme avenues of inquiry as long as they could be covered with a legal figleaf – and this in spite of the fact that the prosecution of Daladier for starting the war would have incensed French public opinion without in any way satisfying the extreme pro-collaborationists and the Germans, both of whom were determined to see Reynaud and Mandel convicted of the non-existent crime of "bellicism." This is not, however, to imply that the Riom magistrates were uncritical supporters of the government. Henri Michel asserted, on the basis of the memoirs of the *Cour Suprême*'s archivist, that they had been shocked by Pétain's decision to anticipate their verdict via the *Conseil de Justice Politique* and that some had contemplated resigning.[45] (Specifically, Barthélemy told Blum's defense lawyer Spanien that Wateau had had to be talked out of resigning.[46] It is typical of Vichy attitudes that the most independent magistrate was a general.) Indeed, given the magistrates' exalted notion of their status, their reaction could hardly have been otherwise.

At the trial itself, too, the magistrates appear to have taken their independence quite seriously, and to have investigated the issues presented to them with the energy of a court whose verdict would be meaningful. Considerable time was devoted, for example, to the question of whether the Popular Front had (as the right-wing press so often alleged) delivered necessary arms and matériel to the Spanish Republican government. To this end, as we have seen, the court called a number of customs officials to testify as to whether they had seen armaments

44 Valière testimony, 4 December 1940, Box 41, Series 496AP, AN.
45 Michel, *Procès de Riom*, 43.
46 Note apparently by Spanien, 20 October 1941, Box 24, Series 74AP, AN.

pass the Pyrenees – a rather crude method, since arms could of course be reshipped.

The case of the investigation of arms deliveries to Spain is of particular interest because it was one of the few charges investigated by the Court which was ultimately dropped for lack of evidence. When the trial was finally held, General Boris, who had raised the question of artillery deliveries to Spain during his *instruction* testimony, was not asked about the issue again because (as Caous noted) the *instruction* had shown that no such deliveries occurred.[47] To be sure, officers who deliberately chose to raise the issue were allowed to do so. General Édouard Requin, for example, commented on a rumor that the shortage of blankets was due to deliveries to Spain.[48] It was, however, clear that such observations were nothing more than hearsay. In such ways, the regime's obsession with legalism occasionally translated into real justice. It was impossible to adhere to the grand French tradition of the *instruction*, even in its modified form, without introducing some regard for truth into the procedure.

These attempts to defend their prerogatives does not, however, suggest that the magistrates were in any way sympathetic or even neutral towards the defendants. In fact, the defendants' requests during the trial were routinely refused. It is understandable that the magistrates did not accede to those defense memoranda that would have entailed having the trial thrown out of court or denying their own jurisdiction. That would indeed have been a bold act of defiance which would require a dramatic revision of the conventional archetype of the hidebound or cowardly magistrate that flourishes in the recent literature on Vichy.[49]

The magistrates, however, went further, throwing out even relatively minor procedural pleas with such regularity that it becomes difficult to explain these events except in terms of ideological allegiance to the Vichy project of condemning parliamentary politics. For example, Blum had requested that a stenographic record be kept of the sessions of the court held under *huis clos* (without the presence of the press). This, surely, cannot be seen as a particularly obtrusive request, since Blum made it clear that he had no intention of demanding that these sessions be made public in the near term, but only that evidence be preserved for the sake of "the preservation of the essential right of the accused to justify themselves when the moment has come, not only before the Court but before opinion and history." Blum accepted as legitimate that some sessions might involve the discussion of military secrets that it would be inopportune to reveal

47 Riom trial transcript, 25 March 1942, Box 25, Series GE, AdHC.
48 Riom trial transcript, 19 March 1942, Box 25, Series GE, AdHC.
49 See, for example, Alain Bancaud's views on the subject, as cited in Kaplan, *The Collaborator*, 102.

to the public – a concession which, given the state of the Army of the Armistice in 1942, must have been difficult to make with a straight face. He pointed out, however, that parliamentary commissions dealing with secret military matters normally kept a stenographic record of their secret sessions, suggesting that this proceeding could not therefore entail security risks.

It was a trivial request, completely meaningless in the near term and relevant only as a source when the inevitable memoirs and recriminations were written after the war. The *Cour Suprême* could have conceded it without in any way compromising or even affecting the legal position of the prosecution, and it is difficult to believe that a minor procedural change would have met with opposition from on high. Instead, however, the Riom magistrates seized on Blum's passing mention of the taboo word "Parliament" to instruct him sternly that "the practices followed in the Parliamentary Assemblies cannot be invoked before Courts of Justice" because of the fact "that the only object of hearings before punitive jurisdictions is the search for truth in light of the penalties attached by law to recognized infractions."[50] In other words, the magistrates, obsessed with the sanctity of their profession, were more than willing to adopt Vichy's belief that debates in court differed from debates in Parliament because only the former aimed at determining the objective truth. They were even willing to go out of their way to make this point when the original mention of parliamentary committees in Blum's note had been a mere example with no bearing on the basic debate about the value of parliamentary practices in general.

Parliamentary debates might lie, but justice was concerned only with determining the unbiased truth. Indeed, the parliamentarian-as-deceiver was also critical to one of the key accusations against the defense: the suggestion that they had deceived the nation regarding its military capabilities. In the circumstances of 1941 and 1942, optimism had almost gained the status of a crime. This accusation formed the centerpiece of the indictment that the *Cour Suprême* drew up hastily after the *Conseil de Justice Politique* had delivered its verdict. It focused on the minutes of the crucial 23 August 1939 cabinet meeting, in which Gamelin and La Chambre had assured the government that their branches of the armed forces were ready for war. In this way, Gamelin, although a military leader, was assimilated to the parliamentarians as a deceiver. The fact that this interpretation was completely incompatible with the notion that Daladier himself had knowingly misinformed the nation was ignored. Instead, the court accused Da-

50 AIV C22, 6 March 1942, Box 1, Series 2W, AN.

ladier of failing to stop his subordinates from misinforming the cabinet[51] – an entertainingly novel concept of legal responsibility.

In other words, the notion of the parliamentarian as a cunning master of words which he used for the purposes of deceit, which we have already seen to be critical to the press coverage to the trial, was also present in the self-perception of the magistrates themselves. They defined themselves by opposition to the political sphere, to which they deemed themselves superior, even when presiding over a trial that to us appears to have been obviously political in nature.

Conclusion: The Suspension of Legal Norms

With these sympathies in mind, it becomes clear why the Riom magistrates were willing to participate in a system in which the normal rules of French jurisprudence were honored in the breach. And there can be little question that they were so honored. For all the government's legalism, its violations of prewar legal norms were many and varied.

Traditionally, the legal process in France includes a period of *instruction* before the trial, in which magistrates, defendants and prosecutors collaborate to assemble the body of evidence (dossier) that would then be presented before the court. This permits a consensus regarding the salience of evidence. The *magistrat d'instruction*, however, is normally dissociated from the final court to avoid an overly great concentration of power, whereas the *Cour Suprême* conducted its own *instruction.* This conflation of *magistrat d'instruction* and trial judge meant that the judges who would preside over the trial would be the same as those who had ascertained that there was sufficient evidence to proceed to a trial in the first place. This removed a crucial protection from the defendants, but it was minor compared to the court's repeated failures to provide the defendants and their lawyers with the full dossier of evidence prior to interrogating the defendants at the *instruction.* Even that paled beside the court's refusal to allow the defendant's lawyers to accompany them during these interrogations.[52] At every stage, the court's procedure, so reassuringly conventional on the outside, was twisted to hinder the defense.

How much of this hindrance was inspired at the highest levels cannot be determined. It seems, however, implausible that the regime micromanaged the con-

51 List of accusations against defendants, 28 October 1941, Box 1, Series 2W, AN.
52 For a discussion of the constraints on the defense lawyers, see Ribet, *Le Procès de Riom*, 16.

duct of the court. Although the various magistrates and officials who periodically received the defense lawyers' complaints were usually willing enough to blame higher authority (or, less plausibly, the Germans) for any and all difficulties imposed on the defendants, this conduct did not obtain when it came to the question of the court's behavior regarding the suspension of their normal judicial rights. At the beginning of the *instruction*, for example, in September of 1940, the defense lawyer Ribet met Caous to discuss the question of procedure. Far from hiding behind the usual excuses, Caous simply responded to Ribet's complaints with the incessant refrain that "The court hasn't talked about the matter yet,"[53] which implied that the court did have power to adjudicate as it chose matters such as the communication of the *dossier d'instruction* to the defense.

It is worth noting that, just as Vichy and its supporters were not alone in seeing treason as the cause of the 1940 collapse or in demanding that the traitors pay the price of their misdeeds, so they were not the only ones to believe that an unusual situation demanded an unusual judicial approach. In June 1941, for example, Roger Genébrier, Daladier's personal secretary, succeeded in securing an interview with Christian Jayle, Barthélemy's *chef de cabinet*. (This was yet another indication that 1940 had not entirely succeeded in rupturing the bonds that united the *république des camarades:* Jayle and Genébrier were old acquaintances, who had been much associated in ministerial cabinets before the war.)

The most extraordinary thing about the meeting, however, was not the individuals involved but the topics discussed. After Jayle had candidly admitted that the question of war guilt was not the ground on which the government wanted to base the trial, a dilemma on which he blamed the failure of the court to begin the trial proper ("The Court of Justice cannot say: 'Daladier is the culprit,' and also, it is not possible for it to say 'It was Hitler'"), the two moved on to the question of how the court had been constituted. One commented that a better approach would have been a jury of *anciens combattants* [veterans]; the other worried that such a jury would have shot Daladier out of hand, "without judgment, without reflection." (Both, meanwhile, agreed that the best possible approach would have been to retain the *Haute Cour* model, if only it had been possible to find some way of incorporating the Senate into the new regime.) It would have been an entirely conventional discussion, had it not been for the fact that it was the friend and ally of the defendants who called for a jury of *anciens combattants*, and the Vichy official who worried about the consequences of such arbitrary and unpredictable justice!

---

53 *Ibid*, 17.

The existence of this consensus regarding the extraordinary nature of the situation does not, of course, exculpate the regime even slightly for its constant sleight-of-hand with legal forms. Vichy's real crime, however, was a failure of justice and not of legalism. Wherever possible, the government sought to misrepresent the grossest of its violations of legal norms as extensions of the French legal tradition and not as breaches with the past. For example, when the president of the court, Henri Lagarde, decided at the last moment to withdraw from the trial and return to the *Cour de Cassation*, the government released a press communiqué that claimed that the change of presidents represented the separation of *instruction* and trial that legal tradition demanded and that the government had tranquilly ignored for a year and a half:

> This important exchange of functions between two of the most eminent journalists [*sic*, corrected to 'personalities' in a later draft] of the judicial world corresponds to the constant desire of the government to assure the most absolute independence to the legal system and particularly to its leaders.
>
> One of the fundamental principles of the good administration of justice is the separation of *instruction* and trial court. He who collected evidence may not judge. That is the principle that was placed at the head of the great law of 1897.
>
> Without a doubt, the organic law of the Supreme Court permitted this confusion [of functions].
>
> The Government, bowing to considerations of clarity and truth, prefers not to use this faculty as much as it could.[54]

It goes without saying that none of this should be taken seriously as evidence of the sincerity of the government's commitment to legal precedent; but it is also clear that there was a segment of public opinion that cared for such precedent and that the government was anxious to conciliate.

The court-as-Parliament rubric, then, was not wished by the government on an unsuspecting France. Rather, the widespread desire, which the government shared, to replace parliamentary debate in whole or in part with legalistic searches for absolute truth conflicted directly with the government's desire to have a successful trial. It was this conflict that caused the trial's failure.

54 *Communiqué à la Presse*, 30 December 1941, Box 1718, Series BB30, AN.

8 The *Massilia* Affair and the Clermont-Ferrand Desertion Trials

Vichy's efforts to prosecute prewar Republican leaders for the crime of being prewar Republican leaders were rarely crowned with success. There was, however, one major exception to this rule. Between 1940 and 1941, the same military tribunal of Clermont-Ferrand that had so signally failed to indict Reynaud convicted three relatively minor Republican politicians of desertion. Jean Zay, who had served as Minister for National Education for the three years before the war; Pierre Mendès France, who had occupied the post of Secretary of State for Finance under the Popular Front government, and who was to become the champion of decolonization after the war; and Pierre Viénot, who had served as Undersecretary of State for the Maghreb and the Near East under Blum, had all joined the French military at the outbreak of the Second World War, even though parliamentarians were exempt from conscription. Their patriotism was rewarded with sentences that varied from deportation for Zay, at the time the most prominent of the three, to an eight-year suspended sentence for Viénot.

The common denominator and the original excuse for prosecuting these individuals was that they were serving military officers who had embarked upon the *Massilia*, a steamer that in June 1940 transported part of the French parliament to Casablanca in Morocco with the aim of continuing the struggle from northern Africa. At the time the policies of the newly-installed Pétain government were still in flux, and the parliamentarians of the *Massilia*, who included all of the Republican political figures we have previously encountered and many others, believed or hoped that General Charles Noguès, the commander of the undefeated French forces in northern Africa, could be prevailed upon to stay in the war. As a result of a series of deliberate or accidental miscommunications, they also believed that the remainder of the French parliament would also be accompanying them. Instead, they found themselves greeted with vilifications and, in many cases, ultimately (or, in the case of Georges Mandel, immediately) arrested.

The *Massilia* affair had a highly polarizing effect on French opinion: for those already inclined to sympathize with those who boarded it, the Vichy regime's reaction proved its duplicity, while those who supported the armistice tended to see departure from France as a betrayal of those who remained behind. Thus, for example, a plethora of rumors swept France to the effect that those who boarded the *Massilia* had been deliberately tricked into doing so – rumors that the Gaullists took seriously enough that, during the post-occupation *épura-*

https://doi.org/10.1515/9783110610161-008

tion (the purge of collaborators), the *Haute Cour de Justice* would investigate them in the course of its *instruction* against Alibert.[1]

Bitterer still were the reactions of those who saw the parliamentarians' decision to embark on the *Massilia* as evidence that they were abandoning France in her hour of need. An anonymous letter sent to the *Cour Suprême* on 13 August claimed, probably spuriously, to offer an eyewitness account. The sailors were said to have initially had no idea of the identities of those they were transporting, and to have reacted in a strongly "national" – that is, conservative – sense when they discovered them: "Very hostile cries such as 'bastards, traitors, Jews, cowards, etc.'" So opposed were the sailors to transporting parliamentarians when Bordeaux was full of refugees, said the letter, that the boat only left after a number of officers had boarded and caused the mission to assume "a different character."

These anonymous letters were not altogether incorrect in noting tensions between the crew and their passengers. The accounts of the parliamentarians themselves acknowledged that some clashes took place. At the same time, however, these letters both exaggerate the probable extent of the problems and overemphasize their political nature as a clash between the politicians who directed the war and the supposedly betrayed and "national" members of the military. This emphasis also appears in the radical right-wing press, in which one can read such contemporary headlines as "The Jew, Jean Zay, pantsed and spanked ... in a public square in Algiers by French aviators."[2] One notes, alongside the emphasis on the national identity of the aviators (they are identified as French, and Zay as "Jewish") and their occupations as members of the military, the rather juvenile emphasis on making the heirs of the Revolution into "real" sans-culottes by pantsing them. Another anonymous letter made this connection explicit: Zay "was literally *déculotté* (pantsed) and he had to spend the whole afternoon with underwear on just one side of his leg, he was a real *sans culotte*."[3] The fact that this letter predates the aforementioned article makes it clear that the press campaign fed on the opinions of a certain segment of the French population rather than simply inspiring them.

In other words, the radical right loved to interpret the *Massilia* affair as a clash between discredited and authentic national ideas. There is, however, no reason to believe that this corresponds to the reality of the affair. Mendès France, reflecting on the incident many years later, thought that the disturbances on

1 The records for this investigation may be found in Box 46, Series 3W, AN.
2 *La France au Travail*, 3 August 1940.
3 Anonymous letter, 28 June 1940, Box 69. Series 2W, AN.

board the boat were simply the result of differing opinions regarding the continuation of the war. In his own words:[4]

> People have greatly exaggerated regarding the signs of ill humor on the part of the crew of the "Massilia" regarding the parliamentarians. The discontentment of the crew predated the embarking of the parliamentarians and had already caused various incidents prior to the 20 June [when they embarked]. In fact, the boat had taken part in a certain number of distant expeditions and the members of the crew had been separated from their families for a long time. A great number of them [wanted?] a relatively long stay at Bordeaux, which would have allowed them to see their families. When they were belatedly told that the boat would leave again soon for North Africa and that there would therefore be no leave, the result was an unarguable tension between the command and the sailors.
>
> Moreover, when the latter were informed that there might be an armistice but that the "Massilia" was heading to North Africa, they concluded that they would again be separated from their families and for an entirely uncertain period.

To be sure, later in the letter Mendès France admitted that the attitude of the sailors worsened "when they saw that the parliamentarians on board of the ship were in favor of continuing the war," so the matter was not merely a politically anodyne question of leave. At the same time, however, Mendès France's account makes it clear that the emphasis the right-wing press placed on the political nature of the incident is exaggerated. It was, in fact, part and parcel of the radical right's effort, which they had in common with virtually all political organizations in France, to hitch the general outrage to their preferred explanation for France's problems.

Radical right wing accounts of the *Massilia* affair, like the one we have cited above, placed great emphasis on the supposedly venal and cowardly nature of those who sailed on the ill-fated vessel. According to one anonymous report, the parliamentarians were supposed to have brought twenty-three new cars and a number of luxury dogs with them, while the Radical politician César Campinchi suggested that the crew would be paid in pounds if they agreed to fly the British flag. (Why on earth the writer thought that Campinchi would want the *Massilia* to fly a British flag to avoid German bombardment is anyone's guess, although it is evident that reason was not his or her strong point.) Zay was

4 Mendès France to Georg Prahl Herbitz [a researcher who had asked Mendès France for various pieces of information on the *Massilia* affair, including the attitude of the sailors], 2 August 1971, Box E1-III, Annexe 2, Fonds Mendès France, Alliance Israélite Universelle, Paris (henceforth AIU).

said to be "green with fear." The anonymous pseudo-informant recounted with great glee the "fright of our Lords of War."[5]

The choice of words may be a mere contrast between the cowardice imputed to the parliamentarians and their responsibility for national defense. It seems likely, however, that the writer of the letter was attacking the war itself – in other words, they were adopting the radical right-wing rhetorical stance of accusing their opponents of encouraging other people to fight their battles. This stance, which the collaborationist radio personality Philippe Henriot adopted in his unauthorized publication of Jean Zay's letters, generally involved an intimation that the person in question was un-French (usually because they were Jewish) and wanted to steer France into war with Germany (because, via a train of logic that probably made more sense to its proponents, only a Jew would have been interested in fighting Hitler's regime).

Henriot would eventually become Vichy's Minister of Information, so it would be inaccurate to characterize this view as being far removed from the mainstream at Vichy. At the same time, however, it would be a mistake to see it as the dominant trend there. If the *Massilia* affair added to Franco-French divisions, it was not because it seemed to correlate well with a certain preexisting pacifist sentiment among a certain section of the French right, but because the defeat had already exacerbated those tensions to the point that any suspicion seemed legitimate.

Henriot himself was well aware of the fact that his viewpoint on the matter had until recently been in a distinct minority. Thus, for example, in the context of an issue of *Gringoire* that discussed the *Massilia* affair extensively, Henriot called upon the government to "name responsible parties in every quarter," and noted that many had only recently come to oppose parliamentarism.[6] For him, what separated him from the majority was the belief that cowardice was endemic in the parliamentary system and could not be limited to the handful of individuals that would finally come to trial under Vichy.

At any rate, there is no reason to believe that any prominent members of the Vichy government thought of the (to us) evidently political scapegoating of Zay, Mendès France and Viénot as political, or as anything other than impartial justice.

5 Anonymous letter, 13 August 1940, Box 69, Series 2W, AN.

6 *Gringoire*, 8 August 1940.

Differentiation of Sentencing

The most obvious aspect of the Clermont-Ferrand trials was that they had markedly different outcomes. Zay was convicted of desertion in the face of the enemy; Viénot and Mendès France were convicted, but of simple desertion only; and Wiltzer, the only conservative parliamentarian to be indicted as a result of the affair, was acquitted. Anne Simonin, who has written the only recent article on the Clermont-Ferrand trials, concluded that Zay's assessment of the matter in his prison memoirs was basically correct: Zay was given a heavier sentence because he was Jewish[7] (unlike Viénot, who only received a suspended sentence) and was prominent in the Blum government (unlike Mendès France and Viénot, who were undersecretaries, and Wiltzer, who was a conservative). Simonin adds to Zay's analysis the suggestion – probably intuitively obvious to Zay's audience, but less so today – that his role as Minister of National Education probably exacerbated the matter, since the education issue went to the heart of French societal divisions.[8] The French Right loathed the secular Republican education system in any case (one remembers Romier's reference to the "mandarinate" of primary educators), and to have the system headed by a Jew was to add insult to injury.

There is no question that Zay had long been loathed by the radical right. One thinks, for example, of Céline's famous comment "*Je vous Zay*" (I Zay you) – a play on Blum's equally well-known (and frequently cited out of context) outburst in 1925, during a stormy parliamentary debate, that "*Je vous hais*" (I hate you). Zay's early political career had been marred by the theft and publication of a pastiche he had written in the style of a well-known anti-war writer. Known as *Le Drapeau*, the pastiche heaped execrations on the French flag in the name of the dead of the recently ended First World War. The fact that Zay himself was too young to have fought in that conflict – he was only forty when he was arrested in 1940 – lends credence to his statement that *Le Drapeau* was a literary exercise rather than an expression of personal conviction. Either way, however, it is worth noting that violent anti-war sentiment was not an uncommon reaction to the Great War's hecatombs – one thinks of Henri Barbusse's *Le Feu* – and nor was it limited to the French left. Indeed, the level of doublethink that must have been required for radical right-wingers who were violently

7 Zay was a practicing Protestant, but was half-Jewish by ancestry. His opponents invariably referred to him as Jewish, and he did not bother to correct them.

8 Anne Simonin, "Quel prisonnier au fond de la cour...Le procès Jean Zay," Journée d'étude: "Les papiers Jean Zay entrent aux Archives nationales," 8 June, 2010.

opposed to the Second World War to criticize Zay for retrospectively opposing the First is extraordinary.

The level of loathing that the far right felt for an individual does not, however, correlate well with how they fared under Vichy. We have seen that the regime failed in prosecuting Reynaud, Mandel, and Auriol, all of whom were at least as distasteful to the pro-German right as the Clermont-Ferrand victims (and far more prominent in prewar French politics). In order to explain why Zay, Mendès France and Viénot were the only Popular Front ministers to be successfully prosecuted by Vichy's courts, we need to turn to other factors.

The Magistrates

Perhaps the most surprising feature of the Clermont-Ferrand accusations was the fact that the court that convicted Zay, Mendès France, and Viénnot, and acquitted the conservative Wiltzer – thereby appearing to show utter subservience to orders – was the same one that so signally refused to convict Reynaud, who was a far more important figure for both the government and the Germans. At the time, Mendès France believed that the court that convicted him was merely demonstrating spineless obedience to Vichy's instructions;[9] but the context afforded by the Reynaud-Leca-Devaux case shows that this cannot possibly have been true. It is evident that the presiding magistrate Leprêtre had considerable room for manoeuver, and the primary blame for the proceedings at Clermont-Ferrand must therefore attach, not to the Germans or even Vichy, but rather to the magistrates themselves.

It is evident that they had no qualms about their work. Zay wrote that they took no more than five or six minutes to condemn him[10] – a quite remarkable speed record, especially given the extremely punctilious example set by the *Cour Suprême*, which, as we have seen, took much more time to do much less. The behavior of the presiding judges, then, is one of the most intriguing aspects of the Clermont-Ferrand trials.

This is doubly the case when one considers that the pressure from above cannot have been nearly so intense in these instances as in the Reynaud case. De Font-Réaulx, who had been Alibert's intimate while in office, later testified that Alibert was opposed to the prosecution of Zay: "He had received several times Me Alexandre Varenne, Zay's defense attorney. If he could not stop the

9 Mendès France, *Liberté, Liberté Chérie*, 216.

10 Zay's notes on the circumstances of his imprisonment, Box 119, Series 667AP, AN.

trial, which was under the Ministry of War's jurisdiction, he made haste, at M. Alexandre Varenne's demand, to stop the deportation of M. Jean Zay to [the prison colony of] French Guyana at the last minute."[11] We must, of course, take this claim – made after the Liberation, and in the context of the preparation of evidence for Alibert's *épuration* trial – with more than a grain of salt. In particular, the effort to shift the blame to another Vichy cabinet member smacks of a very common defense strategy. At the same time, it is evident that someone at Vichy must have intervened on Zay's behalf, since he was not in fact deported.

Anne Simonin has suggested[12] that the reason that Zay was not deported was a purely practical one. Unable to secure transport across the Atlantic in time of war, the government was forced to suspend the deportation until the Greek kalends. This view has the merit of plausibility; in particular, it helps to explain the delay in carrying out the sentence even before it had been commuted. It does not, however, explain why the sentence of deportation was ultimately commuted and not merely delayed. For this we must turn to Zay's own papers, which have recently become available at the *Archives Nationales*.

Part of the reason appears to rest on that old mainstay of Vichy's political prisoners, the old boys' network, which, as we have seen, remained very much in existence during the Vichy years. Even if this network was considerably less in evidence for Zay than for Reynaud, since Zay was both less prominent and much further from the political orientation of most of Vichy's ministers, it unquestionably existed even for him. Thus, for example, Varenne wrote to Zay[13] that he hoped that his condition would benefit from Barthélemy's appointment as Minister of Justice, since Barthélemy was an ex-parliamentarian (albeit, as Varenne failed to remark, one whose lack of electoral success had given him little reason to love the Republic) and – probably more importantly – a personal acquaintance of Varenne's.

This might help to explain why the commutation was not reversed, but it does not tell us why it was originally granted, since the commutation occurred before Barthélemy replaced Alibert. If any Vichy politician wanted to reenact the Dreyfus Affair, it was Alibert, the arch-antisemite. Perhaps Zay was simply not important enough for such a reenactment; but, in any case, the fact that the government did not even use the full latitude the legal decision had afforded them casts doubt on the notion that the Vichy regime cared enough about Zay to force the courts to make him a scapegoat for the defeat.

---

11 Font-Réaulx testimony, Box 47, Series 3W, AN.

12 Simonin, "Quel prisonnier au fond de la cour," 3.

13 Varenne to Zay, Box 119, Series 667AP, AN.

Mendès France

The nominal grounds for the indictment of the four Clermont-Ferrand defendants was that, since they were army officers, their embarkment on the *Massilia* represented either desertion, the abandoning of an assigned military post, or both. Any disinterested party would immediately have seen how obviously factitious such accusations must be at a time when the French Army was disintegrating and separation from one's normally assigned regiment was the norm rather than the exception. The indictment against Mendès France was a particularly egregious example of this problem: Leprêtre, the magistrate in charge of the *instruction* (and the same man who displayed such moral fibre in his treatment of Reynaud in the preceding chapter), changed the date when Mendès France was supposed to have deserted no fewer than three times in the course of the indictment. His initial attempt to prosecute Mendès France for his embarkment on the *Massilia* quickly foundered on a series of objections, the most notable of which was that Mendès France had left his regiment, not in the course of the German advance, but before it – for he was on leave at the time of the collapse of the French front. A similar logical absurdity attached to the accusations against Zay, who was accused of having deserted in the face of the enemy when the enemy was not near his regiment at the time when he left to seek instructions in Paris, and who, in any case, could hardly have been said to have been closer to the enemy than the other individuals who were indicted.

We will see momentarily that the Zay case, factitious though it was, was not quite as ridiculous as it appears at first glance. For the Mendès France case, however, the future prime minister wrote at the time that Leprêtre had decided "once and for all" that he was guilty of desertion,[14] and, while Mendès France is of course not an impartial witness in this regard, Leprêtre's conduct during the *instruction* certainly bears out the claim. We have only Mendès France's word for the bullying attitude Leprêtre adopted in some of their personal interviews,[15] but, given that on three separate occasions Leprêtre changed the supposed period when Mendès France had "deserted," it is evident that he thought that Mendès France's guilt was clear and that the facts were a mere distraction. No evidence could sway him, including the testimony of Mendès France's commanding officer that, when, on 10 June, he had ordered Mendès France to rejoin his unit, he had told the young officer that the execution of the order could be

14 Mendès France to Pétain, 21 June 1941, Box E1-III, AIU.
15 Mendès France, *Liberté, Liberté Chérie*, 217.

delayed. (Indeed, by that point, no further resistance in metropolitan France was possible.)

The text of the indictment against Mendès France is eloquent regarding the prosecution's uncertainty even in their own minds regarding the nature of his offense: he was supposed to have left his corps without authorization "at the beginning of June 1940 [when he went on leave], in any case before the 20th of that month."[16] This particular document is dated not from Clermont-Ferrand, but from Casablanca, indicating that Leprêtre was not alone in his willingness to indict a politically suspect individual despite having no concrete idea of when he was supposed to have deserted. All levels of the French justice system connived in the Clermont-Ferrand cases in ways that they were signally unwilling to do at Riom or in the cases of Mandel or Reynaud.

The future careers of the military magistrates bear out this impression of a group of dedicated and politically motivated individuals whose fates were anchored to that of the Vichy regime. It is well established that, in spite of the *épuration*, there was a remarkable continuity of personnel leading from the Third Republic to Vichy to the Fourth Republic,[17] which makes it all the more surprising that no such continuity existed in the case of the Clermont-Ferrand court. Perré, who presided over the final stages of the trials, was sentenced to twenty years' imprisonment at the Liberation. As for Leprêtre, the *juge d'instruction* in many of the cases we have encountered so far, he was personally targeted by the Resistance even before the end of the Occupation. He was shot in 1943 and left partially paralyzed. After the Liberation, he went underground until the fury of the *épuration* had abated. This decision probably saved his life, but not his career. He never recovered either physically or professionally from his activities in the Vichy years, and sent his former victim Mendès France a bathetic letter[18] after the latter had risen to the Premiership of the Fourth Republic:

> My illness follows its inexorable course and, invisibly, the circle closes. In the face of this threat, my wife and I would like to leave Touraine and retire to Brittany, at Blains, where we have family. We will miss Montlouis, we made friends there, our house was pleasant and I need not vaunt the charms of Touraine, but what would happen, so far from our family, if my wife were suddenly taken ill?
>
> Perhaps we might have the pleasure – before leaving – which will not happen for several months, to see you again in this region where you have relatives and friends?

16 Indictment against Mendès France, 4 September 1940, Box E1-II, Annexe 1, AIU.
17 See, e.g, Gildea, *Marianne in Chains*, on local officials and mayors.
18 Leprêtre to Mendès France, 18 Jan 1955, Box E1-III, Annexe 2, AIU.

It goes without saying that one cannot take the sentiments expressed in this extraordinary letter at face value. The letter begins with a series of excessively fulsome praises of Mendès France, apostrophized as "a Head of Government who governs, a Statesman in the noble sense of the word." By itself, such praise from a political opponent would stamp the letter as duplicitous, but the context makes it even more obvious that Leprêtre was simply begging for assistance. He must have fallen far indeed if his most useful governmental connection was the man he had wrongfully imprisoned. In any case, we certainly cannot credit with any good faith the support he offered for Mendès France's policies, most notably the 1954 withdrawal from Indochina (which he described as a disagreeable necessity in an untenable situation – a possible reference to the armistice of 1940).

At the same time, however, the terminology Leprêtre used is not without interest. Even in a letter designed to beg for help, he could not resist slipping in a sly dig at those who engaged in politics: "How many traps planted for his feet [i.e. Mendès France's, adressed here in the third person]. The beauties of Politics! For my part, I have never engaged in it and I don't regret it." Moreover, while one may with reason doubt the sincerity of his description of Mendès France as a "Head of Government who governs," one must recollect the specific Vichyite tenor of such phrases, which were invariably used to describe the need to step outside the party system and accept personal responsibility for the nation's successes and failures. Indeed, Mendès France's efforts to sidestep the traditional party system (which destroyed the venerable Radical Party, to which he belonged, in the process) were not without their similarities to Vichy's own logic.

In other words, we cannot draw too sharp a distinction between the military magistrates of the Clermont-Ferrand tribunal and the civilian magistrates of the *Cour Suprême*. Both seem to have had similar priorities. Moreover, it is worth noting that, had it wished to, the *Cour de Cassation* (which, as we have seen, had considerable personnel overlap with the *Cour Suprême*) could have reviewed the Clermont-Ferrand cases via the French equivalent of a writ of certiorari. (Mendès France mentioned with some bitterness in a letter to Pétain the fact that they had not done so.)[19] This refusal to reverse the military judgments on appeal shows the solidarity between the military and civilian segments of the French justice system.

It is worth emphasizing, in this connection, that military tribunals were an entirely normal part of the French legal system. In each of the major naval bases in metropolitan France, for example, it was admirals who heard cases affecting their men. Unlike the Riom trials, for which the Vichy government made

19 Mendès France to Pétain, 21 June 1941, Box E1-III, AIU.

its own law (but, as we have seen, without success), the Clermont-Ferrand trials were conducted on the basis of a preexisting crime (desertion) and largely on the basis of preexisting law. This was surely the consequence of the fact that Zay and the others were much smaller fry than the Riom defendants; but, curiously enough, this very circumstance may have rebounded to their disadvantage.

It is hardly unheard of for the small fry to fare worse than the big fish at post-regime-change trials. (Jacques Boudot, Laval's chauffeur, was sentenced to *indignité nationale* at the Liberation while Maurice Papon, a senior police official who helped deport Jews to their deaths in the Holocaust, avoided all punishment until a newspaper exposé in 1981.)[20] In the case of the Clermont-Ferrand trials, however, it seems likely that the difference in outcomes was due to the continuity of legal forms that was the product of the lesser importance of these trials, and not the low priority assigned to the Clermont-Ferrand trials in itself.

This paradoxical result becomes less strange if one contemplates the state of desertion law in occupied France. Although the notion that the French army threw down its arms at the first sign of trouble is entirely mythical – in fact, it suffered as many casualties per day during the May-June campaign as in the worst periods of trench warfare[21] – it was nonetheless the case that, as the Germans pursued their war of envelopment, millions of soldiers were detached from their disintegrating units and left to fight or flee on their own or in small groups.

For this reason, alterations to France's desertion laws in 1940–1941 were solely in the direction of greater laxity. It was clearly impractical, not to mention (one assumes) undesirable, to prosecute every soldier who found himself detached from his unit in the course of the disaster. On 8 July 1940, Vichy's Air Minister, Bertrand Pujo, wrote to the general responsible for the French Air Force in North Africa to explain that, since the permanent military tribunals had reacquired jurisdiction for cases of desertion on July 1, they had become weighted down with an "encumbrance" of cases "which necessitate for the future the greatest circumspection in regard to indictments of soldiers who deserted or were reputed to have done so."[22] It was a truly extraordinary message that clearly amounted to instructions for the military hierarchy to avoid initiating prosecutions for desertion except in the most egregious of cases – a message that would have been utterly inexplicable outside the context of a situation in which sticking to the letter

20 Pierre Assouline, *L'Épuration des Intellectuels, 1944–1945* (Brussels: Complexe, 1985), 134.

21 Julian Jackson, *The Fall of France: The Nazi Invasion of 1940* (Oxford: Oxford University Press, 2003), 179–180.

22 Ministre de l'Air to Général commandant supérieur de l'Armée de l'Air en Afrique du Nord, 8 July 1940, Box E-1, Annexe 1, AIU.

of the law would have meant putting half of France in prison. In other words, precisely as the Vichy government was crafting laws to prosecute the Riom prisoners, an unrelated dynamic was forcing them to relax the enforcement of the laws that would be used to prosecute the Clermont-Ferrand accused.

Once again, what emerges from this analysis is a picture of the increased independence of magistrates under Vichy, who, far from being the passive prisoners of orders from above, had greater freedom of action than ever before because the overburdening of the military justice system had essentially forced the government to offer them greater discretion in the question of who would be prosecuted. This is not, of course, to say that there was no government interference in the trial. The government interfered in abundance, probably not always in ways that left paper trails, but sometimes in extremely obvious and traceable ways; Darlan, for example, had the Mendès France case transferred to Clermont-Ferrand from the Casablanca tribunal that had begun the prosecution,[23] as the message rather disingenuously said, "for reasons concerning the good administration of Justice" (a form statement).

The current chapter will not seek to deny this government manipulation of the trials. It will, however, seek to recast the form of this manipulation. Vichy's magistrates, even its military magistrates, did not receive simple marching orders from Vichy. Rather, the regime played the role of a sympathetic adviser to magistrates who were independent, but who adhered to the same basic beliefs as the government they served. Vichy's method of rule, even in its early years, was force – but force mediated through hegemony.

It is precisely in the Mendès France case that we can see best how this hegemony operated in practice. After Mendès France's commanding officers, General François d'Astier de la Vigerie and Colonel Lucien, had testified in his favor at the *instruction*, Leprêtre took it upon himself to write to Vichy to ask for information regarding the value of this testimony. In response, Jean Bergeret,[24] Vichy's Air Minister, accused both of being political. Astier was "suspected of having lobbied for the post of Air Minister in an illegal government" (i.e. a resistance government). After acknowledging Astier's brilliant First World War record, moreover, Bergeret wrote that "since the end of the war of 1914–1918, it seems that he has always maintained very persistent relationships with political personalities." Bergeret took it upon himself to remind Leprêtre of the substance of the case: "The lieutenant Mendès France is suspected of having neglected

23 Darlan to Commissaire du Gouvernement près le Tribunal Militaire Permanent de Casablanca, 13 September 1940, Box E-1, Annexe 1, AIU.

24 Bergeret to Leprêtre, 23 January 1941, Fonds Pierre Mendès France, Archives de Justice Militaire, Le Blanc, Indre (henceforth AJM).

his duty: to rejoin his post – for which he had indirectly received orders – to 'consult' Colonel Lucien."

As for Lucien, Bergeret insisted that he did not have authority to give Mendès France orders, since the latter depended directly on his commanders in French Syria, where he was normally assigned. Bergeret attached a list of steamers by which Mendès France could have gone to Syria, but this was not enough; he also felt it necessary to discredit Lucien, who "was generally considered as having attachments with representatives of political parties and whose advancement appears to have been due more to his political connections than to his professional value." "One must note," Bergeret added, "that this officer signed a Model 2 Declaration (regarding having ceased to belong to a secret society)" – in other words, he had been a freemason. Bergeret insisted that Lucien had only been promoted because of Cot's influence, and that he lacked the number of hours in the air to be a colonel. In September 1940, Lucien was duly placed on leave because of false rank. "I consequently believe," Bergeret concluded, "that one can accord little credit to the testimony of General d'Astier and Colonel Lucien."

It was a friendly piece of advice, but one whose bias was truly incredible. Yet Bergeret was a minister and not a magistrate; even by Vichy's standards, it was less incumbent on him to be neutral. What is extraordinary about the letter is not that it was written, but that it was solicited. There was no need for Vichy to order its magistrates about when they themselves were willing to write to the government for advice on how to assess witness testimony.

Alex Wiltzer

The primary exception to the rule that the Clermont-Ferrand trials, unlike those at Riom, went poorly for the defendants was the case of Alex Wiltzer, a conservative deputy who had also boarded the Massilia despite being an army officer. Every study of the Clermont-Ferrand trials (not that there are many) has accepted at face value Zay's assertion in his prison memoirs that Wiltzer was acquitted because, alone of the mobilized deputies on the Massilia, he had not supported the Popular Front. While there is no reason to doubt the fundamental truth of this statement, like most such assertions by Vichy's prisoners, it gave the regime both too much and too little credit: too much in assigning a clarity and coherence of purpose that the regime never possessed, and too little in overstating the extent to which the regime controlled the actions of its magistrates.

Rather, the Wiltzer case affords many of the same characteristics we will see in the other Clermont-Ferrand cases, except that on this occasion they worked to the benefit of the defense. The key factor determining the outcome of the trial was the question of good faith. Wiltzer's prewar political background was certainly essential in convincing both the government and Leprêtre of his good faith, but the matter was not so simple as the notion that being a conservative meant governmental instructions to acquit.

The chronology of the Wiltzer trial was somewhat bizarre. Like the other three mobilized deputies, he was listed as a "deserter" in the virulent press campaign of the radical right (although, unlike, say, Zay, he was not singled out for any particular vitriol). He was then arrested as part of the same sweep that targeted his three peers. The whole process almost gives the impression of being unintentional, as if the government had set out to target the other three and Wiltzer was simply swept up in the chaos.

In the course of the summer and early autumn of 1940, Wiltzer's four brothers began a campaign on his behalf, frantically lobbying senior Vichy officials to annul the prosecution that risked bringing shame on the family name. Their pleas did not fall on deaf ears. On 1 August, Admiral Jean Fernet, Pétain's chief of staff, told them, in the words of their own later account, that "we have examined your case and the restricted Council of Ministers has decided to separate your case from the others and at the moment it is 9/10 convinced of the innonence [*sic;* for innocence] of your brother."[25] Even at this early date, then – three and a half months before Leprêtre would deliver his verdict – the government was apparently already largely convinced that Wiltzer was innocent.

When this apparent decision on the part of the government failed to yield fruit in the form of a verdict of *non-lieu* from Leprêtre, the brothers resumed their campaign. Weygand, Pétain, Laval, General Louis-Antoine Colson, Intendant General Joseph Frédéric Bernard, and Chasseras, then the regime's Director of Military Justice, had by mid-August all received near-identical letters from the Wiltzer brothers pleading Alex Wiltzer's innocence. These letters were shrewdly directed towards differentiating Wiltzer's case from the others and presenting it in a light likely to appeal to Vichy. All of them contained a sentence stating that the Wiltzer case had "nothing in common with the others." Several also complained that "the English radio is already exploiting this Wiltzer case against France."

At the same time, however, the brothers were careful to avoid an explicit claim that Alex Wiltzer's conservative record entitled him to Vichy's beneficence. Rather, they cast his career in an anti-German light: Wiltzer was different from the other Clermont-Ferrand cases in part because he had a signed order permit-

25 Note by Captain Paul Wiltzer, 22 August 1940, Fonds Wiltzer, AJM.

ting him to go to Bordeaux to attend the expected session of Parliament, but also because his long history of struggling against the forces of autonomy in his native Lorraine rendered him so unappealing to the Germans that he had risked death if he had allowed himself to be captured. Indeed, as we shall see momentarily, the cause with which Wiltzer's parliamentary career had associated him in most minds was not conservatism in general but a specific opposition to pro-German sentiments in Lorraine.

The Wiltzer dossier contains a long note[26] on the Wiltzer case, apparently handed in by two of the Wiltzer brothers in person. It is undated, but appears to precede the letters discussed above. If this is the case, then the Wiltzer brothers appear to have undergone a learning curve in their dealings with Vichy, for the earlier note rests heavily on the notion that *all* the mobilized deputies were innocent. In place of the insistence that the Wiltzer case was unique, we see instead a determination to show that "The declarations of President Herriot, General Michel, Questeur Barthe [all of which were cited by the defense in the various Clermont-Ferrand cases as indications that the mobilized deputies had governmental permission to board the *Massilia*] are formal." "These instructions concerned *mobilized deputies* [emphasis in original]," proceeds the note; someone (probably Leprêtre) has written an underlined "Non" next to this line. It is worth noting that the apparent change in the brothers' attitudes certainly precedes the condemnation of Zay, which was the first of the Clermont-Ferrand verdicts, and even precedes Zay's formal arrest (on 15 August). Even in the summer of 1940, it was becoming increasingly apparent that there would be no fair trial. The Wiltzer brothers' subsequent efforts to distance Wiltzer from the other defendants can only be explained in this light.

The appeal to acquit the mobilized deputies in general, rather than Wiltzer in particular, would by itself be sufficient to demonstrate that the Wiltzer brothers possessed no intuitive understanding of Vichy and had to learn the correct approach by experience. Almost as bad for their case in Vichy's eyes, however, is the fact that the note proceeds:

> We wish for a decision and we want one before any judicial enquiry. An administrative enquiry by telegram requesting a statement of the existence of an order [to go to Bordeaux] would suffice. This is an appeal to the Government's justice and the problem is absolutely *governmental in nature* (all emphases in original). The Government alone can and must *decide*; we await this from it *immediately*; we await this decision with serenity.

26 *Note sur le Député Alex Wiltzer, Attaché à l'Intendance*, unsigned and undated, but apparently from the Wiltzer brothers, probably in late July 1940, Fonds Wiltzer, AJM.

Decidedly, the Vichy consensus was a strange one. Even conservatives who would ultimately be successful in their efforts to earn their brother an acquittal could be so badly mistaken regarding its nature as to offer an open appeal to extrajudicial methods.

These efforts, however, would take a long time to be crowned with success. We have seen the extremely favorable initial reception of the Wiltzer brothers at Vichy; but these signs of governmental approval did not result in what the brothers wanted – an immediate governmental, rather than judicial, declaration that Alex Wiltzer was falsely accused. To be sure, it should not be surprising by this point to learn that Vichy preferred to act through judicial channels. At the same time, however, the contrast between the outpouring of private statements of encouragement and the lack of progress on the judicial front is striking.

Admiral Fernet, although generally well-informed, was not a senior cabinet member, and he may have been mistaken or exaggerating regarding the extent of governmental approval of Wiltzer. However, as the Wiltzer brothers resumed their campaign in late August, far more senior figures – the most senior figures at Vichy – offered their support. On 22 August, Du Moulin de Labarthète told Paul Wiltzer:

> The Marshal is eager to receive you. He told me to tell you that he believes that *attaché à l'Intendance* Wiltzer is absolutely innocent, because he had an order from his unit to go to Bordeaux and an order to embark for North Africa and that in addition his specific case as a Lorrainer etc ... made it a duty for him to escape captivity.
>
> The Government regrets that the newspapers' publications affected you, but you will all be rehabilitated and made clean, because the Government does not forget the great services that you have made to France and it counts on men like you.
>
> The Government asks you to have a little patience, because it would be inconvenient to intervene right now, during the enquiry, because an indictment has been issued, but it is convinced that your brother cannot be prosecuted.
>
> Personally I am of the opinion that by indicting everyone without distinction and without informing itself of particular cases, the Government has gone a little quickly, but this error excuses itself, because it was a perturbed time.
>
> In any case, I repeat to you that the Marshal and the Government are entirely convinced of the innocence of your brother and you will have complete satisfaction..[27]

In case this was not enough, Paul Wiltzer also received a message from Bernard Ménétrel, Pétain's doctor and confidant, stating that he had heard that he had missed the opportunity to meet him and that "I regret this, because I would

27 Note by P. Wiltzer, 22 August 1940, Fonds Wiltzer, AJM.

have been happy to shake your hand. I believe that M. Dumoulin de La Barthète has told you with much more authority what I could have said myself." [28]

The message could hardly have been more categorical. For a head of state to comment of the subject of an ongoing judicial investigation that the action of which he was accused was merely his duty (and we have seen the role that duty and responsibility played in Vichy's ideology) was truly something extraordinary. Unlike Zay, Mendès France, or Vienot, Wiltzer was being accepted as a "soldier" rather than a "parliamentarian," and therefore as one of the regime's own.

Indeed, the contacts that appeared most enthusiastic about helping Wiltzer were mostly military. At the end of August, the Wiltzer brothers managed to contact General Coudanne, whose response made it still clearer that the Wiltzer brothers' remarkable access, unlike that of many other political prisoners, went through military more than political channels. Coudanne was, of course, supportive: he made the obvious observation that "it was certainly not he that they wanted to touch" (i.e. that the government was not targeting Wiltzer at the Clermont-Ferrand trials). "In any case," Coudanne continued, "and to respond to your wish, I contacted General Colson whom you no doubt knew at Metz and who was promoted along with me; I gave him the pamphlet that you gave me." (This presumably is one of the notes, discussed above, which the Wiltzer brothers circulated regarding their brother's case.) "It is possible moreover, that a favorable intervention will be made to Mr. Alibert by one of his friends on the initiative of a close friend of mine."[29]

It was a grapevine very similar to the ones we have seen in previous chapters, but one which passed through military rather than ex-parliamentary channels. Although military men certainly pullulated at Vichy, we do not need to resort to an argument of numbers to explain the greater success of the military option; after all, we have seen that men like Reynaud, even in prison, were still able to rely on contacts of the highest order. Rather, it was Vichy's ideology that directed it to afford greater consideration to the same individuals when presented as military men rather than as politicians (since Wiltzer, like all of the individuals considered in this chapter, was both).

As we have repeatedly seen, however, the relationship between Vichy and its magistrates was a great deal more complex than that between master and servant; and if Leprêtre would not indict the vastly more important Reynaud on the

---

28 Ménétrel to P. Wiltzer, 24 August 1940, Fonds Wiltzer, AJM.
29 R. Coudanne to Wiltzer, 27 August 1940, Fonds Wiltzer, AJM.

government's suggestion, then he certainly was not about to let Wiltzer go merely because the government was convinced of his innocence.

After the flurry of activity in August, it would not be until October that the Wiltzer brothers would manage to obtain yet more reassurance from Vichy. None other than Font Réaulx, Alibert's *chef de cabinet* and a man regularly invited to Pétain's personal table, assured them that

> The case of your brother is clear and we have already several times expressed our desire to the military justice administration to see this case settled and your brother cleared.
>
> If it had been a matter of civilian justice the case would have been settled long ago.
>
> I promise you that I will speak of it again and will let M. Casseras, Director of Military Justice, know that the Government does not intend to launch a political trial against your brother and that the *Government does not see any objection and even desires a* non-lieu, *because the case doesn't hold water* [emphasis in original; it was probably added by the Wiltzer brothers].[30]

Once again we see the central but complex role played by the soldier in Vichy ideology. Font Réaulx attributed Leprêtre's independence to being a member of the military; indeed, we have seen that this description of Leprêtre as an independent-minded magistrate is far from inaccurate, and the case of General Wateau, who was probably the magistrate at Riom with the least impressive legal resume but who also seems to have reacted the most violently when Vichy threatened to suspend the trial, contributes to this impression.

More importantly, however, it seems that the government was growing frustrated with Leprêtre. (It is worth noting that the months during which Leprêtre dealt with the Clermont-Ferrand cases overlapped with those during which he was involved with the Reynaud case, which may explain part of this impatience.) If, as we have suggested regarding the Mendès France case, the Vichy government's role at the Clermont-Ferrand trials was one of a friendly advisor to Leprêtre, then the government was now faced with the task of persuading him of Wiltzer's innocence as it would later convince him of Mendès France's guilt.

A direct order, or even an indirect one, was out of the question. On 31 October 1940, Captain Wiltzer wrote to Du Moulin de Labarthète, "I am under the impression that the *Juge d'instruction*, Colonel Leprêtre at Clermont-Ferrand, has decided to render it [i.e. the verdict of non-lieu], but it would still be necessary for the judge to know that *the Government has no objection* [emphasis in orig.] to this decision."[31] An angry marginal note next to "impression", signed by Leprê-

30 Note by Capitain Wiltzer, 25 Oct 1940, Fonds Wiltzer, AJM.
31 Captain Wiltzer to Du Moulin de Labarthète, 31 October 1940, Fonds Wiltzer, AJM.

tre, states "Based on what? please." Leprêtre was far too prickly for the government to tell him what to do, especially in such a minor case; and there was probably a risk that such instructions would have backfired.

The way it went about doing so was almost as instructive as in the Mendès France case. A minister at Vichy – it is not clear which one – ordered an investigation of Wiltzer's political antecedents. This had, of course, no conceivable relationship to the question of whether Wiltzer had deserted or not; but it did speak to the question of credibility through which, as we have seen, the regime's more or less unconscious biases were mediated.

Once again, it is worth stressing that this investigation, truly bizarre though it was in terms of every modern legal norm, was nothing so crude as a simple effort to find out if Wiltzer was pro-Pétain or pro-Laval. We have already mentioned that Wiltzer was associated not so much with any particular breed of conservativism (although he had stood for Parliament under the aegis of the conservative, and friend of Reynaud, Louis Marin's *Union Républicaine Démocratique*) as with his longstanding local fight against the forces of autonomism (that is, pro-Germanism) in Lorraine. Nearly all of the testimonies collected by the government insisted on this aspect of his career, usually as its only identifying feature.[32] The same applied to a petition in Wiltzer's favor, signed by Marin among many others, which emphasized Wiltzer's patriotism. Patriotism, on the French right, tended to be a code word referring to conservative sympathies; but in Wiltzer's case it can be taken a little more literally than usual, since the petition also referred to his support for maintaining French traditions and religion in Lorraine[33] against Protestant Germandom.

It was a considerably more ambiguous and less direct method of persuasion than Vichy's political prisoners imagined that the government must employ. Vichy was not usually overt in its pressure on magistrates. Rather, we should conceptualize the inquiry as the government offering a gentle reminder that Wiltzer was on the right side. Leprêtre was free to act as he wished; but it was a reasonable assumption, given his own political leanings, that he would take this information under advisement. Indeed, Wiltzer was released shortly thereafter.

32 In Fonds Wiltzer, AJM.

33 The Fonds Wiltzer at the AJM contains numerous open letters headed "Attestation," most near-identical; it is evidently a form letter circulated in Wiltzer's favor in October 1940, presumably by his ever-active brothers.

Jean Zay

By far the best-known of the Clermont-Ferrand defendants, as well as the first to be convicted, was Jean Zay, whose background we have already briefly sketched. Since Jean Zay's personal archives have only recently been opened, most accounts of his trial (even Simonin's, which was written on the basis of the new archives) have more or less accepted as accurate Zay's own account in his memoirs, which describes him as a scapegoat for the fallen regime (a phrase that recurs with monotonous regularity in the literature on the Clermont-Ferrand trials).

If he was a scapegoat, it was a bizarre choice, given Zay's relative lack of prominence compared to the Riom defendants. Indeed, of all the Clermont-Ferrand cases, Zay's conviction came closest to being juridically legitimate. To be sure, singling out Zay as a deserter – especially as an individual who had deserted in the face of the enemy – was absurd under the circumstances. As we have already repeatedly stressed, being separated from one's unit – voluntarily or otherwise – was the norm rather than the exception in the chaotic circumstances of the French collapse. This was a point that Zay's lawyer, Alexandre Varenne, stressed at the time in his client's defense. Zay had "fewer responsibilities than thousands of other officers, who lacked the same excuse, less than tens of thousands of soldiers of all ranks carried along sometimes but always against their will into a retreat that often degenerated into a rout, and whom [the Government] has had the good wit not to disquiet, and for whom [the Government] even foresaw and applied measures of aid imposed by the extent of the disaster and by the incalculable number of infractions."[34]

Vichy's targeting of Zay was not random, nor was it reasonable by any neutral standard. Nonetheless, it did possess its own logic, which was not simply one of political necessity. In the document we have just cited, Varenne asserted that Zay had left the army for the "highly honorable motive" that he needed to "go fulfill another duty, in the exercise of his parliamentary mandate at a dramatic hour for the country." It was, from our point of view, a reasonable enough excuse; Zay could not possibly have rendered any further assistance to a front that had already collapsed, but he could still serve his country by reverting to his parliamentary duties. It was, however, an excuse that required that Zay be given the benefit of the doubt, since it rested on the question of motivation.

It was this question of the benefit of the doubt on which all the Clermont-Ferrand trials turned. Even leaving aside the fact that no sincere supporter of the National Revolution was likely to see parliamentary duties as trumping military

---

34 Alexandre Varenne, *Note sur la Déposition de M. le Colonel Gilliot*, undated, Fonds Zay, AJM.

duties under any circumstances, the author of *Le Drapeau* was not a person whom Vichy was likely to favor with any lenient presuppositions regarding his actions. It will be objected that considerations of the benefit of the doubt should not play any role in a legal process worth the name, except insofar as it concerns the burden of proof, which always (except in appeals cases) should favor the defendant. This is certainly true; but it was essential to Vichy's project of transferring power to magistrates that they be given greater autonomy in making their decisions, and this autonomy, by a process of thought with which we should by now be familiar, took the form of giving magistrates the freedom to judge based precisely on whether they chose to give or refuse this benefit of the doubt. Just as in the Riom cases, although with opposite effects, this freedom could never be openly acknowledged and was probably not even understood by its proponents as a deviation from a rules-based system; but it was nonetheless very real.

Zay's case involved more emphasis on this question of the benefit of the doubt because the fundamentals of the case were murkier. His assignment had been to serve as a liaison officer, a role that seems to have aroused some jealousy, since it entitled him to the best transportation at a time when transportation was in high demand due to the rout. (The court examined, but apparently dismissed, allegations from an officer who had reluctantly assigned Zay a replacement car and who claimed that Zay wanted to "*jouer Rip*," i.e. escape.)[35] It was apparently not an essential role, as Zay claimed that his colonel had five other officers capable of doing his job.[36]

On the June day in question, Zay had been ordered to retreat with other support staff to Saint-Flour – albeit on a somewhat relaxed schedule, since he does not appear to have had any specific duties to perform once he arrived. During the journey, Zay, whose colonel seems to have given him considerable latitude to choose his own route during his frequent automobile missions across the blocked and chaotic roads near the front, made a brief detour to reassure himself of his family's safety. During the Saint-Flour journey, Zay learned at a roadblock of the widespread rumors that the Assembly was about to be summoned at Bordeaux, the headquarters of the government in retreat. He immediately set out for that city, where the parliamentary session failed to materialize, but where the *Massilia* waited to transport resistance-minded parliamentarians to Morocco.

Zay's failure to show up at Saint-Flour, where his colonel was expecting him, formed the core of the accusations against him. There were excuses for his con-

35 André Géranton testimony, 2 September 1940, Fonds Zay, AJM.
36 Zay testimony, 24 August 1940, Fonds Zay, AJM.

duct, some of which we have already rehearsed: he could not have done any good at Saint-Flour and might have been able to serve his country better at Bordeaux; he was one of innumerable officers whom force of circumstance had prevented from rejoining their units; and, even on the *Massilia* itself, there were numerous officers lacking a parliamentary mandate who were in similarly irregular situations and who were never charged. At the same time, it is difficult to avoid the impression that Zay's situation, from a strictly juridical standpoint, really was problematic. At the very least, his decision, on his own initiative, to use a military vehicle and chauffeur to reach Bordeaux was one that might have raised eyebrows in a less chaotic situation.

It is worth noting that Zay, unlike most of the other Clermont-Ferrand defendants (most notably Mendès France), did not have the support of his commanding officer at the trial. Pointout, who had been Zay's immediate superior, was clearly of the opinion that his failure to report to Saint-Flour constituted desertion. His 3 August testimony[37] to the court explained that Zay was normally given considerable leeway regarding his whereabouts, but, that, in the absence of specific orders, his post was with the General Staff of the 4th Army. Zay had been given "free movement" – that is, he was not supposed to follow any specific route – to get to Saint-Flour, but Pointout believed that he was definitely supposed to be there at noon on the 19th of June. Pointout, moreover, had taken it for granted that he would go to Saint-Flour via Clermont (and not via his family's residence) unless the roads were blocked.

To be sure, Zay had told the truth when he said that he was far from irreplaceable; his job was done by another officer when he failed to arrive. Pointout also testified that Zay had called on the 20th to inform him that he was attending a session of parliament – another example of the crucial role that the question of good intentions played in the trial. Nonetheless, the tenor of the Pointout testimony was clearly unfavorable to Zay; indeed, he stated that the only reason why he had not immediately reported Zay for desertion was that he had a statutory obligation to wait forty-eight hours. Indeed, a telegram from Pointout to Zay from the 24th of June stated that Zay was "currently engaged in an irregular absence" and should immediately return to Saint-Flour unless he could show orders to the contrary.[38]

Pointout's opinion was not, of course, the definitive verdict on the question of whether Zay had deserted. It is pointless to speculate on the reason why the telegram is dated the 24th (the date of the Massilia's arrival at Casablanca),

37 Pointout testimony, 3 August 1940, Fonds Zay, AJM.
38 Pointout to Zay, 24 June 1940, Fonds Zay, AJM.

which is obviously more than forty-eight hours after Zay failed to report to Saint-Flour. Perhaps Pointout was unable to contact Zay prior to that point, or perhaps he sympathized with the tide of right-wing criticism of the *Massilia* passengers. In either case, however, the fact that Zay's commanding officer thought that he had deserted was a legitimate reason to believe that there was merit to the accusation.

The situation that faced the French authorities after the collapse, therefore, was one in which far too many people had committed the crime of desertion to make it possible to punish all of them. This collapse of the rules-based system, combined with Vichy's desire to transfer power to magistrates (on which we have already insisted several times), meant that the question of desertion became a subjective one that revolved around the issue of good faith, which in practice was largely a matter of political affiliation.

This fact was apparent to the defense at the time. Zay adduced in his defense that he could hardly be accused of running away, since his assignment was to retreat.[39] In a letter to Noguès, he made the question explicit: if his "good faith" was being contested, he asserted, then the fact that he left France as being *chargé de mission* for the Minister of the Interior became relevant.[40] In the same category we can place Zay's insistence that, because of the state of his health, he would have been excused from military service in 1939 even if he had not been a parliamentarian. The government took this claim seriously enough to have a doctor examine Zay in September. (He concluded that Zay was in fairly good health.)[41]

In summary, then, the Zay case was not one of a scapegoat accused on grounds that were inherently ridiculous; rather, the government case was an exaggeration of a reasonably legitimate accusation that could, however, have been made against thousands of officers in the special circumstances of 1940. The fact that the government singled out Zay was certainly the product of his political past; however, this singling out expressed itself as a questioning of his good faith as an officer rather than as a directly political accusation.

---

39 Zay testimony, 23 August 1940, Fonds Zay, AJM.
40 Zay to Noguès, 26 July 1940, Fonds Zay, AJM.
41 Report of Dr. Petchot-Baque, 10 September 1940, Fonds Zay, AJM.

Pierre Viénot

In the trials that came after Zay's, the defense was well aware of the need to differentiate their cases from his. No other defendant was foolish enough to think that their parliamentary duty would be accepted by the court as a legitimate excuse for being absent from the army. Rather, Viénot, Mendès France and Wiltzer all sought to convince the court that it was their military duty that brought them to Casablanca, and the fact that it was the *Massilia* that brought them there was merely an irrelevant detail.

In the case of Viénot, his defense made this case explicit, and in direct response to the government's accusations. In their own words, Leprêtre "had expressed the hypothesis that Captain Viénot might have embarked on the Massilia on 20 June, not as a soldier, but as a parliamentarian." If, indeed, Viénot had gone to North Africa as "a politician decided to pick sides," then, the defense admitted, "the conduct of Captain Viénot loses, morally, its justification."[42] This line of defense involved abandoning Zay, which makes one question its sincerity. It seems more likely that Viénot and his lawyer (his brother André Viénot) had determined that there was nothing further that could be done for Zay, who had already been condemned, than that the Viénots had genuinely decided for themselves that Zay's conduct was indefensible. In other words, the prioritization of military over parliamentary responsibility was imposed by the government (or rather, since we have established that this differentiation is important, by Leprêtre), rather than being invented autochtonously by defense and prosecution alike.

Like all of the defendants, Viénot was anxious to establish that his conduct was similar to that of many other officers in the chaotic circumstances of 1940. As the note cited above puts it, "an initiative identical to that of hundreds and perhaps of thousands of other soldiers, of whom none have been prosecuted and some, as it can be proven, have been officially congratulated. For them, who also left without orders, [the Government] did not suggest for an instant an intention to violate the law and, consequently, a crime."

This insistence on intentionality (*intention délictuelle*) had a specific basis in law. Most crimes, including desertion, require *mens rea* – that is, they require the alleged perpetrator to have been aware that he was taking the forbidden action. In none of the Clermont-Ferrand cases, however, could it be shown that the defendants had deliberately set out to desert. There is an obvious analogy with Vi-

42 "Mémoire pour le Capitain Viénot," undated but during instruction, by André Viénot, Fonds Viénot, AJM.

chy's legal quasi-innovation of *trahison des devoirs de sa charge* and with the emphasis on incompetence rather than bad intent at the Riom trial. At the same time, however, the emphasis on *intention délictuelle* was a bad ground for Viénot's stand. In a trial whose bias against the defendants was primarily the consequence of a refusal to grant them the benefit of the doubt that was normally accorded to soldiers separated from their units in the wake of the defeat, Leprêtre was unlikely to assume that Vienot's motives were pure.

This is in spite of the fact that Viénot was far from being a left-wing ideologue. To be sure, he had served under the Popular Front; but, unlike Zay, he had not made himself particularly obnoxious to the right and had in fact made friends on both sides of the aisle. Similarly, the fact that he would later become a prominent member of the Resistance and the Free French, becoming a founding member of the *Comité d'Action Socialiste* and then De Gaulle's ambassador to Great Britain, says little in itself about his political views. Some resistance members were right-wing; some, like Henri Frenay, were even pro-Pétain for a time. Indeed, many right-wing politicians wrote to testify to the character of the accused man, always using similar language: they might not see eye to eye with Viénot when it came to politics, but he was a man of honor who would never have deserted.

Thus, for example, Wladimir d'Ormesson, then the French ambassador to the Vatican, wrote to say that he did not agree with Viénot's political views but that he could testify to "the honor, the duty, the religious devotion to his country" that the accused man had always espoused.[43] André François-Poncet had a similar impression of Viénot: without supporting his political beliefs, he could nonetheless state that Vienot was "a brave man and a patriot" and that his decision to go to Africa, while it might have been misguided, must have been made in good faith.[44] Finally, Noguès, the commander of French forces in North Africa whose decisions had determined that that region would not continue resisting after the armistice was declared in metropolitan France, testified to Viénot's patriotism, as did René de Saint-Quentin.[45]

Indeed, Viénot was no typical member of the Popular Front. To demonstrate this fact, the defense introduced one of its more bizarre pieces of testimony: Viénot's correspondence with the deceased Marshal Hubert Lyautey, of whom he had been the confederate and protegé. Lyautey was an individual who has frequently been cited as an important precursor to the Vichy regime. Like Pétain,

43 D'Ormesson to Pierre Viénot, August 1940 (no day), Fonds Viénot, AJM.

44 François-Poncet to André Viénot, 24 September 1940, Fonds Viénot, AJM.

45 Noguès to Picard, 30 September 1940, Fonds Viénot, AJM; René de Saint-Quentin to André Viénot, 3 November 1940, Fonds Viénot, AJM.

he had reached the highest ranks of the French army and appealed by virtue of that fact to individuals looking for a military strongman to rescue France from its parliamentary stasis. Unlike Pétain, however, he had been the source and not merely the object of right-wing political thought in the 1920s, and his book on *Le Rôle Social de l'Officier* (The Social Role of the Officer) was enormously influential then and later (and provided the inspiration for the title of Vichy's Minister of Youth Georges Lamirand's book *Le rôle social de l'ingénieur* (The Social Role of the Engineer), which espoused many of the ideas on the importance of merit-based hierarchy that we have seen in previous chapters).[46]

It is therefore of great interest to see the bonds of friendship that had evidently united Vichy's inspiration with its future victim. The correspondence between Lyautey and Viénot shows not merely the normal forms of courtesy between superior and inferior (Viénot had served under Lyautey in French North Africa) but also unmistakable personal affection. Significantly, it was precisely Viénot's wilingness to transcend bonds of party (that is, to espouse the belief that Lyautey's ideas were above party) that attracted Lyautey to him. In Lyautey's own words, "There is for me no better criterion of the value of the ideas you express than the way they irk people to the left as well as to the right."[47]

We find here a potent reminder of the way in which 1940 had fragmented society. Under other circumstances, Viénot's relationship with Lyautey and his espousal (at that date) of an anti-ideological ideology might have endeared him to many of those who served Vichy. Viénot was not Zay, and it was far from inevitable that he would come to be hated by the right. 1940, however, had changed everything. Viénot's affiliation with a hero of Vichy did not save him from being convicted.

46 Georges Lamirand, *Le Rôle Social de l'Ingénieur, Scènes de la Vie d'Usine* (Paris: Éditions de la Revue des Jeunes, 1932). I am grateful to Henry Rousso for pointing out the ideological link between Lyautey and Lamirand in a personal conversation.

47 Lyautey to Viénot, 12 February 1925, Fonds Viénot, AJM.

9 Conclusion

The purpose of this book has been to present a new mechanism by which the defeat of 1940 undermined pluralistic politics, over and above the immediate impact of military reverses on the willingness of the French parliament to grant extraordinary powers to Pétain. We have argued that one consequence of the defeat of 1940 was that *no* political viewpoint, be it Gaullist, Vichyist, or any of the other -ists into which French society had fragmented, could reassemble something resembling a French nation unified enough to agree on the basic boundaries of political discourse.

The ideological space that separated Vichy from its victims could be quite narrow. We have seen how Viénot's defense cited his close friendship with Lyautey as proof of his *bona fides*, at precisely the same time that Lamirand[1] was using Lyautey's writings as a reason to try men like Viénot! It was precisely the question of *bona fides* that was insuperable. While overt antisemitism played a limited role in Vichy's political trials, for example, a (supposed) Jew like Zay had to go to much greater lengths to prove his good intentions. In this sense, the Riom and Clermont-Ferrand defendants were caught in a double bind. It was the government's doubt that their heart was in the right place that led to the trials, and everyone knew it – but, at the same time, it was precisely the criterion of intentionality, of *mens rea*, that the government had removed from the definition of treason (and desertion).

Sublimating the role of anti-Semitism into a broader question of perceptions of reliability goes against the aforementioned historiographical consensus that argues that pre-1940 developments, notably the rift caused by exclusionary racial ideas of the French nation, were fundamental to Vichy. One litmus test for the role of anti-Semitism in Vichy's political trials is contemporary mentions of the Dreyfus Affair (1894–1906), an even more famous court case in which a Jewish army officer was falsely accused of espionage. At the time of Dreyfus, antisemitism had been respectable, mainstream, and widespread in influencing attitudes towards the trial on both sides of the political spectrum.[2] Moreover, the nature of the Dreyfus Affair, as a case of the victimization of a Jew for failings in national security that were in fact the fault of the army, makes the comparison

1 See his preface to Patrick Heidsieck, *Rayonnement De Lyautey* (Paris: Gallimard, 1941). Appropriately enough, this book was reprinted in 1947 – with the preface removed and a dedication to the Army of Liberation.

2 Pierre Birnbaum, *The Anti-Semitic Moment: A Tour of France in 1898* (New York, NY: Hill and Wang, 2003), *passim*.

https://doi.org/10.1515/9783110610161-009

seem obvious today. In the 1940s, however, the Dreyfus Affair was still the subject of political division, a point that Maurras made clear upon his condemnation during the postwar *Épuration* by shouting that it was the "vengeance of Dreyfus."[3] An analysis of contemporary references to Dreyfus should therefore make it clear whether the interpretation of Vichy's political trials that we have proposed, that they were an attempt to escape "politics," was a mere figleaf for anti-Semitism. At the very least, we should not expect the victims of these trials to shy away from the comparison, unless they were also under the spell of the anti-political consensus.

All of the political prisoners under discussion here were highly educated men,[4] and many of them made use of their prison stays to expand their knowledge of history still further. This being the case, it is hardly surprising that they made use of a multiplicity of historical examples in their defense. Mandel, for example, took notes on a 1797 trial of a former minister who had commented that if he were tried by an "enlightened, equitable and free tribunal," he would go free, and if otherwise, would merely be the equivalent of being "massacred by bandits."[5]

By far the most popular historical example for the defendants, however, was not that of Dreyfus but that of Marshal François Achille Bazaine, who had been tried in 1873 for having surrendered the fortress of Metz to the Germans. The comparison was evident. The Franco-Prussian War was the last disaster of comparable importance in French history; Bazaine was a military leader; and, fortuitously, he even shared Pétain's rank. It is hardly surprising, this being the case, that the comparison was a common one. Thus, for example, Reynaud, in an understandably exasperated document written during his imprisonment, commented sarcastically that "after our defeat of 1871, Marshal Le Boeuf did not condemn [the former opposition activists and mainstays of the post-1871 regime] M. Thiers and Gambetta to imprisonment in a fortress" and noted that Bazaine was imprisoned in better conditions.[6]

The example of Bazaine was appealing not only for the defendants but also for resisters in general. Over two years after Riom, for example, the resistance journal *Tout pour la Patrie* described Pétain in so many words as "old Bazaine."[7]

3 Heinz-Gerhard Haupt, *Histoire Sociale de la France depuis 1789* (Paris: Maison des Sciences de l'Homme, 1993), 269.

4 Mandel's personal archives contain a note on the theater under Napoleon with a bullet hole through it. He apparently had it in his pocket when he was killed. Box 77, Series 544AP, AN.

5 Undated note by Mandel, circa 1943–4, Box 73, Series 544AP, AN.

6 Note by Reynaud, undated, Box 24, Series 74AP, AN.

7 *Tout pour la Patrie*, undated (after Mandel's murder), Box 77, Series 544AP, AN.

Similarly, the Communist resistance journal *L'Appel au Combat* published an article under the headline "Pétain-Bazaine."[8] For those who supported the defendants, the use of the Bazaine parallel began almost immediately after the defeat; thus, for example, a M. Paul Robert wrote to Alibert in August 1940 to recommend, with heavy sarcasm, that Bazaine be rehabilitated, since his surrender had averted "a useless slaughter of Frenchmen"[9] (the regime's excuse for the armistice).

Bazaine did not merely appear in the private notes of the defendants, but even in their public testimony. Le Troquer, for example, noted in his opening address to the court at Riom that Bazaine had been prosecuted after the liberation rather than during the war – a rather more eirenic use of the example than the defendants were using in private.[10]

Even supporters of the government used the example of Bazaine on occasion. Excusing the government's delay in holding the trial, for example, *Le Temps* noted in April 1941 that Bazaine was not tried until two years after the peace treaty.[11] Similarly, the right-wing Swiss *Gazette de Lausanne*, in the context of an article that offered the highest encomiums to the judges, excused their delay in trying the defendants by noting that "when we remember that the *instruction* of the Bazaine trial, which had only one defendant and one charge against him, lasted over nine months, we must give homage to the speed of the Riom pretrial magistrates."[12]

Another historical analogy that appeared in pro-government sources was that of the trial of the Polignac ministry after the fall of Charles X, which, by a rather tortured process of reasoning, was supposed to have provided a precedent for the trial in that Jules de Polignac was tried for having fired on French citizens and therefore for causing French blood to be shed. Thus, for example, the previously cited *Gazette de Lausanne* article argued that the Riom trial "is related, at bottom, to the trial of Polignac and of the ministers of Charles X: ... brought, on 15 December 1830 before the Chamber of Peers constituted as the High Court of Justice, for having, by making the King sign the ordinances that led to the July Revolution, taken the responsibility of letting French blood flow, having thus *trahi les devoirs de leur charge.*"[13]

8 *L'Appel au Combat,* undated, Box 31, Series 552AP, AN.
9 Paul Robert to Alibert, 21 August 1940, Box 1, Series 2W, AN.
10 Riom Trial transcript, 19 February 1942, Box 25, Series GE, AdHC.
11 *Le Temps,* 23 April 1941.
12 *Gazette de Lausanne,* 10 April 1941.
13 *Ibid.*

In contrast, the Dreyfus Affair was invoked far more rarely than other, more anodyne incidents. It is not entirely absent from the sources; Daladier, for example, mentioned Dreyfus twice in his prison diary.[14] This, however, was the exception rather than the rule.

The only defendant willing to invoke Dreyfus on a regular basis was Reynaud, who wrote an undated declaration from prison whose rhetorical structure was clearly modeled on Émile Zola's famous *J'Accuse* address in defense of Dreyfus. (The address had appeared in Clemenceau's *L'Aurore*, another link to the father of French national unity.) In another note on the French magistrature, written in 1941, Reynaud asked rhetorically "Do we not know, by the sad experience of the Dreyfus Affair that, especially in political matters, *the truth always comes out* and that the backlash is harmful to its renown that has such importance for the country?"[15] Jacques Charpentier, Reynaud's lawyer, went still further by stating in his official conclusions that Reynaud's trial represented "A *coup de force* without precedent in the annals of justice, of which the Dreyfus Affair itself did not offer the spectacle."[16] Reynaud continued to argue along similar lines after the war, asserting that "At the start of the century, it was France's honor to be thrown into turmoil by a government decision to transfer jurisdictions, which was infinitely less serious – because it was a matter of moving the Dreyfus Affair from the Criminal Chamber of the *Cour de Cassation* to the whole of the *Cour de Cassation* – than the actions that Marshal Pétain has committed."[17] By emphasizing the damage to France's reputation and condemning his trial as a "political" one, Reynaud was effectively redirecting Vichy's own rhetoric of national interest and the corroding impact of politics, in much the same way that Daladier's supporters saw him as a "leader" whose claims to unite the nation could be contrasted with those of Pétain.

Occasionally, supporters of the government side in the trial would refer to the Dreyfus Affair from the opposite standpoint. General Charles Grandsard, for example, asserted that Pierre Cot kept files on the political inclinations of Air Force officers "as in the time of the Dreyfus Affair" as part of his program of inserting politics into a previously apolitical army.[18] He was presumably conflating the Dreyfus Affair with that other great turn-of-the-century scandal, the

14 Daladier, *Prison Journal*, 9, 28.

15 Paul Reynaud, *Déclaration*, undated, and note on "La Magistrature Française," 2 January 1941, Box 24, Series 74AP, AN.

16 Conclusions by Jacques Chevalier, 12 January 1943, Box 24, Series 74AP, AN.

17 Report of the *Commission chargée d'enquête sur les evenements survenus en France de 1933 à 1945*, 1951, Box 25, Series 74AP, AN.

18 Testimony of Charles Grandsard, 8 November 1940, Box 39, Series 496AP, AN.

André Affair, when a Republican Minister of War had been caught using freemason records to purge Catholic (and hence presumably anti-Republican) generals. This desire to shift the meaning of the Dreyfus Affair from one of jurisprudence to one of politicization of the army surfaced periodically on the European right; the *Corriere della Sera*, for example, alleged that Gamelin was from the generation of freemasons who had supposedly entered the army after the acquittal of the "Jewish freemason" Dreyfus[19] – another confused reference to the André Affair. The same conflation surfaced in a long unsolicited note forwarded to the court by the government and written by the radical Catholic conservative and retired artillery colonel Léon Maury, who thought that the French army had been at its best between 1871 and 1897, before being ruined by the effort to establish a republican army. Maury thought that Stalin's experience in Finland showed that such an army would necessarily prove ineffective.[20] In fact, it is very difficult to find an example of the kind of moderate conservative who shaped Vichy's political trials referencing the Dreyfus trial at all, and those who did almost invariably conflated it with the André Affair as an example of an attempt to reshape the French Army along political lines while eliding the specifically juridical elements of the Dreyfus reference.

This pattern of historical analogies reveals that contemporaries saw the trial in a very different light from that we now adopt. Vichy's own trials were not conceived as efforts to impose a political reckoning with the Dreyfusards, as the radical right-wing press would have preferred. Rather, they were intended to produce purely juridical statements whose very apoliticism would serve to legitimate the regime. References to still-disputed elements in France's past would only have served to reveal the fact that the regime's claims to apoliticism were a myth.

None of this, of course, is intended to deny the very real anti-Semitism of some members of the regime. Alibert, in particular, was notorious for this characteristic. We do not need the defeat to explain why so much of the French political spectrum hated Blum and Zay. We do need the defeat to explain how that hatred was reconceptualized in a form that led to political trials.

The fact that the defendants also shrank from the Dreyfus comparison is also interesting. One would be tempted to say that they were simply resorting to arguments that were likelier to win over the regime, except that the Bazaine comparison also appears in documents that attack the regime openly, or that were intended for private consumption. In any case, it seems implausible that Blum's

19 Report on foreign press, 6 February 1941, Box 1719, Series BB30, AN.

20 Léon Maury, *Note brève*, 29 July 1940, Box 2, Series 2W, AN.

defense, which openly described the trial as a "trial of the Republic" and asserted that the outcome had already been determined by Pétain's prior sentence of life imprisonment, was avoiding the mention of Dreyfus so as not to antagonize the regime. Rather, it seems that there was a certain consensus between the regime and those it tried regarding the acceptable range of historical metaphor.

Above all, there was a consensus that the Dreyfus Affair was a part of "politics," and that politics were bad. This was both a product of and a break from the apoliticism of interwar movements like the *Redressement Français*. It was a product of that movement in that the Vichyites who directed the trials had emerged from it and had become predisposed, even before the war, to thinking of the political arena in terms of scientific fact instead of pluralistic debate. Much more importantly, however, it was a break from that movement; for that movement had been sincerely liberal in nature, devoted in large measure to defending the Republic, and focused on the maintenance and expansion of rights, democracy and pluralism rather than their elimination. If the notion of a unitary France excluded large segments of the French Left from being considered part of the "French nation" even before the war, so did the Popular Front, even in its name, exclude large segments of the French Right from being considered part of the "French people." Romier was no more a proto-dictator than his friends Herriot and Blum. The supreme irony of 1940 was that it converted a movement focused on expanding Republicanism into an assault on the Republic.

All societies seek to place certain conceptions within, and others outside, the sphere of legitimate political debate, with the law serving as the dividing line between the two. A defendant at a murder trial cannot advance as a valid defense the idea that murder should be legal. At the same time, it is entirely possible for members of a democratic society to hold vehemently opposed definitions even of so basic and universal a concept as murder; consider, for example, the current debates over abortion or euthanasia.

This is the fundamental contradiction of democracy, which is founded on debate, yet which also rests on a common acceptance of fundamental principles. This book has argued that the contradiction is not insuperable. France in the 1930s was engaged in a debate on the composition of the nation; but this debate did not lead directly to the exclusionary policies of the 1940s. Rather, the interwar assault on politics, which proclaimed itself to be apolitical while adopting stances on obviously political issues such as taxation and property rights, contained only the same unacknowledged contradiction as democracy as a whole. These contradictions survived even under Vichy – consider, for example, how the government consistently opposed the idea of "politics" and of a "political" trial, while at the same time allowing the Riom sentences to be limited by the abolition of capital punishment in political cases. 1940, however, had turned the old contradiction into something different and lethal.

From Riom to Human Rights

Throughout this book, we have argued that Vichy's political trials were a case of "necessary" justice – that is, of a situation in which the popular demand for a judicial solution was considerable, and the necessity to resolve this demand in one direction or another was a key task of any new regime. In this sense, Riom was an example, perhaps the first example, of a well-known category in legal studies: transitional justice, or trials intended to mark the transition from one regime to another. To be sure, transitional justice is normally associated with the transition from dictatorship to democracy and not vice-versa.[21] We have, however, argued that law can also be a key instrument for the establishment of an anti-pluralistic regime. This argument naturally invites comparisons with the situation in France after 1944, a much better-known example of transitional justice, when popular demands for a reckoning with those who failed them during the Occupation were at least equally prominent.

In the second situation, the result was the *Épuration*, one of the most controversial moments in modern French history. Assesments of the *Épuration* have varied considerably: some, especially those still nostalgic for Vichy, have described it as terror pure and simple,[22] others have argued that it did not go far enough,[23] and still others have in recent years come to suggest that the *Épuration*, while imperfect, was probably fairly close to the best that could have been done,[24] even if a consensus has emerged that the violence of the *Épuration* was unfairly gendered.[25] In particular, the original criticisms of the *Épuration* – for example, that it focused on the small fry (including, famously, Laval's chauffeur) while sparing the big fish, or that it was mob justice – no longer seem ten-

21 See, for example, Elster, *Closing the Books*; Jon Elster, ed., *Retribution and Reparation in the Transition to Democracy* (Cambridge: Cambridge University Press, 2006).

22 Pétain's lawyer, Jacques Isorni, held this view, and spent much of his life lobbying to revise the sentence against Pétain. See, e.g., Jacques Isorni, preface to *Un Procès Inique*, by Pétrus Faure (Paris: Flammarion, 1973), whose title summarizes its argument.

23 Megan Koreman, *The Expectation of Justice: France, 1944–1946* (Durham: Duke University Press, 1999).

24 Jean-Paul Cointet, *Expier Vichy: L'Épuration en France, 1943–1958* (Paris: Perrin, 2008).

25 Fabrice Virgili, *La France Virile: Des Femmes Tondues à la Libération* (Paris: Payot & Rivages, 2000), distinguishes carefully between this allegation and the notion of mob justice.

able. At the same time, relative to many other European states[26] – and also to the view in France itself in the 1980s and 1990s[27] – it seems likely that the *Épuration* was relatively thorough and severe,[28] even if the nature of circumstances ensured that many officials would remain in office.[29] In particular, the common penalty of *indignité nationale,* a kind of civic death, was sufficiently severe that one of the leading works on the subject compares it to the Terror.[30]

This analysis is not intended to denigrate the *Épuration* by comparing it to Riom, or to elevate Riom by comparing it to the *Épuration.* Rather, the example of the *Épuration* makes it clear that there were alternatives to Riom, even by Vichy's lights. The directors of the *Épuration* shared many concerns with those of Vichy's trials – a concern with legality, a need to cater to public concerns without resorting to lynch law, and a desire to impose one side's views of the nature of treason in the French Civil War – but they handled the results far better, even discounting our greater sympathy for their cause. Consider, for example, Alice Kaplan's study of the trial and execution of the collaborationist writer Robert Brasillach,[31] which makes it clear that the definition of treason in use in 1944 was relatively grounded in provable harm – for Brasillach had encouraged his readers to denounce members of the Resistance. Even if Brasillach ultimately died in part for his opinions, and, in particular, his notorious statement that France would retain a positive memory of "sleeping" with the Germans, the considerably greater concreteness of the venerable charge of *intelligence avec l'ennemi* as opposed to the Vichyite neologism *trahison des devoirs de sa charge* placed a limit on the abuses of the *Épuration.*

The *Épuration* did not fully restore pluralism in France. Between 1946, when elections resumed, and 1981, when the socialist François Mitterrand was elected, the most important change in the political orientation of the government – De Gaulle's coup of 1958 – took place by force. At the same time, however, the counterexample of the *Épuration* shows how a superior administration of justice,

---

26 It is now well known that the denazification process in West Germany, in particular, left much to be desired. See, for example, Norbert Frei, *Adenauer's Germany and the Nazi Past: The Politics of Amnesty and Integration,* trans. Joel Golb (New York: Columbia University Press, 2002).

27 Conan and Rousso. *Vichy : An Ever-Present Past.*

28 Henry Rousso, "The Purge in France: An Incomplete Story," in *Retribution and Repatriation,* ed. Jon Elster, 89–123, offers a detailed statistical reappraisal of the *Épuration.*

29 Many historians have testified to the nature of these continuities. See, e.g., Gildea *Marianne in Chains,* 236.

30 The main thesis of Simonin, *Le Déshonneur dans la République,* is the continuity between these events.

31 Kaplan, *The Collaborator.*

backed by a narrower definition of treason, could restore due process even if it could not restore pluralism. Riom and the *Épuration* were both efforts to impose one side as judicial victors in the French Civil War, but the *Épuration* succeeded where Riom failed, not merely because of events in the world war, but also because the *Épuration* had a much narrower and more workable definition of treason.

This emphasis on the role of specificity and concreteness in differentiating "good" from "bad" transitional justice contrasts with much of the existing literature on the French magistrature under the occupation,[32] which has focused heavily on the importance of general legal principles in determining magistrates' actions. In particular, much has been made of the distinction between the natural-law tradition (which bars legal innovations such as *ex post facto* legislation, so much in evidence at the Riom trial) and the positivist tradition (which treats the letter of the law as sacrosanct and does not seek to interpret it in the light of broader principles).[33] We have seen, however, that one of the central problems with Vichy's justice system was precisely that the "letter of the law" was so vague that it provided magistrates with enormous scope for interpretation, almost certainly as part of Vichy's broader effort to transfer power from politicians to Romier's *prévoyants*.

If Riom's violation of *nulla poena sine lege* (the legal principle that condemns *ex post facto* legislation) contrasts poorly with the *Épuration*, the nature of the contrast with Nuremberg, which also violated this principle, is less obvious. It certainly was not as simple as a Resistance legal paradigm replacing one sponsored by Vichy. Indeed, as we have seen, the ultimate cause of Riom was that a legal paradigm was relevant at all, and that in turn was the consequence of the fact that virtually all of the French came to see responsibility for the disaster in terms of legal culpability.

The French legal position at Nuremberg was an idiosyncratic one. While the French sided with the American position that what was at stake was a crime against human civilization as a whole – hence the court's famous innovation of the "crime against humanity" – what they had in mind was not Nazi mass murder, but the Germans' supposed efforts to suppress the national spirit of their victims by, for example, spreading misleading propaganda and distorting

32 Bancaud, *Exception ordinaire*, and Danièle Lochak, "La Doctrine sous Vichy ou les Mésaventures du Positivisme," *Ressources Documentaires sur le Génocide Nazi et sa Négation*, 5 December 2000, accessed 19 September 2018, http://www.anti-rev.org/textes/Lochak89a/, are two of the major works that adopt this argument.

33 But see, in contrast, Israël, *Robes Noires, Années Sombres*, which argues for the irrelevance of this distinction.

the words of the subject nation's own literary canon in favor of the occupier.[34] (The subsequent literature on France in the occupation years has indeed been morbidly obsessed with the question of the behavior of the French literati towards the occupiers).[35] In other words, the French position was that one legitimate role of the court was to establish a canon of national identity. Logically, if the effort to force the French to diverge from this canon was a crime against humanity, then collaborationist artists' willing divergence from it was, if not treason, then at least highly dubious.

In the end, however, what came out of Nuremberg did not establish as case law the French position regarding violations of national identity as crimes against humanity, nor even the much more influential American position that the greatest Nazi crime was the crime against peace.[36] Similarly, even if legal forms could do nothing to save Zay, the fact that the Riom trial failed to condemn its designated victims (or, in some cases, even to indict them) is perhaps a salutary reminder that, once started, a trial that offers defined, even if limited, protections to witnesses and defendants can develop a momentum of its own.

This ability of trials to escape from their original purpose is a general characteristic of transitional justice, which by definition takes place in circumstances in which competing or previously suppressed visions of social reality exist in the broader society that surrounds the closed space of the courtroom and can at any moment intrude into that space, sometimes in ways that were not initially expected or desired by the parties that arranged the trial. At Nuremberg, for example, Judge Norman Birkett complained in his diary that the endless reiterations of Nazi atrocities whose existence had already been proven a hundred times over served no legal purpose, but "it seems impossible to stop it, or to check the volume of it."[37]

Most theoreticians of Nuremberg have drawn a strict antithesis between its conception of law and those espoused by dictatorships. Judith Shklar, for example, in her study *Legalism*, argued that law itself was incompatible with totalitar-

---

34 For an excellent account of the French position at Nuremberg, see Lawrence Douglas, *The Memory of Judgment: Making Law and History in the Trials of the Holocaust* (New Haven: Yale University Press, 2001).

35 Since virtually every account of the occupation years has at least touched on this question, an attempt to reference this literature adequately would be all but coterminous with a bibliography of Vichy France. There is a good overview of the question in Philippe Burrin, *La France à l'Heure Allemande.*

36 Douglas, *Memory of Judgment.*

37 Michael Marrus, *The Nuremberg War Crimes Trial, 1945–46: A Documentary History* (Boston: Bedford Books, 1997), 164.

ianism and can emerge only in societies that accept common values.[38] There was therefore no need to fear political justice unless it expressed a preexisting repression; it could not create repression. The problem of transitional justice, however, is precisely to create common values where none existed. The fact that the Nazis acknowledged that murder was a crime and that the Holocaust breached conventional morals is irrelevant; the common value that they did not accept was precisely the primacy of law over politics.

If the question of situation cannot resolve the difference between Riom and Nuremberg, much less can the question of procedure. We have seen that many traditional norms of French law were not honored at Riom; but the procedure at Nuremberg was no less problematic, and perhaps more so. Riom and Nuremberg both established new law – or rather, the Constitutional Acts and the Charter of the Nuremberg Tribunal, respectively, had created this new law for them, which they then applied on an *ex post facto* basis. Other unusual aspects of Riom, such as the difficulty in following normal rules of evidence (which the Charter of the Nuremberg Tribunal suspended altogether); the extensive use of witnesses in place of documentation, both to acknowledge the relevance of the trial to society as a whole and to compensate for the lack of hard evidence; the vulnerability of the prosecution to the *tu quoque* argument (that is, the argument that the prosecution was responsible for the same crimes as the accused); and the problem that many of the defendants were symbols of the culpability of a wide group as much as they were deemed culpable in themselves – all these were also factors at both Nuremberg and the Eichmann Trial. Procedure alone cannot differentiate between democratic and dictatorial transitional justice.

It is equally impossible to refer to the attitude of the defendants, which for Shklar was important in differentiating between legitimate and illegitimate trials (since in a legitimate trial the defendant should at least recognize the basic justice of the law imposed, even if they might not want it applied to themselves). Here, too, the list of similarities between Riom and later trials is impressive. We have seen that the Riom defendants maintained an impressive list of contact at Vichy, just as many targets of denazification (Ernst von Weizsäcker comes to mind) had considerable "pull" in the government that was trying them. Similarly, the Riom defendants, like Eichmann and many others, expressed at various times a willingness and indeed a demand to be tried in public and afforded an opportunity to clear their names, especially since both knew that the alternative was administrative justice. Moreover, it would be otiose to emphasize yet

38 Judith Shklar, *Legalism: Law, Morals, and Political Trials* (Cambridge, MA: Harvard University Press, 1964), 144.

again the near-universality of what we have called the "trial consensus" in 1940s France – the general agreement that someone else's bad ideas could be held legally responsible for the defeat. These similarities were the result of a fundamental feature of transitional justice: just as an absolute agreement on basic legal principles never exists in such situations, neither does an absolute disagreement. Transitional justice is civil war in legal form – war, that is, but between spiritual brothers.

There is, however, one important distinction Shklar makes that is useful for our purposes. She attempts to differentiate between Nuremberg and totalitarian show trials on the basis of differing conceptions of treason, which, in her view, was a far more limited conception in democracies than in dictatorships.[39] However, in her view, the category of treason has a tendency to expand over time; and it was therefore crucial that Nuremberg took place in what she believed to be a vacant space of law. This codicil can be ignored; we have already seen that Riom was the result not of judicial creep in the definition of treason, but of an abrupt and violent breach in the political community produced by an external and unforeseeable event (or, rather, of an event that can be considered "external" because it was unforeseeable).

Her emphasis on treason, however, is not misplaced. As long as the *mens rea* requirement of treason is preserved, a Riom-style situation – that is, one in which individuals acknowledged to be patriotic are accused of treason-by-incompetence – cannot occur. That is precisely the distinction that the Genocide Convention makes: it requires, not, to be sure, a conscious attempt to annihilate a protected group as an end goal, but at minimum a conscious attempt to decimate such a group as a means to an end. For an individual to be removed from the political community, she must commit a deliberate act using a forbidden means, and not merely commit an act that results in a forbidden or undesirable consequence. Most crimes allow for a concept of reasonable action – for example, of what forms of child neglect a reasonable person might consider likely to lead to harm. However, crimes that exclude from the community, and which revolve around differing conceptions of right, cannot employ such a concept; for no consensus on which actions are "reasonable" can exist in such a situation. Everyone can tell that leaving a baby in a car in the sun for hours is likely to result in harm; but not everyone agrees that legislation to limit working hours is likely to limit national defense capacity.

Romier had hoped that exposing the Vichy version of rights to public debate would result in the end in a more robust version of *prévoyance*. He was proven

39 *Ibid*, 153.

right in the end, although not in the way he had hoped. The concept of rights Riom represented was, in many ways, so alien to us today that it is difficult to recognize it as rights at all. The few areas where the record of the Popular Front really did expose them to what we would recognize as rights-based criticism – the *vacances de légalité*, for example, which arguably denied equal legal protection to French factory owners faced with sit-in strikes – were largely ignored at the trial in favor of a vision of rights more focused on the nature of the French nation. The fact that we can no longer recognize this vision as representing rights at all is in large consequence of the fact that one side won, and the other side lost, the debate of 1940 – 1950 over what rights should be. This debate in turn regarded the content of rights, not their existence. The great achievement of those years was to limit rights to a concrete form, based in universal ethics (such as the right to exist), that could be handled by a court without the enormous difficulties that arose in the case of Riom.

This interpretation of the origin of rights differs from that of Samuel Moyn, who has argued[40] that what we now recognize as "human rights" (in contrast to individual rights) did not emerge until the 1970s. We argue that many different visions of human rights existed in competition in the 1940 – 1950 period, and that that human rights emerged more or less by accident out of this international debate over rights of which Riom formed a minor part. The process followed a Kantian logic: rights were ultimately defined as that which even the most brutal dictatorships – Stalin's, for example – would not dare to deny *in public;* hence the spectacle of the USSR signing a Genocide Convention designed to prevent a repeat of the Holocaust[41] at the same time as it launched pogroms against "rootless cosmopolitans" at home. In the end, Romier was right to argue that public debate alone could produce a consensus on the nature of right – even if the resulting consensus was not what he would have preferred.

---

40 Samuel Moyn, *The Last Utopia: Human Rights in History* (Cambridge, MA: Belknap Press, 2010).

41 For the purpose of the Genocide Convention, see Johannes Morsink, *The Universal Declaration of Human Rights: Origins, Drafting and Intent* (Philadelphia: University of Pennsylvania Press, 2009).

Bibliography

Printed Sources

Bainville, Jacques. *Two Histories Face to Face: France versus Germany.* Translated by Paul Lefaivre. Paris: Nouvelle Librairie Nationale, 1919.
Barthélemy, Joseph. *Ministre de la Justice: Vichy 1941–1943: Mémoires.* Paris: Pygmalion/Gé rard Watelet, 1989.
Bloch, Marc. *Strange Defeat: A Statement of Evidence Written in 1940.* New York: Norton, 1968.
Coordinator of Information, Western European Section. „Donovan Nuremberg Trials Collection." *French 'War-Guilt' Trial at Riom.* Accessed September 20, 2018. http://lawcollections.library.cornell.edu/nuremberg/catalog/nur:00810.
Daladier, Edouard, and Léon Blum. *Les Grandes Journées du Procés de Riom.* Edited by Roger Genebrier and Pierre Mazé. Paris: La Jeune Parque, 1945.
Daladier, Édouard. *Prison Journal, 1940–1945.* Edited by Jean Daladier. Translated by Arthur Greenspan. Boulder: Westview Press, 1995.
De Beauvoir, Simone. *The Prime of Life.* Translated by Peter Green. New York: World Publishing Company, 1962.
De Coquet, James. *Le Procés de Riom.* Paris: Fayard, 1945.
Du Moulin de Labarthète, Henri. *Le Temps des Illusions: Souvenirs (Juillet 1940–Avril 1942).* Paris: Éditions du Cheval Ailé, 1946.
Heidsieck, Patrick. *Rayonnement De Lyautey.* Paris: Gallimard, 1941.
Heijenoort, Jean Van. „The Riom Trial: The Truth About French „Democracy"." Marxists Internet Archive. Accessed September 23, 2018. https://www.marxists.org/history/etol/writers/heijen/works/riom.htm.
Isorni, Jacques. Preface to *Un Procès Inique*, by Pétrus Faure. Paris: Flammarion, 1973.
Lamirand, Georges. *Le Rôle Social de l'Ingénieur, Scènes de la Vie d'Usine.* Paris: Éditions de la Revue des Jeunes, 1932.
Laure, Auguste Marie Émile. *Pétain.* Paris: Berger-Levrault, 1941.
Mendès–France Pierre. *Liberté, Liberté chérie (1940–1942): Suivi de Roissy-en-France:Recit d'un Vol du Groupe Lorraine (3 Octobre 1945).* Paris: Fayard, 1977.
Pétain, Philippe. *Discours aux Français: 17 Juin 1940–20 Août 1944.* Edited by Jean-Claude Barbas. Paris: Albin Michel, 1989.
Ribet, Maurice. *Le Procès de Riom.* Paris: Flammarion, 1945.
Reynaud, Paul. *Au Coeur De La Mêlée: 1930–1945.* Paris: Flammarion, 1951.
Romier, Lucien. *Catholiques et Huguenots à la Cour de Charles IX.* Lagny: E. Grevin, 1924.
Romier, Lucien. *Explication de Notre Temps.* Paris: Grasset, 1925.
Romier, Lucien. *Qui Sera le Maître, Europe ou Amérique.* Paris: Hachette, 1927.
Romier, Lucien. *Problèmes Économiques de l'Heure Présente; Conférences Données à l'Ècole des Hautes Études Commerciales de Montréal, du 29 Septembre au 25 Octobre 1932.* Montreal: Albert L'Evesque, 1933.
Rousseau, Jean-Jacques, et al. *Rousseau's Political Writings: New Translations, Interpretive Notes, Backgrounds, Commentaries.* Translated by Julia Conaway Bondanella. New York: Norton, 1988.
Schmitt, Carl. *The Concept of the Political.* Translated by George Schwab. Chicago: University of Chicago Press, 2007.

https://doi.org/10.1515/9783110610161-010

Vercors. *Le Silence de la Mer*. London: Les Éditions de Minuit, 1942.

Newspapers

The historian's task is considerably simplified, with regard to newspaper sources, by the fact that several of the Riom defendants assiduously collected press clippings about themselves. Newspapers that reported extensively on the various trials covered in this book include:
Action Française
Combat
Le Cri du Peuple
Le Figaro
La France au Travail
Gringoire
Je Suis Partout
Les Nouveaux Temps
L'Oeuvre
Le Petit Parisien
Le Populaire
Le Temps

Secondary Sources

Agi, Marc. *René Cassin: Prix Nobel de la Paix (1887–1976): Père de la Déclaration Universelle des Droits de L'Homme*. Paris: Perrin, 1998.
Amouroux, Henri. *Quarante Millions de Pétainistes: Juin 1940-Juin 1941*. Paris: R. Laffont, 1977.
Arendt, Hannah. *On Violence*. New York: Harcourt, 1970.
Assouline, Pierre. *L'Épuration des Intellectuels, 1944–1945*. Brussels: Complexe, 1985.
Atkin, Nicholas. *The Forgotten French: Exiles in the British Isles, 1940–44*. Manchester University Press, 2003.
Azéma, Jean-Pierre, and François Bédarida. *Vichy et les Français*. Paris: Fayard, 1992.
Bancaud, Alain. „Le Procès de Riom : Service et Renversement de la Justice." In Baruch, Marc Olivier, and Vincent Duclert, eds. *Justice, Politique et République – De l'Affaire Dreyfus à la Guerre d'Algérie*. Brussels: Complexe/IHTP/CNRS, 2002.
Bancaud, Alain. *Une Exception Ordinaire: La Magistrature en France, 1930–1950*. Paris: Gallimard, 2002.
Baudoui, Remi. „Raoul Dautry, La Conscience du Social." *Vingtième Siècle. Revue d'Histoire*, no. 15 (1987): 45–58.
Bédarida, François, Jean-Pierre Azéma, and Daniel Cordier. *Jean Moulin et le Conseil National de la Résistance: Journée d'Études sur le Conseil National de la Résistance, Sorbonne, 9 Juin 1983*. Paris: Centre National de la Recherche Scientifique, 1983.
Béteille, Pierre, and Christiane Rimbaud. *Le Procès de Riom*. Paris: Plon, 1973.
Birnbaum, Pierre. *The Anti-Semitic Moment: A Tour of France in 1898*. New York, NY: Hill and Wang, 2003.
Blatt, Joel. *The French Defeat of 1940: Reassessments*. New York: Berghahn, 2006.

Bloch, Marc. *Strange Defeat: A Statement of Evidence Written in 1940.* New York: W. W. Norton & Company, 1968.
Bokelmann, Elisabeth. *Vichy contra Dritte Republik: Der Prozess von Riom, 1942.* Paderborn: Schöningh, 2006.
Bracher, Julia. *Riom 1942: Le Procès.* Paris: Omnibus, 2012.
Bredin, Jean-Denis. *L'Infamie: Le Procès de Riom, Février-Avril 1942.* Paris: B. Grasset, 2012.
Brower, Daniel R. *The New Jacobins: The French Communist Party and the Popular Front.* Ithaca, NY: Cornell University Press, 1968.
Butler, Michael. *Selling a „Just" War: Framing, Legitimacy, and US Military Intervention.* Basingstoke: Palgrave Macmillan, 2012.
Burrin, Philippe. *La Dérive Fasciste: Doriot, Déat, Bergery: 1933–1945.* Paris: Seuil, 1986.
Burrin, Philippe. *La France à l'Heure Allemande : 1940–1944.* Paris: Seuil, 1995.
Chomienne, Christian, and Maurice Olender. *Juger sous Vichy.* Paris: Seuil, 1994.
Clément, Jean-Louis. „La Hiérarchie Catholique et les Principes de la Révolution Nationale." *Guerres Mondiales et Conflits Contemporains* 218, no. 2 (2005): 27–36.
Clinton, Alan. *Jean Moulin, 1899–1943: The French Resistance and the Republic.* Houndmills, Basingstoke: Palgrave, 2002.
Jean-Paul Cointet, *Expier Vichy: L'Épuration en France (1943–1958)* (Paris: Perrin, 2008).
Conan, Eric, and Henry Rousso. *Vichy: An Ever-Present Past.* Hanover: University Press of New England, 1998.
Coutau-Bégarie, Hervé, and Claude Huan. *Darlan.* Paris: Fayard, 1989.
Curtis, Michael. *Verdict on Vichy: Power and Prejudice in the Vichy France Regime.* New York: Arcade Publishing, 2002.
Diamond, Hanna, and Simon Kitson. *Vichy, Resistance, Liberation: New Perspectives on Wartime France.* Oxford: Berg, 2005.
Douglas, Lawrence. *The Memory of Judgment: Making Law and History in the Trials of the Holocaust.* New Haven: Yale University Press, 2001.
Dudink, Stefan, Karen Hagemann, and John Tosh. *Masculinities in Politics and War: Gendering Modern History.* Manchester: Manchester University Press, 2004.
Durand, Bernard, Jean-Pierre Le Crom, and Alessandro Somma. *Le Droit sous Vichy.* Frankfurt Am Main: Klostermann, 2006.
Duroselle, Jean-Baptiste. *France and the Nazi Threat: The Collapse of French Diplomacy, 1932–1939.* New York, NY: Enigma, 2004.
Duroselle, Jean-Baptiste. *La Décadence, 1932–1939.* Paris: Imprimerie Nationale, 1979.
Elster, Jon. *Closing the Books: Transitional Justice in Historical Perspective.* Cambridge: Cambridge University Press, 2004.
Elster, Jon, ed. *Retribution and Reparation in the Transition to Democracy.* Cambridge: Cambridge University Press, 2006.
Ezra, Elizabeth. *The Colonial Unconscious: Race and Culture in Interwar France.* Ithaca, NY: Cornell University Press, 2000.
Fields, Karen Elise. *Revival and Rebellion in Colonial Central Africa.* Princeton, NJ: Princeton University Press, 1985.
Frank, Robert. *Le Prix du Réarmement Français: 1935–1939.* Paris: Publications de la Sorbonne, 1982.
Frapet, David. *Le Socialisme selon Léon Blum.* Nonette: Créer, 2003.

Frei, Norbert. *Adenauer's Germany and the Nazi Past: The Politics of Amnesty and Integration.* Translated by Joel Golb. New York: Columbia University Press, 2002.

Frenay, Henri. *L'Énigme Jean Moulin.* Paris: R. Laffont, 1977.

Furet, François. *Penser la Révolution Française.* Paris: Gallimard, 1985.

Gildea, Robert. *France since 1945.* Oxford: Oxford University Press, 1996.

Gildea, Robert. *Marianne in Chains: Daily Life in the Heart of France during the German Occupation.* New York: Picador, 2004.

Glasner, David. „Eureka! Paul Krugman Discovers the Bank of France." Uneasy Money. November 04, 2013. Accessed September 21, 2018. https://uneasymoney.com/2013/11/03/eureka-paul-krugman-discovers-the-bank-of-france/.

Glasner, David. „Hawtrey's Good and Bad Trade: A Centenary Retrospective." SSRN. December 19, 2013. Accessed September 21, 2018. http://ssrn.com/abstract=2369028.

Halls, W. D. *Politics, Society and Christianity in Vichy France.* Oxford: Berg, 1995.

Haupt, Heinz-Gerhard. *Histoire Sociale de la France depuis 1789.* Paris: Maison des Sciences de l'Homme, 1993.

Hellman, John. *The Knight-Monks of Vichy France: Uriage, 1940–1945.* Montreal: McGill-Queens University Press, 1993.

Hoffmann, Stanley. „Aspects du Régime de Vichy." *Revue Française de Science Politique* 6, no. 1 (1956): 44–69.

Hoffmann, Stanley. „Collaborationism in France during World War II." *The Journal of Modern History* 40, no. 3 (1968): 375–95.

Horne, John N., and Alan Kramer. *German Atrocities, 1914: A History of Denial.* New Haven: Yale University Press, 2001.

Israël, Liora. *Robes Noires, Années Sombres: Avocats et Magistrats en Résistance pendant la Seconde Guerre Mondiale.* Paris: Fayard, 2005.

Jäckel, Eberhard. *La France dans L'Europe de Hitler.* Translated by Denise Meunier. Paris: Fayard, 1968.

Jackson, Julian. *France: The Dark Years, 1940–1944.* Oxford: Oxford University Press, 2001.

Jackson, Julian. *The Fall of France: The Nazi Invasion of 1940.* Oxford: Oxford University Press, 2003.

Kaplan, Alice. *The Collaborator: The Trial & Execution of Robert Brasillach.* Chicago: University of Chicago Press, 2000.

Kitson, Simon. *Vichy et la Chasse aux Espions Nazis: 1940–1942: Complexités de la Politique de Collaboration.* Paris: Autrement, 2005.

Koreman, Megan. *The Expectation of Justice: France, 1944–1946.* Durham: Duke University Press, 1999.

Kuisel, Richard F. *Ernest Mercier; French Technocrat.* Berkeley: University of California Press, 1967.

Laborie, Pierre. *L'Opinion Française sous Vichy.* Paris: Seuil, 1990.

Lackerstein, Debbie. *National Regeneration in Vichy France: Ideas and Policies, 1930–1944.* Farnham: Ashgate, 2012.

Latour, Bruno. *Nous n'Avons Jamais Été Modernes: Essai d'Anthropologie Symétrique.* Paris: La Découverte, 1991.

Lefort, Claude. *The Political Forms of Modern Society: Bureaucracy, Democracy, Totalitarianism.* Edited by John B. Thompson. Cambridge: Polity Press, 1986.

Lochak, Danièle. „La Doctrine sous Vichy ou les Mésaventures du Positivisme." Ressources Documentaires sur le Génocide Nazi et sa Négation. December 5, 2000. Accessed September 19, 2018. http://www.anti-rev.org/textes/Lochak89a/.

Maier, Charles S. *Changing Boundaries of the Political: Essays on the Evolving Balance between the State and Society, Public and Private in Europe*. Cambridge: Cambridge University Press, 1987.

Maier, Charles S. *Recasting Bourgeois Europe: Stabilization in France, Germany, and Italy in the Decade after World War I*. Princeton, NJ: Princeton University Press, 1988.

Marrus, Michael Robert. *The Nuremberg War Crimes Trial, 1945–46: A Documentary History*. Boston: Bedford Books, 1997.

Marrus, Michaël R., and Robert O. Paxton. *Vichy France and the Jews*. New-York: Basic Books, 1981.

Martinez, Gilles. „Joseph Barthélemy et la Crise de la Démocratie Libérale." *Vingtième Siècle. Revue d'Histoire* 59 (1998): 28–47.

Maury, Jean-Pierre. „Constitution de la IIIe République." Constitution de 1875, 3e République. 1998. Accessed September 19, 2018. http://mjp.univ-perp.fr/france/co1875.htm#senat.

Maury, Jean-Pierre. „Le Gouvernement de Vichy." Acte Constitutionnel N° 7 du 27 Janvier 1941. Accessed September 21, 2018. http://mjp.univ-perp.fr/france/co1940.htm#7.

Merleau-Ponty, Maurice. *Sense and Non-Sense*. Translated by Patricia Dreyfus and Hubert Dreyfus. Evanston, IL: Northwestern University Press, 1964.

Merleau-Ponty, Maurice. *Humanism and Terror: An Essay on the Communist Problem*. Translated by John O'Neill. Boston: Beacon, 1969.

Michel, Henri. *Le Procès de Riom*. Paris: Michel, 1979.

Michel, Henri. *Vichy, Année 40*. Paris: R. Laffont, 1966.

Millington, Chris. *From Victory to Vichy: Veterans in Inter-war France*. Manchester: Manchester University Press, 2012.

Monnet, François. *Refaire la République: André Tardieu, une Dérive Réactionnaire (1876–1945)*. Paris: Fayard, 1993.

Morsink, Johannes. *The Universal Declaration of Human Rights: Origins, Drafting and Intent*. Philadelphia: University of Pennsylvania Press, 2009.

Moyn, Samuel. *The Last Utopia: Human Rights in History*. Cambridge, MA: Belknap Press, 2010.

Mouffe, Chantal. „Deliberative Democracy or Agonistic Pluralism?" *Social Research* 66, no. 3 (Fall 1999): 745–758.

Muel-Dreyfus, Francine. *Vichy and the Eternal Feminine: A Contribution to a Political Sociology of Gender*. Translated by Kathleen A. Johnson. Durham: Duke University Press, 2001.

Noiriel, Gérard. *Les Origines Républicaines de Vichy*. Paris: Hachette, 1999.

Paxton, Robert. *Vichy France: Old Guard and New Order, 1940–1944*. New York: Columbia University Press, 2001.

Pedroncini, Guy. *Pétain: La Victoire Perdue (1919–1940)*. Paris: Perrin, 1995.

Pedroncini, Guy. *Pétain: Le Soldat et la Gloire 1856–1918*. Paris: Perrin, 1989.

Pollard, Miranda. *Reign of Virtue: Mobilizing Gender in Vichy France*. Chicago, IL: University of Chicago Press, 1998.

Pottecher, Frédéric. *Le Procès de la Défaite: Riom, Février – Avril 1942*. Paris: Fayard, 1990.

Rawls, John. *A Theory of Justice*. Cambridge: Belknap, 1971.

Rhodes, Anthony, and Cyril Buffet. *La Propagande dans la Second Guerre Mondiale*. Translated by Henri Gueydon. Paris: Presses De La Cité, 1989.

Roussel, Christine. *Lucien Romier, (1885–1944): Historien, Économiste, Journaliste, Homme Politique*. Paris: France-Empire, 1979.

Rousso, Henry. *Le Syndrome de Vichy: De 1944 à nos Jours*. Paris: Points, 1990.

Ruiz, Julius. *Franco's Justice: Repression in Madrid after the Spanish Civil War*. Oxford: Oxford University Press, 2005.

Scott, James C. *Seeing like a State: How Certain Schemes to Improve the Human Condition Have Failed*. New Haven, CT: Yale University Press, 1998.

Sherwood, John M. *Georges Mandel and the Third Republic*. Stanford: Stanford University Press, 1970.

Shklar, Judith. *Legalism: Law, Morals, and Political Trials*. Cambridge, Massachusetts: Harvard University Press, 1964.

Schuker, Stephen A. *The End of French Predominance in Europe: The Financial Crisis of 1924 and the Adoption of the Dawes Plan*. Chapel Hill: University of North Carolina Press, 1976.

Simonin, Anne. *Le Déshonneur dans la République*. Paris: Bernard Grasset, 2008.

Simonin, Anne. „Quel prisonnier au fond de la cour...Le procès Jean Zay." Journée d'étude: „Les papiers Jean Zay entrent aux Archives nationales," 8 June, 2010.

Soucy, Robert. *French Fascism: The First Wave, 1924–1933*. New Haven: Yale University Press, 1986.

Soucy, Robert. „French Fascism and the Croix de Feu: A Dissenting Interpretation." *Journal of Contemporary History* 26, no. 1 (January 1991): 159–188.

Soucy, Robert. *French Fascism: The Second Wave, 1933–1939*. New Haven: Yale University Press, 1995.

Sowerwine, Charles. *France since 1870*. London: Palgrave, 2001.

Sternhell, Zeev. *Ni Droite, Ni Gauche: L'Idéologie Fasciste en France*. Paris: Fayard, 2000.

Sweets, John F. *Choices in Vichy France: The French under Nazi Occupation*. New York: Oxford University Press, 1986.

Thuillier, Guy. „La Réforme de l'Administration Vue par le Redressement Français en 1927." *La Revue Administrative* 43, no. 253 (January/February 1990): 21–31.

Tooze, J. Adam. *The Wages of Destruction: The Making and Breaking of the Nazi Economy*. New York: Penguin Books, 2006.

Tronel, Jacky. „Pierre Béteille, Un Magistrat Sous Surveillance..." Histoire Pénitentiaire et Justice Militaire. August 28, 2010. Accessed September 20, 2018. https://prisons-cherche-midi-mauzac.com/des-hommes/pierre-beteille-un-magistrat-sous-surveillance-4356.

Vergnon, Gilles. *L'Antifascisme en France de Mussolini à Le Pen*. Rennes: Presses Universitaires De Rennes, 2009.

Vinen, Richard. *The Politics of French Business: 1936–1945*. Cambridge: Cambridge University Press, 1991.

Virgili, Fabrice. *La France Virile: Des Femmes Tondues à la Libération*. Paris: Payot & Rivages, 2000.

Walton, G. Charles. *Policing Public Opinion in the French Revolution: The Culture of Calumny and the Problem of Free Speech*. Oxford: Oxford University Press, 2011.

Weisberg, Richard H. *Vichy Law and the Holocaust in France*. New York: New York University Press, 1996.

Winock, Michel. *Nationalism, Anti-semitism, and Fascism in France*. Translated by Jane Marie Todd. Stanford, CA: Stanford University Press, 2000.

Index

www.ingramcontent.com/pod-product-compliance
Lightning Source LLC
Chambersburg PA
CBHW051401240926
51852CB00002B/76